A Collector's Guide to

Rock, Mineral, & Fossil Localities of Utah

by
James R. Wilson
Geology Department
Weber State University

A Collector's Guide to
Rock, Mineral, & Fossil
Localities of Utah

Miscellaneous Publication 95-4
UTAH GEOLOGICAL SURVEY
a division of
DEPARTMENT OF NATURAL RESOURCES
ISBN 1-55791-336-8

1995

STATE OF UTAH
Michael O. Leavitt, Governor

DEPARTMENT OF NATURAL RESOURCES
Ted Stewart, Executive Director

UTAH GEOLOGICAL SURVEY
M. Lee Allison, Director

UGS Board

Member	Representing
Russell C. Babcock, Jr. (chairman)	Mineral Industry
D. Cary Smith	Mineral Industry
Richard R. Kennedy	Civil Engineering
E.H. Deedee O'Brien	Public-at-Large
C. William Berge	Mineral Industry
Jerry Golden	Mineral Industry
Milton E. Wadsworth	Economics-Business/Scientific
Scott Hirschi, Director, Trust Lands Administration	*Ex officio member*

UGS Editorial Staff

J. Stringfellow	Editor
Vicky Clarke, Sharon Hamre	Graphic Artists
Patricia H. Speranza, James W. Parker, Lori Douglas	Cartographers

UTAH GEOLOGICAL SURVEY

The **UTAH GEOLOGICAL SURVEY** is organized into three geologic programs with Administration, Editorial, and Computer Resources providing necessary support to the programs. The **ECONOMIC GEOLOGY PROGRAM** undertakes studies to identify coal, geothermal, uranium, hydrocarbon, and industrial and metallic resources; to initiate detailed studies of the above resources including mining district and field studies; to develop computerized resource data bases, to answer state, federal, and industry requests for information; and to encourage the prudent development of Utah's geologic resources. The **APPLIED GEOLOGY PROGRAM** responds to requests from local and state governmental entities for engineering geologic investigations; and identifies, documents, and interprets Utah's geologic hazards. The **GEOLOGIC MAPPING PROGRAM** maps the bedrock and surficial geology of the state at a regional scale by county and at a more detailed scale by quadrangle. The Geologic Extension Service answers inquiries from the public and provides information about Utah's geology in a non-technical format. The Paleontology and Paleoecology Section maintains and publishes records of Utah's fossil resources, provides paleontological recovery services to state and local governments, and conducts studies of environmental change to aid resource management.

The UGS Library is open to the public and contains many reference works on Utah geology and many unpublished documents on aspects of Utah geology by UGS staff and others. The UGS has several computer data bases with information on mineral and energy resources, geologic hazards, stratigraphic sections, and bibliographic references. Most files may be viewed by using the UGS Library. The UGS also manages a sample library which contains core, cuttings, and soil samples from mineral and petroleum drill holes and engineering geology investigations. Samples may be viewed at the Sample Library or requested as a loan for outside study.

The UGS publishes the results of its investigations in the form of maps, reports, and compilations of data that are accessible to the public. For information on UGS publications, contact the Sales Office, 2363 South Foothill Drive, Salt Lake City, Utah 84109-1497, (801) 467-0401.

The Utah Department of Natural Resources receives federal aid and prohibits discrimination on the basis of race, color, sex, age, national origin, or handicap. For information or complaints regarding discrimination, contact Executive Director, Utah Department of Natural Resources, 1636 West North Temple #316, Salt Lake City, UT 84116-3193 or Office of Equal Opportunity, U.S. Department of the Interior, Washington, DC 20240.

Printed on recycled paper

PREFACE

Although written by one person, this publication tries to present several different viewpoints. As a professional geologist, I recognize the importance of minerals and fossils to scientific research; as an educator, I feel the need to present the public with information about geology rather than just listing some collecting locations; and, as a collector, I am aware of the thrill of discovery, as well as the service that collectors can render to the professional geologic community if proper methods of collecting, curation, and documentation are observed. In trying to serve these different groups, I may not have completely pleased everyone, but perhaps all can find something of value herein.

With the tremendous growth of population in this and neighboring states, there are more collectors than ever before and with the rapidly escalating prices for mineral and fossil specimens in the retail market, there is a great demand for displayable material. It has become necessary for professional geologists, hobby collectors, and commercial collectors to recognize each others' existence and to try to work together within a framework of regulation, courtesy, and common sense so that material of scientific value is not lost and undue restrictions are not placed upon collecting. There is a continuing need for collectors and professionals to work together with resource managers and legislators to develop workable laws and rules affecting the collecting of minerals and fossils.

Of particular concern is the development of management plans for wilderness areas which take a very restrictive approach to collecting. In essence, policies are being formulated which would allow the collection of material loose on the land surface, but which would prohibit any excavation. Since very little fossil or mineral material of any worthwhile quality can be found without digging, this effectively prohibits collecting in wilderness areas.

I appreciate the assistance I have had from a number of people who took the time to contribute information and ideas to this book, but, in all cases, the final decision as to what to include or leave out was mine. I have deliberately left out locations where I was aware of access problems or where the amount of material was not sufficient for large numbers of collectors to visit. I have left out some sites because of their scientific value or because the person discovering the site requested its location not be revealed. In some cases I was not able to visit the location for myself and have had to rely on written or verbal reports from others, therefore, there may be problems with some of these sites of which I was not aware. As mentioned elsewhere in this volume, the listing of a site does not constitute permission for anyone to collect material or trespass on private property. It is each individual's responsibility to determine if access is legal and to obtain permits or landowner permission where necessary.

Persons who made significant contributions of time and information to this book include: Lloyd and Val Gunther, Richard Kennedy, Richard Moyle, Bob Randolph, and Steve Robison. Photographs were contributed by Joe Marty, David Richerson, and Val Gunther. Frank DeCourten, geologist, formerly with the Utah Museum of Natural History, and William W. Wray, geologist and attorney, reviewed the manuscript and made helpful suggestions. David Gillette, the Utah State Paleontologist, and personnel at the Utah Geological Survey also reviewed the manuscript.

TABLE OF CONTENTS

Chapter 1 MINERALS 1
    Introduction 1
    Minerals and Properties 1
    Crystallography 5

Chapter 2 ROCKS 10
    Introduction 10
    Igneous Rocks 10
    Sedimentary Rocks 15
    Metamorphic Rocks 18

Chapter 3 FOSSILS 23
    Introduction 23
    Geologic Time 23
    Fossils 24
    The Variety of Life 29

Chapter 4 COLLECTIONS 34
    Personal Collecting 34
    Public Collections 37

Chapter 5 SUGGESTIONS FOR FURTHER READING 39
    Introduction 39
    Publications 39

Chapter 6 A GUIDE TO COLLECTING SITES 48
    Collecting in Utah 48
    The Guidebook Section 55
    Beaver County 58
    Box Elder County 65
    Cache County 68
    Carbon County 71
    Daggett County 72

Davis County	73
Duchesne County	74
Emery County	75
Garfield County	79
Grand County	83
Iron County	86
Juab County	89
Kane County	94
Millard County	96
Morgan County	105
Piute County	106
Rich County	109
Salt Lake County	110
San Juan County	114
Sanpete County	116
Sevier County	118
Summit County	119
Tooele County	120
Uintah County	125
Utah County	127
Wasatch County	130
Washington County	131
Wayne County	133
Weber County	135
Glossary	137
References Cited	144
Index	147

CHAPTER 1
MINERALS

INTRODUCTION

What is the difference between a rock and a mineral? This is a fairly basic question, but it causes considerable problems for students in an introductory geology class and may be confusing to the person who has been collecting one or the other for many years. You can think of minerals as the building blocks from which rocks are made and, likewise, atoms are the building blocks of minerals. Some rocks are composed of only one mineral (limestone, for example, is wholly calcite) and a few minerals, the native elements, are composed of only one species of atom. It is more common, however, to have several minerals in a typical rock, just as it is common to have several different atoms making up each mineral. For simple definitions, you could say that a mineral is a chemical compound that occurs in nature. A rock is a relatively hard, cohesive, aggregate of minerals. A more precise definition of a mineral is investigated in the following section. Rocks are treated in more detail in Chapter 2.

MINERALS AND THEIR PROPERTIES

What is a Mineral?

A **mineral** is a naturally occurring, homogeneous, solid that is formed by inorganic processes, has a definite chemical composition, and has an orderly arrangement of atoms. If this definition is examined in detail it is seen that a mineral is a chemical compound that occurs in nature. Synthetic materials, even when chemically identical to a naturally occurring substance, are not minerals.

The word "homogeneous" as used here, means that the mineral cannot be separated into its components by any physical process. As an example, quartz (SiO_2) can be pulverized to a fine powder, but each of those grains of powder will still be quartz. It does not break down into silicon and oxygen as a result of being pulverized.

The definition also states that minerals are solids, for example, water is not a mineral, but ice is. Native mercury, which may occur as liquid droplets oozing from a rock, would be excluded by this definition, although most geologists would accept it as a mineral. Petroleum is also excluded.

These solids must be formed by inorganic processes. This means that $CaCO_3$ which precipitates from sea water is mineral, but the same material, when formed by an oyster as part of its shell or as a pearl, is not. Coral reefs are made of $CaCO_3$, material that is secreted by coral polyps and algae, and, likewise, cannot be considered to be a mineral. This is a gray area of some dispute between mineralogists and other geologists since this same type of material, shells and reef detritus, is an important component of the biogenic sediment that makes up some limestones.

Minerals have a definite chemical composition, but this does not mean that the composition is fixed. Many minerals have some degree of variability in their composition which is usually indicated in their chemical formula by a series of elements or ionic groups enclosed in parentheses and separated by commas, such as topaz, $Al_2SiO_4(F,OH)_2$, where fluorine and hydroxyl substitute for each other.

Finally, the definition indicates that minerals have an orderly internal structure, that is, the atoms are arranged in specific positions relative to one another. It is this arrangement of atoms that affects the crystal form of the mineral and other properties such as cleavage and hardness.

Figure 1-1 illustrates a simplified view of these last two concepts. Figures 1-1a and 1-1b illustrate the pure substances calcite and magnesite in which the calcium atoms (open circles) and magnesium atoms (shaded circles) are in specific positions relative to the carbonate layers (rectangles). In magnesian calcite (Figure 1-1c), a certain amount of magnesium substitutes for calcium in a random fashion. If both calcium and magnesium are present, but each has a specific location in the structure, then the mineral would be dolomite as shown in Figure 1-1d.

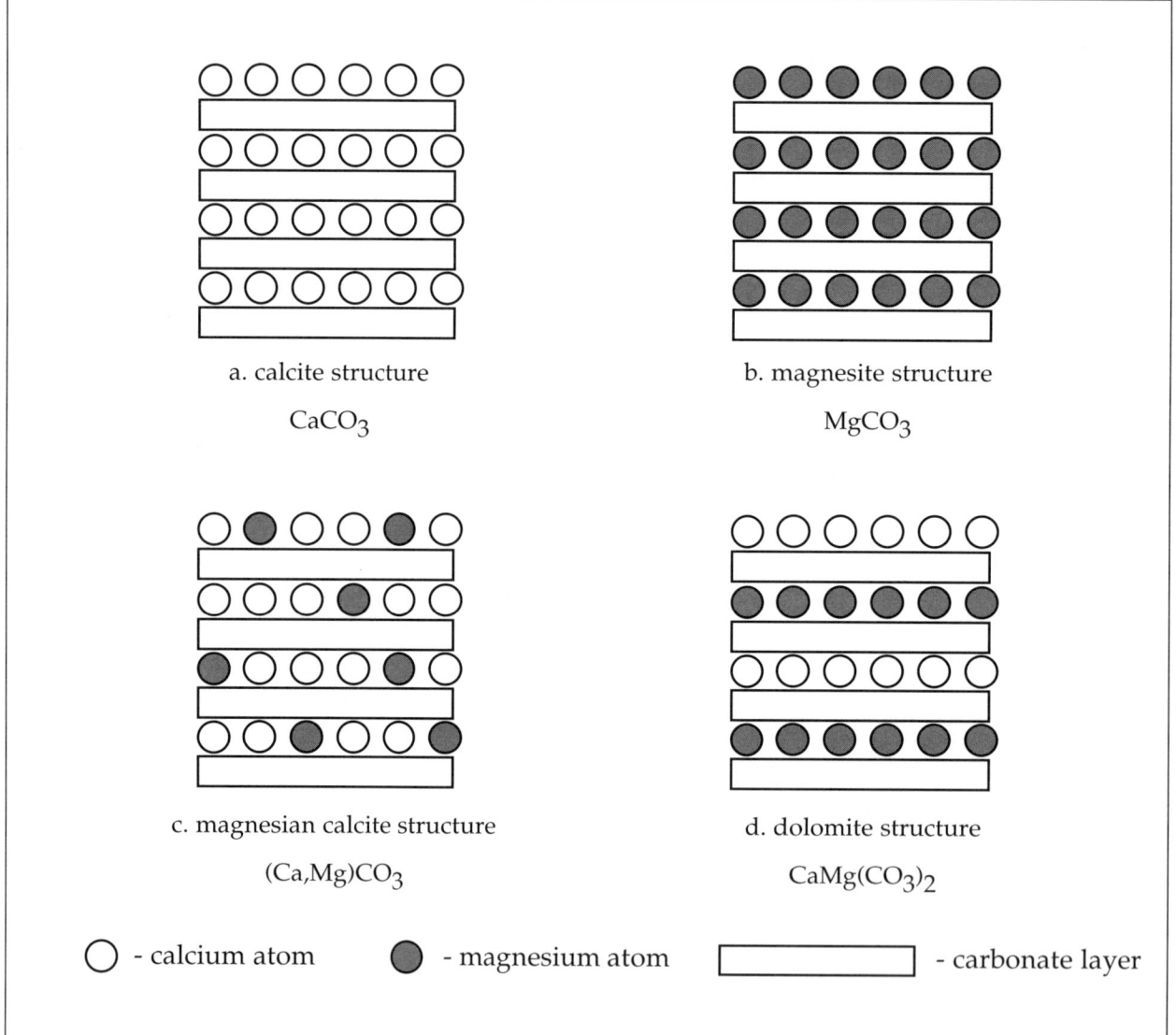

Figure 1-1 This diagram illustrates the difference between order (a, b, and d) and randomness (c) with regard to the cation positions in simple carbonates. When there is only one cation position (a, b, c) then it is filled by either Ca or Mg or a random mixture of the two. Dolomite has two separate cation positions which are occupied by Ca and Mg respectively.

Classification of Minerals

Minerals are commonly classified on the basis of their chemistry as is listed below:

1. *Native Elements*
2. *Sulfides* (includes antimonides, tellurides, arsenides, and selenides)
3. *Sulfosalts* (a metal and semi-metal with sulfur)
4. *Oxides and Hydroxides*
5. *Halides* (compounds of the halogen elements, principally Cl and F)
6. *Carbonates*
7. *Nitrates*
8. *Borates*
9. *Phosphates, Arsenates, and Vanadates*
10. *Sulfates and Chromates*
11. *Tungstates and Molybdates*
12. *Silicates*

Silicate minerals are those which contain the silicate structural group $(SiO_4)^{-4}$. Because there are so many silicate minerals and their properties depend upon the specific manner in which the silicate structural groups are arranged, the silicates are further subdivided on the basis of their structure. For a detailed discussion of silicate structures, the reader should refer to a mineralogy book such as one of those listed in Chapter 5. Names of the structural categories of silicate minerals and examples of each are given below:

   a. *isolated silicate groups* (examples: topaz, olivine, garnet, staurolite, and zircon)
   b. *double silicate groups* (examples: epidote and hemimorphite)
   c. *silicate rings* (examples: beryl and tourmaline)
   d. *chain structures* (examples: pyroxene, amphibole, wollastonite)
   e. *sheet structures* (examples: muscovite and biotite mica, talc, chlorite, and kaolinite)
   f. *three-dimensional framework structures* (examples: feldspar, quartz, zeolites)

Properties of Minerals

The mineral collector commonly makes use of the physical properties of individual minerals to identify them. A few chemical tests are also effective in identifying minerals or a specific element contained within a mineral. The following section briefly defines some of the common properties used in mineral identification.

Luster is the manner in which the mineral reflects light. Since we see most objects by reflected light, this property is one that is quite familiar. In mineralogy, luster is divided into metallic and non-metallic groups. Minerals with a metallic luster are those which reflect light as if they were a metal object. Many sulfide and some oxide minerals (as well as others) have a metallic luster. The great majority of minerals have a non-metallic luster and because so many minerals are of this type, specific types of non-metallic luster are often used. Some of the more common of these terms are: vitreous (reflects light like glass), dull, pearly, silky, glistening, resinous, adamantine (hard bright luster common to diamond and some lead minerals), and other

Table 1-1
Moh's Hardness Scale
1. talc
2. gypsum
3. calcite
4. fluorite
5. apatite
6. orthoclase
7. quartz
8. topaz
9. corundum
10. diamond

similarly descriptive terms.

Hardness of a mineral is usually related to Moh's Scale in which 10 minerals are numbered from 1 to 10 in order of increasing hardness.

Moh's Scale is an arbitrary listing and there is some overlap in actual hardnesses particularly in the 3 to 4 range. It is usually sufficient to establish the hardness of a mineral within a range of values and for this purpose several common objects are useful tools. A fingernail is 2.5, a penny is 3, a piece of glass is 5.5, and a knife blade is 5.0 - 6.0. A useful division for identification purposes is to group minerals into the following classes: 1 - 2.5, 2.5 - 5.5, and greater than 5.5. This requires no more than a fingernail and a piece of glass.

Cleavage is one of the most difficult properties to explain by words and pictures and is best learned by studying minerals with different types and qualities of cleavage. Cleavage is the tendency of a mineral to break along specific directions creating relatively smooth, usually lustrous, surfaces. Cleavage is named on the basis of the number of directions of cleavage (which, if absolutely perfect, would form a geometric shape) and is described in terms of its quality. Quality terms are perfect, very good, good, fair, and poor with these last two unlikely to be observed by casual inspection. Directions and forms of cleavage are listed in Table 1-2.

Table 1-2

Types of Cleavage

Number of Directions (Descriptive Term)	Examples
1 direction (basal, pinacoidal)	micas, talc, graphite
2 directions (prismatic)	feldspars, pyroxenes, amphiboles
3 directions (cubic, directions at right angles)	galena, halite
3 directions (rhombohedral, not at right angles)	calcite, dolomite
4 directions (octahedral)	fluorite
6 directions (dodecahedral)	sphalerite

Some minerals have more than one type of cleavage present which may cause confusion. Gypsum, for example, has both a basal and a prismatic cleavage which may mimic rhombohedral cleavage. In all cases, cleavage results from the atomic bonds being weaker along certain planes and is the external evidence of the orderly arrangement of atoms within the mineral.

Habit is the shape or occurrence of the mineral and/or its aggregates. Habit can be a particular crystal form, for example, a cube, which is a common habit for pyrite crystals. Besides crystal forms, which are discussed in more detail later, common terms for habit are as follows: oolitic (small round particles), pisolitic (pea size round particles), botryoidal (rounded masses similar to a bunch of grapes), reniform (kidney shaped), fibrous (composed of fibrous minerals), acicular (slender, needle-like crystals), tabular (flattened crystals), stalactitic (like a stalactite), earthy, granular, and massive.

Streak is the color of a mineral's powder when observed on a streak plate (a piece of unglazed porcelain such as the back of a ceramic tile). This is mainly useful for dark-colored metallic minerals which may have a streak somewhat different from their apparent color. The streak plate has a hardness of about 6, and attempts to streak hard minerals result in a white powder which is only the pulverized ceramic material.

Color is usually an untrustworthy property unless you have had enough experience in examining minerals to recognize the wide range of colors exhibited by them. As an example, fluorite is a relatively common mineral which occurs in various shades of purple, blue, green, yellow, and colorless. Sphalerite is another mineral whose color is often misleading since it can be green, yellow, brown, red, or black.

Magnetism is a rare property, but is quite useful in identifying magnetite and pyrrhotite, the only common minerals that exhibit strong magnetism.

Fluorescence is the emission of light from a mineral while it is being exposed to ultraviolet radiation (black light). Many minerals such as calcite and fluorite may be fluorescent, but the property is highly variable. Fluorescence is a useful identifying property for some minerals, notably scheelite (which fluoresces blue-white under short-wave ultraviolet and does not fluoresce under long-wave ultraviolet) and some uranium minerals.

Phosphorescence is a property similar to fluorescence, but in this case the light continues to be emitted from the mineral after the exciting radiation has been turned off. This is usually of short duration and quite weak, so a completely darkened room is usually necessary to observe phosphorescence. The property is fairly common in calcite.

Specific gravity (a unitless ratio) or **density** (mass per unit volume) can be measured fairly accurately by anyone with access to a beam balance or analytical balance (commonly available in schools). For field identification, it is often enough to make use of **heft**, that is, to estimate the specific gravity in terms of light, average, or heavy for a non-metallic or metallic mineral. With practice, this can be done fairly accurately for preliminary identification. Barite is a notably heavy non-metallic mineral while halite and sulfur are quite light. Graphite is a low specific gravity metallic mineral while galena and gold have very high specific gravities even for metallic minerals.

CRYSTALLOGRAPHY

Crystals

A **crystal** is any substance composed of a regularly repeating arrangement of atoms which results in plane surfaces (faces) forming as the crystal grows, creating a more or less well-developed geometric figure. Any material, whether organic or inorganic, that has an orderly internal arrangement of atoms is said to be **crystalline** and has the potential to form a crystal. In actual practice, however, crystals are not so common, and well-formed crystals are particularly rare. For a crystal to be created there must be the proper supply of fluid and chemical substances needed for that particular mineral and there must be sufficient space for it to assume the geometric shape determined by its arrangement of atoms. Other factors also will affect the likelihood of a mineral forming as a crystal. Thus, some minerals (such as pyrite) have a strong tendency to form crystals whereas other minerals (bornite and chalcopyrite, for example) rarely occur as crystals. Very well-formed crystals with well defined faces are described as **euhedral**. Less well-developed crystals are referred to as **subhedral** and crystals that have poorly developed faces are said to be **anhedral**.

Mathematical and geometrical factors constrain the number of possible arrangement of objects (in this case atoms or groups of atoms) to 32 point groups or crystal classes that can be identified on the basis of their external symmetry. Operators known as symmetry elements relate groups of crystal faces to one another creating visible symmetrical arrangements such as the 3-fold, 4-fold, and 6-fold patterns of faces seen on some crystals. The 32 crystal classes are grouped into six **crystal systems** based on symmetry elements that are present in each. For example, all crystals with one unique axis and 4-fold symmetry associated with that axis are in the tetragonal system, whereas if the unique axis has 3-fold or 6-fold symmetry, the crystal is in the hexagonal system. A detailed discussion of crystallography is beyond the scope of this book, but a summary of the different crystal systems and some clues to their recognition are given in Table 1-3. The reason that a collector should study crystallography is that being able to identify the crystal system of an unknown mineral is a major help in determining the identity of the specimen.

Table 1-3
The Crystal Systems and Their Recognition

System	Characteristic Features
Isometric	cubes, octahedrons, and ball-shaped crystals; many similar faces; equidimensional crystals.
Tetragonal	four-sided and eight-sided crystals; square cross-section; usually one dimension is distinctly elongated.
Hexagonal	three-sided or six-sided crystals; triangular or hexagonal cross-sections; rhombohedrons; pyramidal terminations may be prominent.
Orthorhombic	box-shaped, rectangular crystals; rectangular or diamond-shaped cross-section; tabular crystals; much less symmetry than isometric or tetragonal.
Monoclinic	box-shaped with a pronounced slant in one direction; very little symmetry is evident.
Triclinic	often as wedge- or water-shaped crystals; almost total lack of symmetry.

Distribution of Minerals in the Crystal Systems

The minerals are not distributed equally among the six crystal systems as can be seen from the data in Table 1-4. Almost half of all minerals fall into either the monoclinic or the orthorhombic systems, with a smaller, but significant, number of isometric minerals. Although some common as well as important minerals occur in the other systems, these systems are represented substantially less abundantly. This table may offer some crude guidelines when attempting to determine the crystal system of an unknown mineral. For example, if you are unable to decide whether a crystal you have collected is tetragonal or orthorhombic, you might choose tentatively to label it as orthorhombic while you investigate further.

Table 1-4
Distribution of Minerals by Crystal System

Crystal System	Number of Minerals	Percent of Total
Triclinic	19	3.1%
Monoclinic	148	24.3%
Orthorhombic	153	25.1%
Tetragonal	64	10.5%
Hexagonal (trigonal division)	69	11.3%
Hexagonal (hexagonal division)	53	8.7%
Isometric	103	16.9%

- data from Donnay and Nowacki (1955)
Subsequent data show no different pattern.

Twin Crystals

A crystal is said to be twinned when it occurs as two or more intergrown individual crystals in a well-defined symmetrical relationship. Twins may often be recognized by the unusual symmetry they seem to possess or by the occurrence of re-entrant angles between the twinned individuals.

Twins are related by a symmetry operation such as a twin plane or rotation axis that is not present in the individual crystal. The surface along which the crystals are joined is known as the **composition plane** and may or may not be the same as the twin plane. The specific twin plane or rotation axis defines the twin for a given crystal system and constitutes what is known as a **twin law**. Some twins are so common and well known that the twin law is given a common name as in Carlsbad twins. Examples of twinned crystals are shown in Fig. 1-2.

It is common to find crystals that have intergrown in some manner to yield a random arrangement of individuals or a pseudo-symmetrical arrangement that might be mistaken for twinning. Some crystals may occur as parallel intergrowths having the appearance of twinning, but they will usually have slightly random contacts with each other.

Twins may be classified on the basis of the relationship between individuals as follows:

1. *Contact Twins* — individuals are joined along a single plane
   examples: calcite, rutile, gypsum, pyroxenes
2. *Penetration Twins* — one crystal appears to penetrate another
   examples: pyrite, fluorite, staurolite, orthoclase
3. *Polysynthetic Twins* — repeated twinning with parallel planes
   example: plagioclase
4. *Cyclic Twins* — repeated twinning at a constant angle between planes
   examples: cerussite, chrysoberyl, aragonite

Figure 1-2 Twinned crystals. Top row (left to right) spinel twin (spinel, galena), Japenese twin (quartz), fishtail twin (gypsum). Bottom left, cyclic twin (chrysoberyl). Bottom center, contact twin (calcite scalenohedron). Bottom right, Carlsbad twin (orthoclase).

Unusual Features of Crystals

Most minerals are deposited by the relatively steady flow of chemical fluids during a single mineralizing episode or during a single stage within a multi-stage event. It is not unusual, however, to see evidence of several periods of mineral growth within a single crystal. This can create interesting features for the collector.

Most commonly you will observe color zonation within the crystal. Because color is often the result of trace amounts of foreign elements trapped in the mineral structure, relatively minor changes in the fluid chemistry can create remarkable color variations in some minerals. Fluorite is particularly noteworthy in this regard, and color banding is a common feature.

Changes in fluid composition or, more likely, several stages of growth may create color patterns or shading in the crystal that outline earlier crystal faces. This creates what are called **phantoms** in the crystal. Sometimes the effect is enhanced by having small grains of a different mineral deposited on the early-formed faces, and subsequently enclosed by the renewed growth. Phantoms are common in quartz, calcite, and fluorite.

More rarely a second stage of growth forms around only one end of a pre-existing crystal. This subsequent growth produces a **sceptered** crystal in which the original small crystal now forms a stem or handle to the larger crystal. Well-formed sceptered crystals are highly prized. Quartz is the most common mineral to exhibit this habit. Small quartz scepters are sometimes found in geodes from the Dugway area. Quartz scepters are also known from the Wah Wah Mountains and the Tushar Mountains

The mineralizing fluid that formed the crystal is sometimes trapped within microscopic pockets in the growing crystal. These are known as **fluid inclusions**. On rare occasions the pocket is large enough to be seen with the unaided eye and the drop of fluid with an air bubble can be seen moving as the crystal is tilted. These are usually labeled as "water bubbles" when noticed. Analyses have shown these fluids to be highly saline and sometimes microscopic salt crystals have precipitated from the fluid in the pocket. Large fluid inclusions are a curiosity for the collector, but the microscopic study of fluid inclusions is very important to geologists because they yield information about the composition of the ore-forming fluids and may allow the geologist to make estimates of the pressure and temperature at which the mineral formed. Quartz and halite are two minerals which may have visible fluid inclusions.

Sometimes a mineral that forms late in the sequence of minerals may cover or enclose earlier minerals. Rutile needles enclosed by quartz and sprays of tourmaline in quartz are not uncommon. Other minerals sometimes seen in quartz include hematite, chlorite, and hedenbergite.

A common occurrence is to have an early mineral completely replaced by a later mineral as a result of multi-stage mineralization or changes in chemical conditions such as a change from a reducing to an oxidizing environment. Replacement textures are widespread, but primarily of interest to the collector only when replacement has affected crystals. When a crystal of one mineral is replaced by a second mineral, the crystal form of the first mineral may be retained and the result is known as a **pseudomorph**. Limonite pseudomorphs after pyrite are ubiquitous and may be found at many Utah localities. Stibiconite replacing stibnite and quartz replacing stibnite (Mercur area, Tooele County), agate replacing barite (Moab area), malachite replacing azurite (many areas), and goethite replacing siderite (Cactus Mine, Beaver County) can be found. There are sufficient examples of pseudomorphism that it is possible to build a specialized mineral collection on this basis.

Gemstones

To most of the general public, and to many collectors as well, the only minerals or rock materials that they think of as valuable are those that can be described as gemstones. Although precious gems are rare and may not be found by the average collector, there are many materials that can be considered semi-precious gemstones. In general, these are substances that have some degree of transparency or translucency and can be cut, polished, and/or faceted.

The two most significant gemstones in Utah are topaz, the state mineral, and red beryl. Topaz can be collected by anyone willing to spend a little time and effort at Topaz Mountain in the Thomas Range. Red beryl, although found in the Thomas Range, occurs as a high-quality gem material only in the Wah Wah Mountains where it is under private claim. Material from this site can be seen at the claimholder's jewelry store in Delta, Utah, and at major mineral shows.

CHAPTER 2
ROCKS

INTRODUCTION

Rocks are consolidated aggregates of one or more minerals, i.e., they are made of individual grains of minerals which are held together by some means. It is important to note that it is not unusual to have a rock composed of only one mineral. Limestone is composed of the mineral calcite, sandstone may be composed of the mineral quartz, marble is composed of the mineral calcite, to cite a few examples. There may or may not be any other minerals present in these rocks. On the other hand, some rocks may contain 5 or 6 readily visible minerals that can be recognized in the specimen.

Rocks are grouped in three categories (**igneous, sedimentary,** and **metamorphic**) depending upon their origin. Definitions and examples important to the collector are discussed below.

IGNEOUS ROCKS

Definitions

Igneous rocks are those rocks which cool and solidify from hot, molten, rock material. This molten material is referred to as magma when it is below the earth's surface and is referred to as lava when it is erupted onto the surface of the earth. The reason for having two different names for the same substance is that the rocks produced by the molten material are different depending upon how the material cooled and solidified.

Texture

Rocks that form below the earth's surface by the slow cooling of magma tend to have a coarse or phaneritic texture. This means that the individual mineral grains are easily discernible to the unaided eye. This coarse-grained texture in an igneous rock is usually an indicator that the rock formed by cooling over a long period of time that allowed the mineral grains to attain significant size. These rocks are known as intrusive (or plutonic) igneous rocks. An igneous rock with a very coarse-grained texture (all grains > 0.37 inch) is known as a pegmatite. Pegmatites represent special cases of cooling during which the magma becomes water-saturated and a vapor phase evolves. Rapid diffusion of elements through the vapor phase allows crystals to grow rapidly, creating the large grains typical of pegmatites.

When the magma is erupted onto the earth's surface, it is then referred to as lava and since the lava is exposed to the relatively cool environment of the exterior of the earth, it cools rapidly. The rapid cooling does not allow time for minerals to grow to very large size, so the resulting rock has a very fine-grained or aphanitic texture. This textural term would be applied to any igneous rock whose grains were so small that they could not be easily distinguished by the unaided eye. Fine-grained igneous rocks that formed on the earth's surface are referred to as extrusive (or volcanic) igneous rocks. Shallow intrusive bodies may also have an aphanitic texture.

There are a number of other textural terms which are applied to special types of igneous rocks. (1) It may be that you will find an igneous rock which has two distinctly different sizes of mineral grains present. This is particularly common with extrusive rocks where there may be scattered, easily visible, grains within a very fine-grained matrix. Two different grain sizes indicate two different cooling rates and in extrusive rocks it most likely results when a magma begins cooling at depth (developing large grains by slow cooling) and then is erupted onto the land surface (where rapid cooling of the remaining liquid results in a fine-grained matrix). This texture is referred to as **porphyritic** and the individual large grains are **phenocrysts**. (2) **Glassy** is a word used to describe an igneous rock that formed by such rapid cooling that few if any mineral grains formed, i.e., the rock is a glass. Obsidian is the most obvious example of this. (3) **Fragmental** is used to describe rocks that are composed of fragments of other rocks, usually indicating violent, explosive volcanism.

Composition

While cooling rate determines the size of mineral grains that will occur in a given igneous rock, the mineral species that form are controlled by the chemical elements present in the original magma and the chemical reactions that occur. Although there are 92 naturally occurring chemical elements, it develops that only a few elements account for almost 99% of any magma. The 12 most abundant elements in the earth's crust (which is considered to be about 95% igneous rock) are shown in Table 2-1.

As can be seen from Table 2-1, oxygen and silicon together represent almost three-fourths of the earth's crust which is about 95% igneous rock. The amount of silicon and oxygen, commonly referred to as **silica** (SiO_2), present in many rocks and minerals is a key to their naming and classification. When a magma crystallizes the silica combines with the other common elements in an orderly pattern of crystallization controlled by the temperature of the magma and the availability of the constituents. This sequence is referred to as Bowen's Reaction Series and results in the major minerals of most igneous rocks. The sequence is illustrated in Figure 2-1.

In this sequence, olivine reacts with silica in the magma to form pyroxene, the pyroxene reacts with any remaining silica in the magma to form amphibole, and the amphibole reacts with any remaining silica in the magma to form biotite mica. These are the **ferromagnesian** minerals, i.e, those minerals with iron and magesium and which are commonly green or black in color. At the same time that these minerals are crystallizing in the magma, plagioclase feldspar is also forming. The early plagioclase is rich in calcium, but as the magma cools and its composition changes, the plagioclase becomes more

Table 2-1

Abundance (Wt %) of the Chemical Elements in the Earth's Crust

Element	Symbol	Abundance
oxygen	O	46.6%
silicon	Si	27.7%
aluminum	Al	8.1%
iron	Fe	5.0%
calcium	Ca	3.6%
sodium	Na	2.8%
potassium	K	2.6%
magnesium	Mg	2.1%
titanium	Ti	0.4%
hydrogen	H	0.1%
phosphorous	P	0.1%
manganese	Mn	0.1%

- from Mason and Moore (1982)

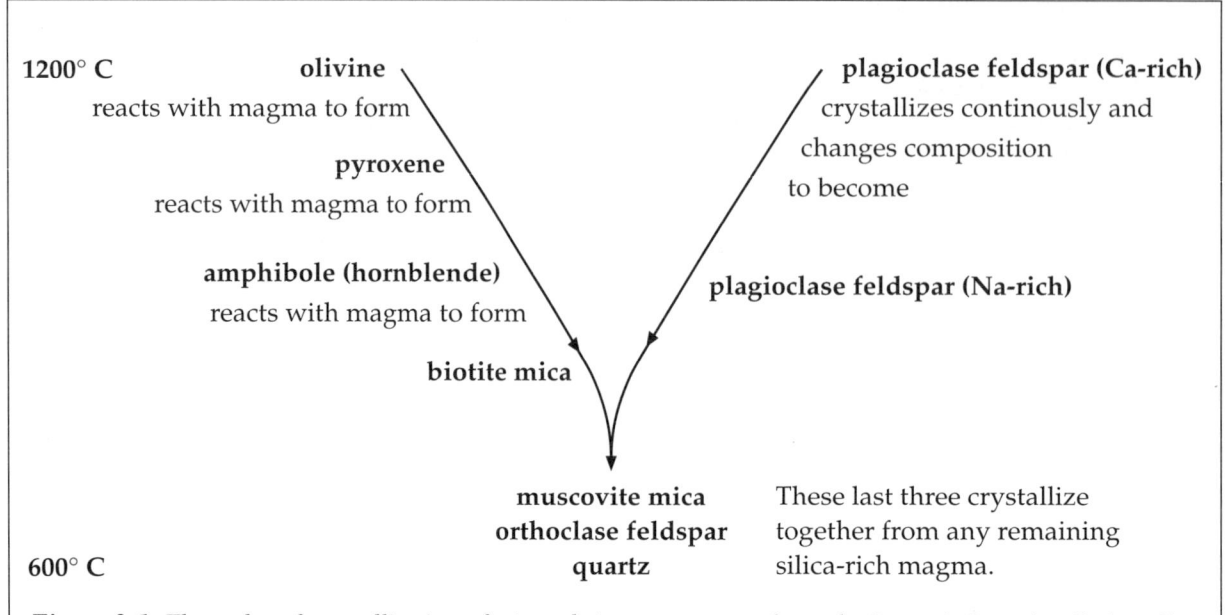

Figure 2-1 The order of crystallization of minerals in a magma as shown by Bowen's Reaction Series. See text discussion for further details.

enriched in sodium. At approximately 600° C any remaining liquid magma crystallizes to form the silica-rich minerals muscovite mica, orthoclase feldspar, and quartz.

Minerals that are close together, either vertically or horizontally, in the figure illustrating the reaction series, will commonly occur together in an igneous rock. For example, if an igneous rock contains olivine or pyroxene, then any plagioclase in the rock is almost certain to be a calcium-rich plagioclase. As a further example, olivine and pyroxene may occur together in a rock, but olivine and biotite are unlikely and olivine and quartz are virtually impossible. Exactly which minerals will occur and how abundant they will be in a given rock is limited by the original composition of the magma from which it formed. As examples, (1) a silica-rich magma will probably produce a rock that is rich in quartz and has very few dark-colored (Fe and Mg) minerals; (2) a magma that has abundant magnesium will result in a rock rich in olivine but without any quartz; (3) a magma intermediate in composition to the first two examples will produce a rock of intermediate composition such as one with amphibole, biotite, and plagioclase which will give the rock a "salt and pepper" appearance or overall gray color.

There are, of course, many other minerals that occur in igneous rocks, but Bowen's Reaction Series illustrates the major rock-forming minerals and provides clues as to what the major minerals may be. The tiny fraction of the magma that is composed of other elements may result in scarce, but interesting minerals for the collector. This is best exemplified in pegmatites which usually represent rocks that form from late stage, water-saturated, volatile-rich, magmatic fluids that cool slowly, and that develop a vapor phase before crystallization is far advanced. Pegmatite mineralization is largely quartz and feldspar, but there may be unusual minerals resulting from concentration of certain elements in the vapor phase. For example, lithium (Li) and beryllium (Be) are very tiny atoms and, if present in the magma, cannot be accommodated in the structures of the common rock-forming minerals. As a result they tend to remain in the magma until the very last fluid crystallizes and then they form their own minerals, commonly spodumene for Li and beryl or phenakite for Be. In addition to the water forming the vapor phase, minerals may be created by other volatiles such as fluorine (topaz or fluorapatite), boron (tourmaline), and chlorine (chloroapatite). Other elements such as lathanum, cerium, niobium and tantalum may result in unusual minerals in pegmatites.

Names of the Igneous Rocks

The names of the igneous rocks are based on texture and mineral and/or chemical composition. Although exact compositions can only be determined in the laboratory, field identification of rock type is usually possible for most coarse-grained rocks. Volcanic rocks are much more difficult to identify because of the smaller grain size, but it is possible to make some deductions as to the specific rock type. Table 2-2 gives a simple classification of igneous rocks that would be useful for the collector. In particular, the rock names granite, diorite, gabbro, and their volcanic equivalents, are convenient for field use.

Form of Intrusive Igneous Rocks

Intrusive rocks that form below the earth's surface create **plutons** or intrusive bodies which have names based on their size and general shape. The largest of these are **batholiths** which usually form the core of present or past mountain ranges and are typically granitic in composition. The name batholith is applied to those bodies which are greater than about 40 square miles in areal extent, have steeply dipping sides, and are "bottomless". Studies indicate that batholiths actually have relatively flat bottoms at depths of 4 to 6 miles although they may have roots extending as deep as 9 miles (Philpotts, 1990, p. 68). Some, but not all, batholiths have associated pegmatites. Most large batholiths are a result of many intrusive episodes during an **orogenic** (mountain-building) period and may exhibit a range of composition. Small batholiths, such as the Mineral Mountains between Beaver and Milford, Utah, probably formed in a post-orogenic environment, in the case of the Mineral Mountains, about 9 million years ago (Stokes, 1986, p. 205). Minerals of collector interest may occur within the massive rock of batholiths, but the better specimens will probably occur in **miarolitic** cavities or "pockets" where the minerals had room to grow into well-formed crystals. Smoky quartz and occasionally topaz, aquamarine, and tourmaline may occur in this manner.

Plutons smaller than 40 square miles are known as **stocks** and these are common in the state. Stocks are commonly more mafic than batholiths and may be diorite, quartz monzonite, or granodiorite. In Little Cottonwood Canyon, Salt Lake County, there are three stocks, with the first encountered near the mouth of the canyon.

Intrusive bodies similar to a stock, but with shapes somewhat like a bowl turned upside down so that they have flat bottoms, are **laccoliths** and were first described from occurrences in the Henry Mountains of Utah. Even today there is some controversy about the shape and nature of these intrusions since our view of these features is necessarily limited by the topography.

The most common plutons are **dikes** and **sills** which are tabular or book-shaped bodies. Dikes are defined as cutting across existing layers or structures in the rock, whereas sills are parallel to such layers or structures. Because these plutons are relatively small offshoots of larger bodies they may not be as mineralogically interesting to collectors, but they may cause some metamorphism of adjacent rocks that could be of interest.

Features Associated with Volcanic Rocks

Igneous rocks may occur on the land surface as lava flows in which case minerals of interest to collectors may occur as phenocrysts (such as the labradorite plagioclase feldspar at Sunstone Knoll near Delta) or as minerals in hollow features such as **vesicles** or **lithophysae** (such as zeolites at Marysvale and topaz in the Thomas Range). Vesicles are the result of gas bubbling out of the lava and are often filled with minerals that formed from hot water circulating through the cooling lava. Either agate or chalcedony is a common material filling vesicles. Lithophysae are openings that often are filled with a spherulitic growth of

Table 2 - 2 Classification of the Igneous Rocks

Essential Minerals	Potassium Feldspar (K-Spar) is Dominant Feldspar			Potassium Feldspar Approx. Equal to Plagioclase	
	quartz 20% - 60%	no quartz or feldspathoids	feldspathoids (usually nepheline)	quartz 5% - 20%	no quartz
Additional Minerals that may be present	biotite, hornblende, muscovite	hornblende, pyroxene, biotite		biotite, hornblende	biotite, hornblende, pyroxene
Color Index (% ferromagnesian minerals)	0 -15	10 - 35	0 - 30	10 - 35	15 - 45
Phaneritic (coarse-grained)	granite	syenite	nepheline syenite	quartz monzonite (adamellite)	monzonite
Aphanitic (fine-grained)	rhyolite	trachyte	phonolite	quartz latite	latite
Common Phenocrysts in aphanitic porphyritic rocks	quartz, orthoclase	sanidine	sanidine, orthoclase	quartz, plagioclase	plagioclase, biotite, glass

Essential Minerals	Plagioclase Feldspar more abundant than Potassium Feldspar (K-Spar)				No Significant Feldspar
	Intermediate Plagioclase			ca-plagioclase dominant	pyroxene and/or olivine
	quartz and k-spar	quartz (5 - 20%)	no quartz		
Additional Minerals that may be present	hornblende, pyroxene, biotite		hornblende, pyroxene, biotite	pyroxene, olivine	serpentine
Color Index (% ferromagnesian minerals)	5 - 25	20 - 45	25 - 50	35 - 60	95
Phaneritic (coarse-grained)	granodiorite	quartz diorite	diorite	gabbro (ca-plag. & pyroxene) anorthosite (only ca-plag.)	peridotite (pyroxene & olivine) dunite (olivine only)
Aphanitic (fine-grained)	dacite	dacite	andesite	basalt	no common aphanitic rocks
Common Phenocrysts in aphanitic porphyritic rocks	plagioclase, pyroxene, biotite	plagioclase, pyroxene, biotite	plagioclase, pyroxene, hornblende	pyroxene, olivine	

- modified from Travis (1952), Dietrich and Skinner (1979), and Spock (1962)

mineral material. They are usually associated with rhyolite and obsidian and are quite plentiful in the rhyolites of the Thomas Range.

Because volcanic rocks cooled rapidly, the individual mineral grains are very small in most cases. However, the porphyritic texture created by the presence of phenocrysts may result in rocks with interesting patterns that can be seen when slabbed and polished. Rocks from the Henry Mountains have large phenocrysts of hornblende (often twinned) which display well on cut surfaces. The identification of the phenocrysts in a volcanic rock may enable the observer to tentatively assign a name to the rock itself, although, in general, it is difficult to identify volcanic rocks without the benefit of a chemical analysis or detailed petrographic descriptions from the microscopic study of thin sections.

Basaltic lava flows sometimes exhibit **columnar jointing** when circumstances were such that the lava flow was dammed to allow cooling without appreciable movement. During cooling, shrinkage cracks develop in a polygonal pattern. Spectacular examples occur at Devil's Tower in Wyoming and the Devil's Post Pile in California. Examples can also be seen at Yellowstone and at Mt. Rainier National Parks. In Utah an interesting example of columnar jointing occurs south of Eureka at a location known as Paul Bunyan's Wood Pile, so named because the columns are arranged horizontally, giving the impression of logs.

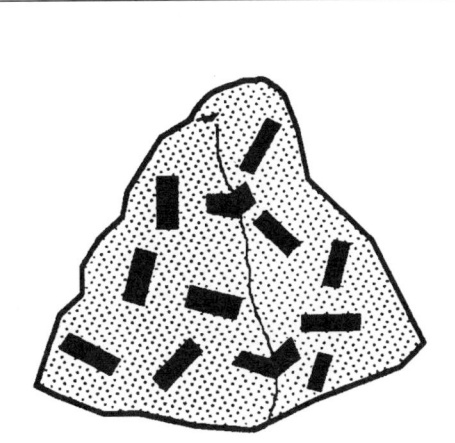

Figure 2-2 An example of a porphyritic texture. The black grains represent the phenocrysts, for example, hornblende crystals in a fine-grained matrix.

Obsidian is a material that is often of interest to rock collectors and, in particular, snowflake obsidian is highly sought. The "snowflakes" are areas where cristobalite, a high temperature polymorph (same composition, but different structure) of quartz, has formed in the dark glass matrix of obsidian. Obsidian is a natural glass and, like all glasses, is formed by the sudden cooling or "quenching" of the molten material. This quenching does not allow time for atoms to bond to form mineral grains so, other than the cristobalite "snowflakes", obsidian is a rock barren of minerals. Small rounded masses of obsidian are often referred to as "Apache tears".

SEDIMENTARY ROCKS

Introduction

Sedimentary rocks, as the name implies, are formed from sediment through physical and chemical changes (**diagenesis**) and eventual **lithification** of the sediment to make it a rock. Sedimentary rocks may be broadly separated into two groups, the **clastic** and the **non-clastic** sedimentary rocks.

Clastic rocks are those which are formed from clastic sediment which consists of fragments of earlier, pre-existing, rocks. **Weathering** weakens rocks and allows forces of erosion to transport the particles that are broken loose. These particles may eventually be deposited, undergo diagenesis and lithification, and become part of a rock once again. The resulting rock is a clastic rock. Clastic rocks rich in quartz (such as sandstone) and clastic rocks rich in clay (such as shale) are common because quartz and clay are often the residual products of weathering of earth materials. Quartz is very resistant to weathering and therefore remains after other minerals have been destroyed while clay is common because it is a result of the destruction of other minerals, particularly feldspar, during weathering.

Non-clastic rocks are formed from **chemical** or **biogenic** sediments, that is, newly created sediment. The most common non-clastic rock created from a chemical sediment is limestone which typically forms by the accumulation of calcite ($CaCO_3$) particles which precipitate in warm shallow ocean waters. Salt and gypsum also accumulate as chemical sediments and result in non-clastic rocks. Biogenic sediments are those which have a relationship to organisms. Numerous marine organisms secrete calcite or aragonite or else create a chemical change in the water which may cause calcite to precipitate. Radiolarians and diatoms generate siliceous sediments which may form chert layers within limestones. Limestones, themselves, are often a mixture of both chemical and biogenic sediments.

Names of the Sedimentary Rocks

Clastic rock names are largely based on grain size of the clastic fragments with varietal names reflecting composition. The most common non-clastic rocks tend to be either carbonates, silica, or evaporites. Names and brief descriptions of the sedimentary rocks can be found in Table 2-3.

Characteristics of the Sedimentary Rocks

One of the primary means by which sedimentary rocks are recognized is that they occur in layers referred to as **beds** or **strata**. The surfaces between individual beds are known as **bedding planes** and allow us to determine the attitude (horizontal, inclined, vertical) of the rock. With the exception of some volcanic rocks, you can be reasonably certain that when you see layers of rock, you are seeing sedimentary rock. (You should be aware that the banding seen in some metamorphic rocks is different from sedimentary layering.)

Cross-bedding is a feature seen in sedimentary rocks, primarily sandstones, that formed from sand dunes, stream channel deposits, or deltaic deposits. Cross-bedding occurs when sediments are deposited on a sloping surface such as the front face of a sand dune. In Utah, fantastic examples of cross-bedding can be seen in the Navajo Sandstone which is well exposed in Zion National Park. This cross-bedded rock is also seen in the area around Escalante, at Capitol Reef National Park, and in the San Rafael Reef west of Green River.

Ripple marks, **mud cracks**, and **rain drop imprints** are all features that may sometimes be found on rock surfaces and indicate the environment in which that particular sediment was deposited. Ripple marks are generally taken as indicative of shallow, moving water such as a stream current or a tidal current. However, deep sea submersibles and cameras have revealed that ripple marks can occur on the deep ocean floor so a shallow water origin of ripple marks is not assured. Many ripple marks occur in red-colored rocks which indicates that the iron in the sediment was oxidized and that would be proof of an oxygenated, probably shallow water, environment, rather than the deep ocean floor. Mud cracks and rain drop imprints both imply an environment where the sediment was wet and then exposed to air where it either dried and cracked or was still soft when sprinkled with rain drops.

Salt casts are cube-shaped holes in rocks that are interpreted as representing where cubes of halite formed as saline water evaporated from sediments. The halite was later dissolved by circulating ground water and removed from the rock, but the shape of the crystal remains preserved in the rock. This feature would imply an environment similar to the salt flats of the Great Salt Lake. It should be noted that pyrite will occur in cube-shaped crystals in rocks, but usually some remnant of the pyrite will remain, perhaps in the form of limonite.

Tracks, trails, and **fossils** are common and important characteristics of sedimentary rocks. With the exception of some volcanic ash deposits, the occurrence of fossils or related features is virtual assurance

Table 2 - 3 The Sedimentary Rocks

NAME	COMPOSITION	COMMENTS
Clastic Rocks		
Conglomerate	pebbles, cobbles, or boulders with a fine-grained matrix	Names such as quartz pebble conglomerate refer to specific textures and composition.
Sandstone	sand-size particles, usually quartz, but may include feldspar and mica, as well as resistates such as rutile, magnetite, and others	Varieties include: quartzose - pure quartz sand; ferruginous - red iron-stained sand; arkose - quartz + feldspar; graywacke - quartz + clay + other minerals
Siltstone	silt-size particles of quartz, mica, and clay	Usually a soft, weak rock without the fissility of shale.
Shale	clay-size particles of clay minerals, mica and quartz	A weak rock that typically exhibits fissility (breaks into flat pieces).
Non-Clastic Rocks		
Limestone	calcite; may include minor dolomite, quartz, or clay, and layers or nodules of chert. Fossils are common.	Effervesces in dilute hydrochloric acid. Varieties include: fossiliferous - abundant fossils; oolitic - small round grains; chalk - soft, white, and marks paper; lithographic - very fine-grained and uniform; coquina - mostly shell fragments; travertine - spring deposited, tufa.
Dolomite/ Dolostone	dolomite; may include minor calcite, quartz, or clay, and layers or nodules of chert	Slow effervescence in dilute hydrochloric acid, Powdered rock reacts more vigorously. Fossils are usually poorly preserved.
Chert/Flint	microcrystalline or cryptocrystalline quartz	Commonly gray, brown, or black (flint), but other colors occur as well. Flint and chert are generally synonymous although flint often refers to black material.
Chalcedony	microcrystalline or cryptocrystalline quartz	Usually transparent to some degree. May be botryoidal and nodular in habit. Varieties include: agate - concentric bands; chrysoprase - green; carnelian - red; sard - brown; heliotrope/bloodstone - green with spots of red.
Jasper	microcrystalline or cryptocrystalline quartz	Usually red, yellow, or orange. Some petrified wood and horn corals have been replaced by jasper.
Siliceous Sinter	opaline silica	Usually white, porous material associated with geyser and hot spring deposits. Sometimes referred to as geyserite.
Rock Salt	halite	Translucent, white, or colored.
Rock Gypsum	gypsum and/or anhydrite	Massive, banded, or fibrous. Usually white, occasionally transparent or colored.
Diatomite	silica	Chalky material; does not effervesce in acid.

that you are seeing a sedimentary rock. Because these features are of such interest to collectors, they are discussed more fully in a later chapter.

Geodes, **concretions**, and other nodular forms, are objects of considerable interest and speculation. Geodes are spherical, hollow, nodules normally 3-6 inches in diameter, but may be much larger. Most commonly they are filled with either quartz or calcite, although other minerals as well as petroleum are known to occur. They are commonly associated with sedimentary rocks, but also occur in volcanic rocks. In either case, there must be a hollow area in the rock in which fluids can deposit mineral material, often forming concentric bands of agate. Individual crystals of quartz or calcite often radiate into the central cavity. The best known geodes in Utah occur at the Dugway geode beds of western Utah.

Septarian nodules are a particular kind of concretion which sometimes occurs as a geode (well known from the Orderville area) in which the original nodular concretion dried and cracked upon shrinking. The cracks and interior were later filled with calcite or chalcedony. The pattern of cracks, the calcite crystals and veins, and the colors make cut and polished nodules very attractive.

There are many and diverse concretions that can be found in Utah rocks. These may take the form of iron nodules ("Moqui marbles") or they may be rounded masses of calcite or quartz. Often these concretions have a nucleus around which deposition began, usually a rock fragment but in the Monte Cristo area there are concretions with well preserved gastropod (snail) shells as the nuclei.

Wonderstone or **picturestone** and other similar rocks result from deposition of iron or manganese oxides along certain surfaces or throughout some zones in a rock. Manganese oxides frequently form **dendrites** (moss-like patterns) on bedding plane or fracture surfaces. These are often mistaken for plant fossils by inexperienced collectors.

METAMORPHIC ROCKS

Introduction

Metamorphic rocks are those rocks which form from pre-existing rocks as a result of the application of heat, pressure, or chemically active fluids to a degree beyond that which occurs in near-surface sedimentary environments. Depending upon the degree of metamorphism and the nature of the original rock material, rocks may be little changed or profoundly altered through metamorphism. In many cases it may not be readily apparent what the original rock was prior to the metamorphic event.

Types of Metamorphism

There are three major classes of metamorphism: (1) **contact metamorphism** in which heat is dominant, (2) **burial metamorphism** in which pressure is dominant, and (3) **regional metamorphism** in which heat and pressure are both significant. These three are discussed in detail below and diagrammed in Figure 2-3. There are other forms of rock alteration that the reader may find mentioned elsewhere or may find examples of in the field. These would include: **metasomatism** - the alteration of minerals by pore fluids, commonly discussed in connection with ore deposits; **spilitization** - alteration of seafloor basalts, usually classified with igneous rocks; **deuteric alteration** - where hot fluids from a cooling magma alter the newly formed minerals; and **cataclasis** or cataclastic metamorphism wherein rocks are crushed and pulverized by fault movement.

(1) Contact metamorphism is associated with the intrusion of a magma and is a result of the heat from the magma affecting the rocks surrounding the intrusive body. Contact metamorphic effects occur over a wide range of temperatures since the temperature is a function of proximity to the intruding magma. Rocks that are adjacent to the intrusion will be heated to approximately half the original temperature of the magma, whereas rocks that are several hundred feet away will be heated significantly less (Philpotts, 1990, p. 77). Reactivity of the rock material to the intruding magma is also an important factor. In general, carbonate rocks such as limestone and dolomite are strongly affected because they will readily react with the fluids associated with the magma. On the other hand, sandstones which are dominantly quartz will show little reaction because quartz is relatively unaffected by any of the metamorphic agents.

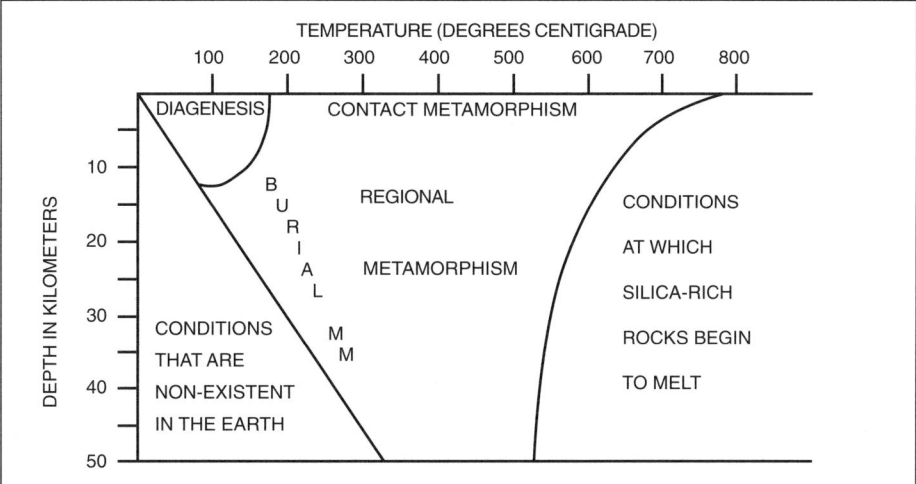

Figure 2-3 Pressure-Temperature relationships between the different types of metamorphism as well as sedimentary processes (diagenesis) and igneous processes (melting) are shown in this graph. Lines dividing different areas are approximate and variable.

Contact metamorphism of carbonate rocks, such as limestone or dolomite, produces a **skarn**. The carbonate rock is changed to marble and any impurities in the original rock or materials introduced during metamorphism will result in a variety of minerals such as: wollastonite, vesuvianite, epidote, spinel, garnet (usually grossular), magnetite, specular hematite, diopside, tremolite, and serpentine. Some of these minerals may occur in well-formed crystals and will be of interest to the collector. The rock itself, whether pure or impure marble, often takes a nice polish and exhibits interesting patterns. Industry attention has lately turned to the occurrence of gold in skarns, resulting in considerable exploration and claim-staking activity. Some of the locations mentioned in this book may have restricted access because of ongoing exploration programs.

2) Burial metamorphism results from the deep burial of sediments in a basin or trough which results in relatively high pressures at comparatively low temperatures. There are unique minerals associated with this type of metamorphism, such as jadeite and lawsonite, but these are generally microscopic and detectable only in thin section with a petrographic microscope. Utah is not known to have any rocks characteristic of this class of metamorphism.

(3) Regional metamorphism, as the name implies, affects large areas (hundreds of square miles) and is usually associated with episodes of mountain building. Along the northern Wasatch Front, the rocks of the Farmington Canyon Complex are an example. At the type locality at Farmington Canyon, Davis County, incipient melting of the rock during metamorphism produced pegmatitic bodies which are readily apparent as white streaks in the otherwise dark-colored rocks. Unfortunately for the collector, pegmatites of this type, produced by extreme metamorphism, usually contain only massive quartz and feldspar.

Metamorphic Minerals

There are a number of minerals that are unique to metamorphic rocks and these are usually of greatest interest to the collector. Minerals of metamorphic rocks are summarized in Table 2-4. In addition to the minerals in the table, many metamorphic rocks will also contain quartz, orthoclase feldspar, and plagioclase feldspar. Common amphiboles and pyroxenes may also occur. The list of minerals is not all-inclusive, as a variety of less common minerals may occur depending upon the conditions of metamorphism and the nature of the original rock material.

Table 2-4

Metamorphic Minerals

Mineral Name	Comments
talc	results from the metamorphism of dolomite or other magnesium-rich rocks
kyanite	an aluminum silicate of regionally metamorphosed rocks
andalusite	a polymorph of kyanite, may occur as andalusite hornfels
sillimanite	another polymorph of kyanite, a very high-temperature mineral
serpentine	alteration mineral of magnesium-rich rocks
garnet (grossular)	contact metamorphic mineral of impure limestones and dolomites
garnet (andradite)	contact metamorphic mineral of iron-rich rocks or introduction of iron
garnet (spessartine)	manganese-rich garnet; also occurs in rhyolite and pegmatites
garnet (almandine)	the common garnet of regionally metamorphosed rocks
garnet (pyrope)	magnesium-rich garnet; also associated with ultramafic igneous rocks
chlorite	green micaceous mineral of low-grade regional metamorphism
actinolite-tremolite	common amphiboles of metamorphic rock, usually acicular crystals
wollastonite	fibrous, acicular mineral found in some marbles
forsterite	results from the metamorphism of dolomite
staurolite	product of regional metamorphism; often as twinned crystals ("fairy cross")
biotite mica	common to both igneous and metamorphic rocks
muscovite mica	common to both igneous and metamorphic rocks
epidote	often found as well-formed, slender green crystals with prismatic habit
vesuvianite	a common mineral of contact metamorphism
diopside	a product of the metamorphism of dolomite
jadeite	a result of burial metamorphism; one of the minerals known as "jade"

Metamorphic Index Minerals

As a rough guide to the degree of metamorphism that has occurred, the concept of the metamorphic index minerals is sometimes useful. This is a list of minerals in generally increasing pressure-temperature conditions, most applicable to aluminum-rich, regionally metamorphosed rocks. The minerals are (from low- to high-grade): chlorite, biotite, garnet, staurolite, kyanite, and sillimanite. All of these minerals may not occur in a specific case because of the original rock chemistry and the particular pressure-temperature path the rock followed during metamorphism.

The Metamorphic Rocks

Metamorphic rocks are divided into two broad categories based on the occurrence of a distinct structure or texture in the rock or the lack of any such feature. Rocks that have such a texture are referred to as **foliated** whereas those that do not are said to be **non-foliated** or massive. Minerals that are present in the rocks are used as qualifying names. A descriptive chart of the metamorphic rocks is shown in Table 2-5.

Table 2 - 5 The Metamorphic Rocks

TYPE OF FOLIATION	ROCK NAME	COMMENTS
Foliated Rocks		
schistosity	schist	Fine layers of platy minerals such as micas create the schistosity. Many varieties, including: biotite schist, muscovite schist, chlorite schist, and rocks with more diverse mineralogy such as garnet-kyanite-biotite schist.
banding	gneiss	Alternating bands of light and dark minerals create the foliation. Varieties such as quartzo-feldspathic gneiss and granitic gneiss are common.
slaty	slate	Slate and phyllite are formed by the metamorphism of shale and break into flat pieces. Slate has a flat, smooth surface and is usually black, but red and green varieties occur.
	phyllite	Phyllite usually has a distinct sheen and surfaces that are curved or wrinkled. Phyllite is considered to be intermediate between slate and schist. The sheen is a result of the growth of mica grains during metamorphism.
cataclastic	mylonite	Mylonite is a fine-grained rock created from rock pulverized by fault movement.
	augen gneiss	A gneiss with large "eyes" or rounded grains in a finer grained matrix.
Non-Foliated Rocks		
massive	marble	Marble results from the metamorphism of a carbonate rock; the type of rock and impurities will determine the mineralogy of the marble. Varieties include: marble (pure calcite), dolomitic marble, brucite marble, forsterite marble, serpentine marble.
massive	quartzite	This rock contains few minerals other than quartz. The grains are strongly bonded together and the rock breaks to give a smooth surface, which distinguishes it from sandstone. Metaquartzite refers to a metamorphic quartzite whereas orthoquartzite is a name given to a strongly bonded sandstone.
massive	hornfels	This is a fine-grained metamorphic rock with no directional structure and is usually the result of contact metamorphism. Dark varieties may resemble basalt. Varieties include: calc-silicate hornfels, andalusite hornfels.
massive	soapstone	A rock composed mostly of talc with chlorite and serpentine as common accessories.
massive	serpentinite	A rock composed of the mineral serpentine.
massive	greenstone	A fine-grained rock with an overall green color resulting from green minerals such as chlorite, epidote, and serpentine.

CHAPTER 3
FOSSILS

INTRODUCTION

Fossils are the remains of organisms or some evidence of their presence preserved in rocks. Fossils are not only the major line of evidence for evolution of lifeforms, but are also important in oil exploration and in many aspects of geologic mapping.

Through the use of fossils it is possible to correlate rock units in different locations. **Correlation** is the process whereby rock units from different geographic areas are matched on the basis of the occurrence of distinct fossils and by comparable stratigraphic position and lithology. Fossils allow us to attribute an age to rock units.

GEOLOGIC TIME

Earth History

When the word "history" is mentioned, most people think in terms of human history, a time span of less than 10,000 years of which only the last 4,000 years are known in any detail. Geologists, however, speak of "Earth history" or "geologic time", which spans approximately 4.6 billion years from the time that the Earth condensed as solid matter from the gaseous material of the solar system. This vast expanse of time that encompasses the history of the Earth and the life upon it is almost incomprehensible to the human mind. For this reason it may be useful to consider the following analogy.

If it had been possible to make a time-lapse movie of the Earth's history by exposing one frame of movie film for each year of the Earth's existence, then the resulting movie, run at a normal speed of 24 frames per second, would take slightly more than 6 years to show in a theater that ran it night and day. Our 6-year movie of the Earth could be summarized as follows:

During the first five years the Earth condensed out of gaseous material and assumed a solid form. This period of time was characterized by the evolution of the solid Earth into core, mantle, and crust, and then, gradual filling of the ocean basins with water. The water originated from volcanic eruptions as did most of the Earth's atmosphere. The early atmosphere of the Earth had very little oxygen and the small amount that was produced combined with iron and was removed from the atmosphere, creating the large iron deposits of Minnesota, Michigan, Canada and elsewhere. Early in the sixth year of Earth history single-celled, then multi-celled, organisms appeared in the oceans. This proliferation of lifeforms in the oceans, particularly stromatolites, a form of algae, led to a more oxygen-rich atmosphere through photosynthesis.

In late May of the sixth year the first vertebrates, the fishes, appeared and by June the first land plants evolved. By mid-summer, amphibians crawled out of the ocean and, within a month, reptiles appeared and were soon dominated by a particular group, the dinosaurs. The dinosaur's dominance ended in late November as the Rocky Mountains began to rise. By December, birds appeared and mammals became the dominant lifeform. At Christmas, of this sixth year of Earth history, the Colorado River began to cut the Grand Canyon. On the morning of December 31 a creature that resembles man is first glimpsed and dur-

ing that afternoon ice sheets moved back and forth across the land. By 11 p.m. people are seen quite often and at 11:45 p.m. these people learn how to make simple tools that can be used to cultivate the soil. This was the beginning of what is called Civilization. At 1 minute and 22 seconds before midnight, the Christian Era began; at 20 seconds before midnight, Columbus discovered America; and in the final 3 seconds occurred World War I, World War II, and all the developments of modern science and technology.

When put in this perspective it is easy to see that "history", when used to refer to human history, represents only a very small part of Earth history. It is also useful to keep in mind that most surface features of the Earth, i.e., canyons, mountains, rivers, etc., are all relatively recent in origin, even though the rocks from which they have been formed may be quite ancient. For example, the Grand Canyon is little more than 10 million years in age although the rocks exposed in the canyon are as much as 2 billion years old.

Geologic time is divided into units of varying length known as **eras, periods, and epochs**. Eras and periods are common units of reference for the entire time scale, but epochs are in common usage for only the most recent era. The eras, their literal definition, and relation to the evolution of life are shown below in Table 3-1. The complete geologic time scale, along with events of significance to Utah, is shown in Table 3-2.

Table 3-1

Geologic Eras

Name of the Era	Literal Definition	Dominant Lifeforms
Cenozoic	"Recent Life"	Mammals
Mesozoic	"Middle Life"	Reptiles
Paleozoic	"Ancient Life"	Invertebrates
Precambrian		
(Proterozoic)	("Earliest Life")	Primitive Lifeforms
(Archeozoic)	("Initial Life")	Beginning of Life

FOSSILS

Fossilization

It would seem, with the vast amount of geologic time and the almost countless number of individual organisms that have existed during the history of the Earth, that the rocks would be overflowing with the fossilized remains of these plants and animals. Instead, we find that the majority of rocks have few if any fossils and only some rocks contain abundant fossils. How can this be?

The basic requirements for fossilization are that the organism possesses hard parts such as bone or shell which can be readily fossilized and that the organism experiences rapid burial to prevent destruction of material by decay or predation. The requirement of hard parts is fairly obvious although there are occurrences of soft tissues being preserved in special circumstances. Without rapid burial, however, even large bones are cracked by predators and gnawed by rodents and soon disappear. Thus the fossil record of the oceans is much more complete than that of the land because it is much easier for an organism to be fossilized in the soft sediment of the ocean bottom than it is to be preserved on the forest floor or desert sands. As a result, there may never be a land fossil record so complete as to convince everyone of the evolution of modern lifeforms, including humans, but the marine record is quite complete and convincing.

Just as living animals can be sought and found in certain habitats with which they are known to be associated, fossils can often be found in rocks representing particular environments. A simplified listing of environments of deposition and their relationships to lifeforms is presented in Table 3-3.

Table 3-2 The Geologic Time Scale

ERA	PERIOD	EPOCH	FROM	TO	ANIMAL LIFE AND EVENTS	GEOLOGIC OCCURRENCES IN THE UTAH AREA
CENOZOIC	QUATERNARY	HOLOCENE	11,000 YA	PRESENT		Complete (?) dessication of the Great Salt Lake as water level fluctuates.
CENOZOIC	QUATERNARY	PLEISTOCENE	1.8 MYA	11,000YA	Mammoth, ground sloth, native horse, bison, pecarries, giant bears, musk oxen, mountain sheep were large animals in Utah.	Lake Bonneville reaches maximum area and depth, then drains catastrophically. Glaciers exist in the Wasatch, Uinta, and La Sal Mountains, and also on the Wasatch and Aquarius Plateaus. Rhyolite lavas of the Sevier Desert.
CENOZOIC	TERTIARY	PLIOCENE	5.3 MYA	1.8 MYA	Climatic change leads to the extinction of animals that had evolved early in the period.	Volcanic activity in the St. George area produces olivine basalt.
CENOZOIC	TERTIARY	MIOCENE	23.7 MYA	5.3 MYA	Extensive grasslands give rise to numerous grazers and evolution of a variety of carnivores. This is the high point of mammalian diversity.	General uplift of the Rocky Mountain area.
CENOZOIC	TERTIARY	OLIGOCENE	36.6 MYA	23.7 MYA	Increase in grazing animals. Many mammals very similar to their modern forms have evolved. Titanotheres became extinct.	Volcanic rocks of the Oquirrh Mountains. Little Cottonwood stock. Keetley volcanics were extruded.
CENOZOIC	TERTIARY	EOCENE	57.8 MYA	36.6 MYA	Rich fauna of the Green River Formation representing a lake environment. Fossils of plants, fish, and non-marine invertebrates.	Intrusive rocks and mineralization at Bingham. Alta stock and mineralization. Expansion of fresh water lakes such as Green River Lake, Uinta Lake, and Lake Flagstaff. Laramide Orogeny ends.
CENOZOIC	TERTIARY	PALEOCENE	66.4 MYA	57.8 MYA	Placental mammals from the riverine deposits of the North Horn Formation. Pelecypods, gastropods, and fish from the Flagstaff Formation.	Erosion of the highlands of western Utah and the Uinta Mountains.
MESOZOIC	CRETACEOUS		144 MYA	66.4 MYA	Pelecypods, gastropods, and ammonites occur in the Mancos Shale. Dinosaur tracks left in the coal beds of Emery, Grand, and Carbon Counties. Fossils of sauropods, ornithopods, and stegosaurs occur in the North Horn Formation of the Wasatch Plateau. Associated with coal beds are fossilized plant material from sequoia, palm, waterlily, fig, cypress, and magnolia.	The sea floods into eastern Utah, while in the west the Sevier Orogeny creates a highland area from which sediment is rapidly derived and delivered to the east. The Laramide Orogeny begins as the Uinta Mountains are formed.
MESOZOIC	JURASSIC		208 MYA	144 MYA	Abundant dinosaur fossils of the Morrison Formation seen today at Dinosaur National Monument and the Cleveland-Lloyd Quarry. Cone-bearing trees and cycads are common.	The Navajo Sandstone, seen at Zion Nation Park and Capitol Reef National Park, was deposited as sand dunes. The Entrada Formation, in which the arches of Arches National Park are found, was deposited. The uranium deposits of southern Utah occur in the Morrison Formation of this period.
MESOZOIC	TRIASSIC		245 MYA	208 MYA	Large cephalopods occur near the base of the Thaynes Formation. Tracks of dinosaurs, other reptiles, and amphibians are found in several formations. Fish fossils occur in the Chinle Shale of San Juan County. Abundant petrified wood is found in the Chinle Shale.	A sea covered western Utah and mud flats extended to the east, then a highland gradually emerged to the west and created a land-locked basin. As the period ended, dune sand covered much of the state.

Table 3-2 The Geologic Time Scale (continued)

ERA	PERIOD	EPOCH	FROM	TO	ANIMAL LIFE AND EVENTS	GEOLOGIC OCCURRENCES IN THE UTAH AREA
PALEOZOIC	PERMIAN		286 MYA	245 MYA	World-wide extinction of many organisms including trilobites, and many forms of crinoids and coral. First mammal-like reptiles. Brachiopods, mollusc, and sponge fossils are common.	Continued deposition in the Oquirrh Basin. Phosphate rock of the Phosphoria Formation is deposited.
	PENNSYLVANIAN		320 MYA	286 MYA	First reptiles appear. Also the first conifers and ferns. Fusulinids, brachiopods, bryozoans, and coral are common fossils.	Tremendous thicknesses of sediment accumulate in the Oquirrh Basin of northern Utah. Salt deposits of the Paradox Basin in southeastern Utah form. Ancestral Rockies are formed as the Uncompahgre Uplift rises along the present Utah-Colorado line.
	MISSISSIPPIAN		360 MYA	320 MYA	First seed-bearing plants. Brachiopods, bryozoans, crinoids, and coral are abundant.	Enormous amounts of limestone are formed throughout the world. All but the northwestern corner of the state is covered by warm shallow seas during the early part of the period. Eastern Utah emerges during the latter part of the Mississippian, but western Utah continues to subside.
	DEVONIAN		408 MYA	360 MYA	"Age of Fishes". First land-living vertebrates. First ammonites appear and the first forest spread across the land. Fish fossils are found in the Water Canyon Formation. Other Utah fossils are brachiopods and corals.	Shallow seas cover western Utah early in the period and become deeper and extend to the east as the period progresses.
	SILURIAN		438 MYA	408 MYA	First vegetation on the land. Brachiopods and corals are common fossils, although dolomitization of these rocks has destroyed many.	A narrow seaway stretches across western Utah to the Idaho border.
	ORDOVICIAN		505 MYA	438 MYA	Trilobites, brachiopods, graptolites. bryozoans, and corals are among the fossils occurring in rocks such as the Garden City Formation of northern Utah and the Pogonip Group of western Utah.	Abundant sedimentation in the Confusion Basin of southwestern Utah, but formations are much thinner to the east. No outcrops of Ordovician rock occur east of the Wasatch Front.
	CAMBRIAN		570 MYA	505 MYA	First appearance of abundant, varied lifeforms, including trilobites, gastropods, pelecypods, cephalopods, corals, and many others. "Age of Trilobites". Abundant and varied trilobites found in the Wheeler Shale of western Utah. Brachiopods are also common.	Subsidence of the Cordilleran geosyncline creates a deep-water environment across western Utah that lasts into the Ordovician. The sea transgresses eastward during the period, eventually covering most of the continent.
PRECAMBRIAN			4.8 BYA	570 MYA	Early forms of life were in existence late in the Precambrian. Stromatolites, a blue-green algae, are commonly found as rounded columnar forms. Organisms without hard parts, such as worms, were probably in existence although not preserved as fossils.	A long time period in which many diverse geologic events occurred resulting in the metamorphic rocks of the Raft River Range in northwestern Utah, the metamorphic rocks of the Farmington Canyon Complex, and the glacial deposits of the Mineral Fork Tillite in the Wasatch Range.

MYA = millions of years ago
BYA = billions of years ago

- adapted from Stokes (1986) and Hintze (1988)

Table 3-3
Environments of Deposition and Associated Fossils

I. **Continental** (above high tides)
    A. **Glacial** (ice deposits) — few animal fossils; logs in recent glacial deposits
    B. **Eolian** (wind deposits) — few animal fossils; some tracks and trails
    C. **Fluvial** (stream deposits) — fossils of animals and plant material
    D. **Colluvial** (gravity deposits) — seldom fossiliferous
    E. **Lacustrine** (lake deposits) — fossils of plants, fish, other animals may be found
    F. **Paludal** (swamp deposits) — abundant plant fossils
    G. **Spelean** (cave deposits) — often trap recent animals, seldom fossilized

II. **Mixed Continental and Marine Environments**
    A. **Littoral** (between the high and low tides)
        1. Beaches — abundant marine fossils, but often broken by waves
        2. Tidal Lagoons — some marine fossils, usually bottom-dwelling animals
    B. **Delta** (river deposition in body of water) — few fossils, some bones and plant material
    C. **Estuaries** (river deposition in bay or inlet) — few fossils, some bones and plant material

III. **Marine (below the tidal limit)**
    A. **Reefs** — very abundant invertebrate marine fossils
    B. **Continental Shelf** — (shallow marine) invertebrate marine fossils common
    C. **Continental Slope** — (intermediate marine) relatively few fossils
    D. **Abyssal Plain** — (deep marine) microfossils

The discussion above ignores the occasional presence of fossils in non-sedimentary rocks. In fact, fossils are so common to sedimentary rocks that their presence is often a reliable indicator to the amateur that the rock is sedimentary. There are, however, occurrences of fossils in other types of rocks. It is fairly common to find fossils in volcanic ash beds, where the plants or animals were smothered by the ash fall from a sudden, violent, volcanic eruption, such as the recent eruption of Mt. St. Helens. Intrusive igneous rocks and lava flows would not be expected to have fossils. Most metamorphic rocks will not have fossils because the heat and pressure that created them will have destroyed the fossils, but relatively low-grade metamorphism may allow some fossils to survive in recognizable form.

Types of Fossilization

Depending upon the material and the circumstances during and after burial, fossilization can occur in several ways or the material can go through a series of changes before reaching the final form that is seen by the collector.

Actual remains of an organism may be preserved in somewhat unusual circumstances such as those instances where the carcasses of mammoths and wooly rhinoceroses were found frozen in the permafrost of Alaska and Siberia. One Siberian mammoth was found when natives noticed that their sled dogs were disappearing during the day and returning later in the day looking well fed. The dogs had unearthed a mammoth from its frozen grave and were devouring it as it was defrosted.

It is also possible that actual remains may be preserved by mummification which occurs naturally when an organism dies in a sheltered location in a very dry climate and is gradually dessicated. Some caves and rock shelters have preserved specimens of late Cenozoic animals and early man in this fashion.

Unaltered shells or bones are sometimes found in rocks. Shells may be calcite, aragonite, tri-calcium phosphate, or opal. Shells of aragonite and opal are seldom found in rocks older than the Cenozoic because their composition tends to change; aragonite becomes calcite and opal alters to a form of quartz such as chalcedony.

Carbonization is a common process of alteration that leaves a carbonized film of the original material on a surface of the rock. Graptolites, abundant fossils of Ordovician to Mississippian rocks, are preserved in this manner. Extensive carbonization of thick masses of plant material leads to the formation of coal beds.

Permineralization is a process whereby the pore spaces within bone or wood are filled with mineral material deposited by ground water circulating through the rock. The fossil may appear unaltered, but is usually distinctly heavier than one would expect. The deposited mineral may or may not be the same as the original material.

Recrystallization occurs when new crystals form at the expense of old and the original material is changed either in texture or atomic structure (polymorphism). For example, fibrous calcite originally deposited in some shells may recrystallize as granular calcite. Many shells are originally formed as aragonite and may recrystallize to the polymorph calcite. Material formed as opal (hydrated silica) is usually amorphous and may recrystallize and dehydrate to one of the cryptocrystalline varieties of quartz such as chalcedony.

Replacement involves the removal of the original substance with its simultaneous replacement by a mineral. This process is also known as petrifaction. Replacement usually does not preserve the original microstructure of the organic material although exceptions are common.

A typical example of replacement is silica replacing calcite resulting in fossils that stand out on weathered surfaces of limestone. The limestone (calcite) is being dissolved by slightly acidic precipitation or runoff and the fossils, having been replaced by silica, are insoluble and stand out in relief. This circumstance allows the collector to dissolve the enclosing carbonate rock and obtain well-preserved fossils.

Other forms of replacement include carbonatization wherein original minerals are replaced by calcite or other, less common, carbonate minerals. Pyritization is a seldom seen, but often spectacular, replacement of organic material by pyrite or marcasite. Many rock shops carry examples of brachiopods replaced in this manner. Other minerals known to replace fossils include hematite and glauconite.

Traces of Plants and Animals

A **mold** is an impression left by the organism in the soft sediment, which is now lithified. When the original fossil is dissolved and removed by ground water a **cast** may be formed by some material filling the created void.

If a mold is left when a fossil is removed from its matrix, then it is possible to make a cast using plaster of Paris or modeling clay. These casts are often useful for study and plaster and plastic casts of exceptional fossils are a standard part of most paleontological collections.

Tracks, **trails**, and **borings** are common traces found in rocks, but the information that they provide is often quite limited. Today, anyone with even a modest knowledge of outdoor lore could recognize the tracks of many common animals when seen in the soft sediment along a stream. Tracks left by insects and rodents form distinctive trails on the surface of sand dunes and can be examined by hikers who chance upon them. The problem with tracks found in rocks is that there is seldom any living animal to which they can be matched and thus confirm the identification.

Dinosaur tracks are found in many places in Utah, but may provide very little information about the animal that left the tracks. The general size and shape of the foot can be observed (although often distorted by soft sediment), depth of the track may indicate weight, and distance between tracks tells something of the animal's gait and size. Even so it is probably impossible to determine which particular species of dinosaur left the tracks.

Even more problematical than tracks are borings and tubes left by worm-like organisms. Sediments are often disturbed after deposition by the feeding and burrowing activities of organisms and this bioturbation is obvious in many former sediments, now preserved as rocks, but very little can be said about the animals responsible. Features of this type have been found in Precambrian Era rocks and offer indirect evidence of the existence of living organisms at that early time.

Coprolites are fossilized excrement of animals. These may be of importance to paleontologists if they contain undigested remains that can be identified. Coprolites may also yield information about the size of the animal and its anatomy. However, not every odd-shaped stone is a coprolite.

Gastroliths are smooth, rounded, highly polished stones which were presumably swallowed by an animal, dinosaurs in some cases, and used to help grind food that it had eaten. They are sometimes found with the fossilized remains of dinosaurs. The collector should be aware, however, that most smooth, round, stones were shaped and polished by the action of streams and are not gastroliths. In sandy areas, movement of sand particles by the wind can sandblast rocks into smooth objects with polished surfaces.

Pseudofossils are naturally occurring objects which are commonly mistaken for fossils. A familiar pseudofossil is the occurrence of lacy manganese oxide dendrites on the bedding planes or fracture surfaces of rocks. These dendrites are often mistaken for fossil "moss". Various forms of cryptocrystalline quartz such as chert and jasper occur in shapes and with textures that may suggest fossilized material, but this is often problematical. Concretions are objects which commonly have odd appearances and have been mistaken for gastroliths, coprolites, or dinosaur eggs.

THE VARIETY OF LIFE

Classification of Organisms

Anyone who is serious about collecting fossils must have at least some rudimentary knowledge about the various types of lifeforms and their relationships to one another. Table 3-4 presents an abridged classification of organisms. In the section which follows, the major phyla are briefly described with the emphasis on those classes of plants and animals which the collector is most likely to encounter.

The More Common Phyla

In this section, the phyla whose representatives are most likely to be found by the average collector are discussed with regard to some of the characteristic features. This is not meant, however, to replace detailed study with a good paleontological reference book. (See Chapter 5 - Suggested Readings).

Phylum Tracheophyta includes those land plants with a well-developed system and structural differentiation into roots, stems, and leaves. Of these, the most important are those of the Subphylum *Pteropsida* (see Table 3-4) which are most commonly found as fossils.

Table 3-4
Classification of Lifeforms
(adapted from Stokes, 1982 and Moore et al., 1952)
asterisks (*) denote extinct forms

Kingdom Monera
    Phylum Schizophyta .... bacteria
    Phylum Cyanophyta .... blue-green algae
Kingdom Protista
    Phylum Chrysophyta .... diatoms, coccoliths
    Phylum Sarcodina .... foraminifera, radiolarians
Kingdom Plantae
    Phylum Chlorophyta .... green algae
    Phylum Tracheophyta.......................... vascular plants
        Subphylum Psilopsida .... psilophytes
        Subphylum Lycopsida .... club mosses
        Subphylum Sphenopsida .... horsetails
        Subphylum Pteropsida .... ferns and seed plants
            Class Filicae .... ferns
            Class Gymnospermae .... conifers, cycads, ginkgoes
            Class Angiospermae .... flowering plants including deciduous trees, cactus, palms, and grasses
Kingdom Fungi
    Phylum Eumycophyta .... few fossils
Kingdom Animalia
    Phylum Porifera .... sponges
    Phylum Archaeocyatha .... sponge-like organisms*
    Phylum Coelenterata .... polyps and medusae
        Class Anthozoa .... sea anemones and corals
    Phylum Bryozoa .... small colonial animals
    Phylum Brachiopoda .... marine bivalves with one valve larger than the other
        Class Inarticulata .... chitinophosphatic shells
        Class Articulata .... hinged calcareous shells
    Phylum Mollusca .... mostly shelled animals
        Class Gastropoda .... most abundant class of molluscs; most have cap-shaped or coiled shell
        Class Bivalvia (Pelecypoda) .... bivalved molluscs such as clams, oysters with valves that are mirror images
        Class Cephalopoda .... most fossil forms have a flat spiral-shaped shell
    Phylum Annelida .... segmented worms
    Phylum Arthropoda .... abundant forms with segmented body and exoskeleton
        Class Trilobita .... extinct segmented forms with trilobate exoskeleton
        Class Chelicerata .... eurypterids*, spiders, and scorpions
        Class Crustacea .... crabs, lobsters, barnacles
        Class Myriapoda .... centipedes and millipedes
        Class Insecta .... insects, rare as fossils
    Phylum Echinodermata .... animals with 5-fold symmetry
        Class Cystoidea .... cystoids, stemmed forms*
        Class Blastoidea .... blastoids, stalked forms*
        Class Crinoidea .... crinoids, usually stalked
        Class Steelleroidea .... starfish and brittle stars
        Class Echinoidea .... sea urchins
    Phylum Hemichordata .... colonial marine organisms
        Class Graptolithina .... graptolites*
    Phylum Chordata .... animals with spinal cords
        Subphylum Vertebrata .... animals with a backbone and highly developed nervous system
        Class Osteichthyes .... bony fishes
        Class Chondrichthyes .... cartilaginous fish, such as sharks
        Class Amphibia .... amphibians
        Class Reptilia .... reptiles
        Class Aves .... birds
        Class Mammalia .... mammals

Land plants first appear in the very late Silurian but are not common until the Devonian. Therefore, plant-like fossils collected from Cambrian, Ordovician, or Silurian rocks are most likely to be the remains of marine algae or one of the branching forms of marine invertebrates or dendrites.

During the Devonian period land plants developed varied morphology with many being the size of shrubs and small trees. The following Mississippian-Pennsylvanian periods witnessed tremendous strides in plant development with giant forms of club mosses (*lepidodendrons*) and horsetails (*calamites*) reaching heights of 100 feet or more before they became extinct during the Permian. Ferns and seed ferns also appeared during the Devonian and reached their peak of development in the Pennsylvanian. The gymnosperms arose in the Devonian but didn't reach their peak until the Permian. Low-lying forests and swamps of the Mississippian-Pennsylvanian periods were periodically buried by sediment to create the coal beds that are common to this strata in many areas of the world. Small coal beds of this age occur in Utah.

The Permian period marked the extinction or near extinction of many lines of plant development, but conifers prospered and two new types of gymnosperms appeared during or at the end of the Permian, the cycads and ginkgoes. Cycads are characterized by a short trunk crowned by palm-like leaves whereas ginkgoes are best recognized by their distinctive fan-shaped leaves.

Conifers were abundant during the Cretaceous and began to decline in numbers while cycads and ginkgoes nearly became extinct. Angiosperms, the flowering plants, evolved during this period and rapidly expanded to dominate the Cenozoic Era. Angiosperms have complex reproductive organs which involve flowers and fruit. Transfer of pollen by insects and the wind and transport of seed by birds and mammals probably had much to do with the rapid expansion of the flowering plants. Angiosperms are divided into two groups: (1) dicotyledons which have two seed parts and wide multi-veined leaves and (2) monocotyledons which have one seed part and narrow parallel-veined leaves. Dicotyledons include deciduous trees, cacti, sagebrush, and most garden plants. Monocotyledons are such plants as grasses, palms, lilies, and orchids. The development and rapid spread of grasses during the Tertiary period was a factor in the explosive evolution of a wide variety of grazing mammals during that time.

Phylum Coelenterata. Coelenterates are almost exclusively marine animals with a very simple anatomy characterized by radial symmetry and a body which is basically a sack-shaped digestive cavity. They generally lack hard parts, but many, such as the corals, are able to secrete calcium carbonate to form a cup which the individual, a polyp, occupies. The three major types of fossil corals are: (1) Tabulate corals, such as *Halysites* (the "chain" coral) and *Favosites* (the "honeycomb" coral), are colonial organisms with tube-like arrangements which may be widely spaced or densely packed. They are found exclusively in Paleozoic rocks. (2) *Rugose* corals are horn corals which lived as both solitary and colonial types during the Paleozoic. They are characterized by the horn shape and radial partitions known as septa. (3) *Scleractinians* are modern corals and may be either colonial or solitary. These are found as fossils from the Triassic to recent time.

Phylum Bryozoa. Bryozoa are tiny aquatic animals which grow together to form colonies that commonly are about one inch in diameter. Fossil bryozoans may exhibit lacy or reticulated patterns such as *Fenestrellina* and other *fenestellids*, stem-like forms such as *Tubucellaria*, and screw-shaped colonies such as *Archimedes*. Many of these may be mistaken for corals by the beginning collector. Bryozoa are abundant in Paleozoic marine rocks from the Ordovician to recent time. *Archimedes* and *fenestellids* are common to Mississippian rocks of Utah such as the Great Blue Limestone.

Phylum Brachiopoda. Brachiopods are one of the major invertebrate animal groups and may be found as fossils in all but Precambrian rocks although many early orders died out at the end of the Paleozoic. These marine bivalves are distinguished by the different sizes of their valves and the bilateral symmetry of each. The smaller valve indicates the top of the animal. The bilateral symmetry, which means that each shell could be cut through the valves to give mirror images, distinguishes them from clams (pelecypods) whose bilateral symmetry derives from each valve being a mirror image of the other but each is unequally developed from left to right (Fig. 3-1). The majority of brachiopods have hinged calcareous shells and are said to be articulates. Some small brachiopods have chitinophosphatic shells and are unhinged. These are known as inarticulate brachiopods.

Phylum Mollusca. Molluscs are divided into three large classes: gastropods, bivalves (pelecypods), and cephalopods (Fig. 3-2). Gastropods (snails) include a wide variety of marine, freshwater, and terrestrial forms which are characterized by a broad flat foot and a shell that is generally coiled into a conical shape. Pelecypods (clams, oysters) are bivalves which, in most cases, have shells that are equal in size and are mirror images of each other. Cephalopods (nautiloids, ammonoids) generally have a shell in the shape of a flat spiral, but straight and slightly curved types are known as well. A particularly important group, the ammonoids, developed in the early Paleozoic and became very prominent during the Mesozoic. They became extinct at the end of that era. All three types of molluscs are found as fossils from the Cambrian to recent time. The Mancos Shale in Utah is particularly noted for its molluscan fauna including the oysters *Ostrea* and *Gryphaea*, ammonoids such as *Baculites* and *Scaphites*, and the clam *Inoceramus*.

Phylum Arthropoda. Arthropods are those animals which usually have a segmented body covered with a hardened exoskeleton. It is estimated that up to 75% of all known animals, vertebrate and invertebrate, belong to this phylum. Arthropods include the crustaceans (crabs, shrimp, and barnacles), scorpions, spiders, millipedes, centipedes, eurypterids, trilobites, and insects. Most of these have a relatively limited fossil record, but there are exceptions, such as the trilobites.

The eurypterids, extinct marine animals related to spiders and scorpions, are sometimes found as fossils. They are best known from the Silurian and Devonian when they were particularly abundant and became extinct during the Pennsylvanian. Some of these animals reached lengths of nearly 10 feet.

Trilobites are the most collectible of the arthropods and Utah is well known for the abundant trilobite fossils that occur in the Cambrian Wheeler Shale near Antelope Springs in Millard County.

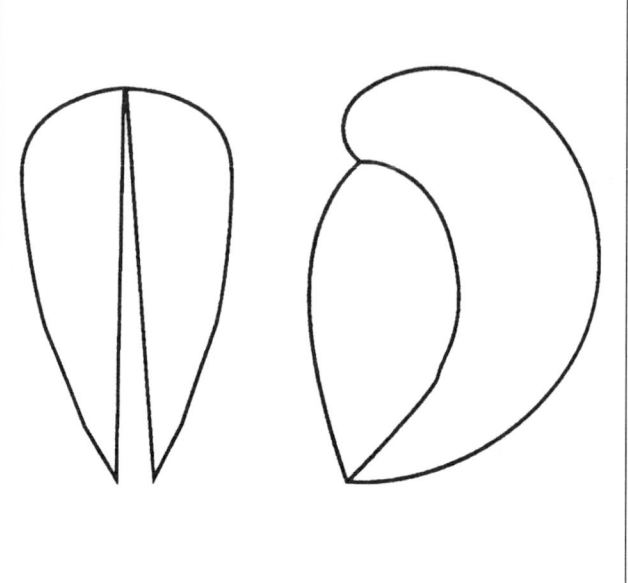

Figure 3-1 Profile of Bivalvia (Pelecypoda) (left) showing valves are mirror images, whereas Brachiopoda (right) have valves of different sizes.

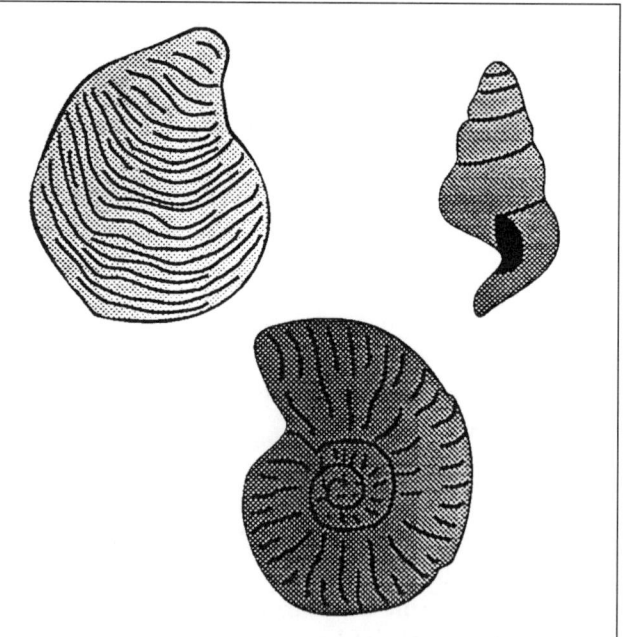

Figure 3-2 The three most common classes of Mollusca, clockwise from top left, Bivalvia (Pelecypoda), Gastropoda, and Cephalopoda.

Trilobites existed throughout the Paleozoic Era but were most abundant in the Cambrian and Ordovician Periods, gradually declining in numbers thereafter. The name refers to the threefold, longitudinal, division of the body into a central axial lobe and two pleural lobes (Fig. 3-3). There is also a threefold division of the body into (1) the cephalon or head region, (2) thorax or stomach area, and (3) the pygidium or tail section. Adult trilobites ranged in size from 0.25 inch (*Agnostus*) up to 30 inches (*Isotelus*) (Moore, et al., 1952, p. 478). Most trilobites are assumed to have been bottom-dwelling organisms and many may have been scavengers. A few trilobites may have been planktonic (based on their elaborate spines) and may have been filter feeders.

Phylum Echinodermata. The echinoderms are a group of exclusively marine animals which have five-fold symmetry. This phylum includes the crinoids, starfish, sea urchins, and sea cucumbers, all of which survive in modern oceans, as well as a number of extinct classes. Most of the echinoderms that survive today are bottom dwellers and it seems likely that most of the fossil forms had a similar lifestyle. Stemmed forms such as crinoids, cystoids, and blastoids were widespread during the Paleozoic Era and, much like modern echinoderms, appear to have lived in large groups or colonies, therefore, fossils of these animals are quite abundant in some rocks. In many of these animals the individual plates or spines were loosely held together by soft tissue so that the parts often become separated and scattered during burial and fossilization. From a mineralogical standpoint, it is interesting to note that each plate, spine, or other hard part of these animals is a single crystal of calcite rather than an aggregate of small grains as seen in other phyla

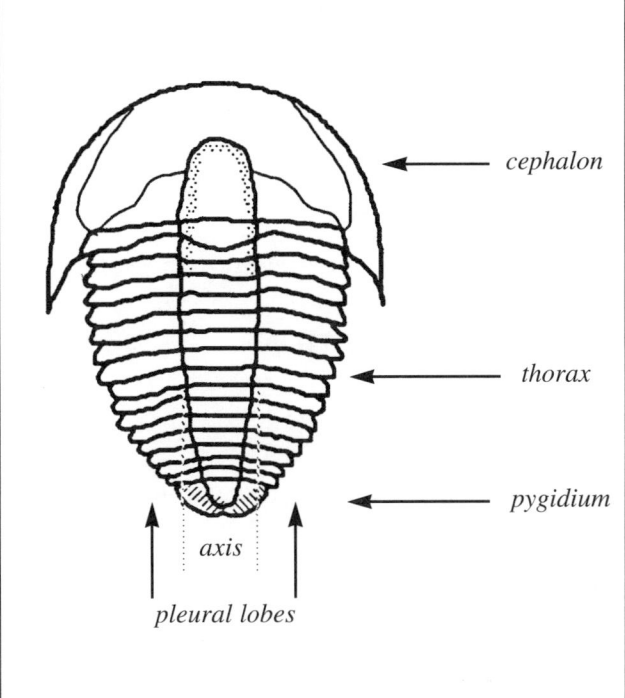

Figure 3-3 Main divisions of the trilobite exoskeleton. The name trilobite is derived from the three longitudinal divisions, the axis and pleural lobes. Disarticulated cephalons, thorax segments, and pygidiums are found quite commonly in rocks.

Phylum Hemichordata. This phylum includes the graptolites, a floating colonial organism, that is most often preserved as films of carbon flattened on a rock surface. The carbon films form dendritic or sawtoothed patterns and are most commonly found in black shales of the Ordovician and Silurian Periods. Because their floating lifestyle allowed them to become widespread in the world's oceans in a relatively short span of geologic time, they are important index fossils for rocks of this age.

Phylum Chordata. This phylum contains those animals with a backbone and a highly developed central nervous system and includes the animals with which most people are familiar such as fish, amphibians, reptiles, birds, and mammals. In the fossil record, there are numerous occurrences of vertebrate fossils, from fish to dinosaurs to Ice Age mammals. The collection of vertebrate fossils is legally restricted because of their relative scarcity and importance to paleontologists in reconstructing the evolution of life. For that reason, there are no mammal or dinosaur fossil locations mentioned in this book. Readers interested in learning more about the vertebrates, their evolution, and fossil record are directed to the section in this book on museums and also should consult the suggested readings.

CHAPTER 4
COLLECTIONS

PERSONAL COLLECTIONS

Collections with a Theme

As each person begins collecting, there is a tendency to collect anything and everything that looks interesting. This usually results in huge amounts of oddly shaped and colored rocks, mineral specimens collected because of a show of color or shiny surface, or fragments of fossil shell; all accumulating dust in boxes in the garage. This initial period of fascination with everything seems inevitable, but it often leads to frustration and dissatisfaction. Many people lose interest at this point and move on to other interests, but those who stay with the hobby must develop specific interests and direction to govern their collecting.

Minerals may be collected with several themes in mind. Many collectors specialize in a certain size specimen. Generally, the common size terms as used by collectors are (from smallest to largest): micromount, thumbnail, miniature, small cabinet, and large cabinet specimen. Micromounts as the name implies are specimens of very small size that are best seen using a microscope. Reasons for collecting micromounts are (1) the cost of obtaining specimens is greatly reduced as micromount material can be readily self-collected or traded and (2) many minerals occur as exquisite, perfect crystals of microscopic size whereas they may seldom occur in large crystals. The cost of a microscope is an initial expense, but you can begin with just a hand magnifier and can often make arrangements to use microscopes available at schools or at club meetings.

Thumbnail specimens are very popular with many collectors. These specimens fit into a small, cube-shaped, plastic box that measures 1⅜ inches on a side, therefore the typical specimen will be somewhat less than 1 inch in greatest dimension. Again, cost and perfection of specimen are governing factors, plus these are minerals that are large enough to be studied with the unaided eye, although use of a magnifier or microscope reveals even more interesting details.

Miniatures are approximately 2-3 inches, small cabinet specimens are approximately 4-5 inches, and specimens of larger dimensions are considered cabinet specimens. Collections of specimens of these sizes require special cabinets and display shelves, which, when added to the cost of the specimens themselves, represents a substantial investment. One may insist upon having nothing but self-collected material in a collection (which is another basis for a collection), but it is difficult to collect moderate- to large-size mineral specimens of high quality. Most collectors will eventually purchase or trade for material to upgrade their collection.

Many collectors combine size with other criteria to limit their collection. Possibilities are (1) geologic occurrence, such as skarn minerals, porphyry copper minerals, or metamorphic minerals; (2) geographic occurrence, such as collecting only Utah minerals, or Arizona minerals, or western states; (3) chemistry, such as collecting only sulfides, or oxides, or silicates, etc.; (4) a single species, such as calcite or quartz, minerals that occur in many different forms and varieties in many different locations; (5) crystals, although all minerals can potentially occur as crystals, good crystals of many minerals are rare; (6) unusual habits or crystal forms, such as twinning.

Collections   35

A rock collector could make a collection of all the different types of rocks (much more feasible than attempting to collect all minerals). Individual examples of the common igneous, metamorphic, and sedimentary rocks can be collected in a casual afternoon at Alta, along the Wasatch Front in Davis or Weber Counties, or elsewhere in the state. There are several hundred varieties of rock, many of which can be found in Utah. A collection of this type is relatively inexpensive and an attractive display can be arranged. Some rock specimens may display better after having been cut and polished, but many collectors may prefer to leave them in their natural state.

A fossil collector might build a collection by concentrating on a particular phylum or an important class within that phylum. For example, a collector could specialize in Mollusca or in the class Bivalvia. Here in Utah, because of the famous trilobite locality near Antelope Springs, there are many collectors who are interested in trilobites. One might also choose to limit a collection to a particular geologic era or period.

Sources of Information

Whether you collect minerals, rocks, or fossils, it is important that you have some understanding of the material so that you can properly prepare, evaluate, and curate your specimens. This guidebook is a simple introduction to the subject and from here you can go on to numerous other books, some of which are referenced in the text and others that are discussed in the annotated bibliography in Chapter 5. You should have some type of field guide to rocks and minerals and/or a field guide to fossils to help you with identification. Many versions of these are available and can be found at any bookstore in the science or nature section. As you become more experienced you will probably want to acquire a college-level textbook in mineralogy, petrology (rocks), and paleontology (fossils). These can be purchased at campus bookstores throughout the state and older editions can be obtained at reduced prices from used book dealers.

You may find that these textbooks are difficult to understand when reading them on your own so you might consider taking a class through a community college program or by enrolling in a class at your local college or university. Senior citizens, in particular, may find discounts available to reduce tuition. Most colleges and universities have a general education rocks and minerals course, often without any prerequisites, that would be suitable for anyone who has a serious interest in rocks and minerals. Likewise, there may be a course in fossils available at an introductory level. In addition, there are the professional-level courses taken by geology majors which usually have prerequisites such as chemistry for the mineralogy/petrology courses and zoology for the paleontology course. These should be undertaken only by the most dedicated collectors, but they will give you the best possible preparation.

Another means of learning more about rocks, minerals, and fossils is to visit some of the museums in the state that have collections of interest. There are a number of public and a few private museums that have significant collections that allow you to see some of the material that has been collected in Utah. A list and brief comment about the various museums in Utah appears at the end of this chapter.

Field Collecting

When you go on a collecting trip you should be properly equipped to collect material and transport it safely home. In general, you should have a rock hammer with either a pick or blade on one end. For fossil collecting in sedimentary rocks, the blade is preferred as it may be used to split rocks along bedding planes. The pick end is useful in harder igneous or metamorphic rocks where it can be used to pry at cracks. You may choose to carry a small maul instead of a rock hammer. The greater weight is useful in breaking larger rocks. In some cases, a sledgehammer may be best if you plan on breaking very large or tough rocks. Several chisels of different sizes are useful for prying and cracking rock. A very useful tool is a small mattock or hoe-pick that can be used for rapid excavation of soil or sediment, digging through mine dumps, and prying at rocks. It also makes a handy walking stick while hiking to the collecting location. For some collecting, such as the topaz in the Thomas Range, a steel pry bar about 5 feet long is extremely useful for levering large slabs of rock from their resting place. This tool is heavy to carry and should only be taken when you have prior knowledge of the type of rock you will be working. Sometimes a sieve or screen is useful for collecting small loose crystals from excavated material or from sediment in a stream bed. This is a common tool when looking for loose topaz or red beryl in the Thomas Range. Other, more specialized equipment, might be a gold pan for panning for gold or other heavy mineral grains in sediment, or a battery powered ultraviolet light (black light) when searching for fluorescent minerals at night. Eye protection should be worn at all times when working with rock.

You need various packs and collecting bags to carry your equipment and the specimens that you hope to collect. You will almost certainly need a bottle of water and some food items as well as a small first aid kit and sun protection. Strong durable hiking boots are an essential requirement if you plan to be scrambling around on old mine dumps or rough terrain. Tennis shoes do not offer ankle protection, quickly fill with uncomfortable rock fragments, and usually suffer serious damage from the sharp rocks. If you are working along a cliff face or quarry wall, particularly if there are others in the immediate area, you should be wearing a hard hat. A fist-sized rock that falls on your head can easily fracture your skull. Your hard hat should have a chin strap to make sure it remains on your head if you fall. A hard hat that comes off when you fall is of no use to you while your head bounces off rocks as you tumble down the slope.

Care should be exercised in extracting specimens from the rock as a bruised or fractured crystal is greatly diminished in value and esthetic appeal. Generally speaking, you should try and remove groups of crystals on matrix if at all possible. These will provide the more attractive specimens and if they need trimming to a smaller size, this can be done at home in a more careful manner than you can do in the field. The same idea applies to fossils. Remove the specimen with sufficient matrix material so that it can be properly exposed and displayed. The matrix helps protect the mineral or fossil from damage during transport. Once extracted, the specimen should be carefully wrapped in tissue, paper towels, or newspaper. Small boxes of different shapes and sizes are useful in that one or more specimens can be packed in them after wrapping for additional protection. Extremely fragile specimens, such as the pseudobrookite needles from the Thomas Range, may require special precautions. Egg cartons, foam rubber, and even embedding specimens in shaving cream may be useful. Experience will dictate what is necessary or works best for you. If this seems to be a lot of trouble, most experienced collectors would reply that if the specimen is not worth wrapping then it's probably not worth collecting in the first place.

Cleaning Specimens

Cleaning procedures will vary depending upon the nature of the specimen, its fragility, and its susceptibility to various chemicals. Simple methods should be attempted before resorting to more drastic measures. It also should be remembered that some specimens may have more esthetic appeal in their more natural, unscrubbed state. A specimen which shows obvious signs of having been cleaned, particularly with acids, will be diminished in value. Water and an old soft toothbrush are often all that is necessary to clean clay and dirt off the surfaces of a mineral. A little detergent may be helpful, but gentle scrubbing is most important. Specimens can be left to soak in a bucket for several days to loosen thick coatings of clay or weathered rock. An ultrasonic cleaner may be helpful if there is one available but this may damage fragile specimens so you should test other specimens before you endanger your prize crystal. Dental picks are invaluable tools for removing particles of dirt from small openings around a crystal or for carefully exposing a fossil. These tools may be found as a set in hobby and craft shops or from dealers in lapidary equipment at their shops or tables in rock and mineral shows.

Acids are commonly used to clean minerals, but these should be used with considerable caution. Hydrochloric acid is commonly used to dissolve carbonate minerals such as calcite from non-reactive minerals such as quartz, but you should be cautious since many minerals may be etched and lose their luster from acid attack. Oxalic acid can be used to remove iron stains from quartz. Specimens can be set to soak overnight in the acid, but faster results can be obtained by heating the solution on a hot plate. Be careful not to boil and splash the acid. Specimens treated in acids should be neutralized by rinsing them in water and then placing them in an alkaline solution such as sodium bicarbonate for a few hours. This will prevent redeposition of the iron on the specimen. Hydrofluoric acid is used to remove quartz or silica from specimens that are impervious to acid, such as fluorite, but this is an extremely dangerous acid and should not be used except under strictly controlled conditions with a fume hood and splash guard.

Curating Specimens

Once a specimen has been collected, trimmed, and cleaned so that it is ready to become part of your collection, it should be carefully labeled. Your label should minimally specify the name of the mineral, rock, or fossil, and the specific location where it was collected. Most labels also include the chemical formula (for minerals), the date collected or purchased, or the formation name for fossils.

While having the correct name is important, the most critical piece of information on the label is the location. A specimen without a location is so diminished in value as to be virtually worthless. Very general locations are almost as bad because for common specimens there is no way to pinpoint a location. As an example, a specimen labeled as "Pyrite, Utah" is inadequately described. A more accurate and useful location label would be "Pyrite, Four Metals Mine Dump, North end of the Dugway Range, Tooele County, Utah". At the very least a county should be specified for anything collected in the United States. Material that is purchased at shows or in dealer shops is sometimes poorly labeled and the dealer may or may not know more about it. You should always ask the dealer, if you feel the location is not specific. Material from some locations is so distinctive that knowledgeable collectors can identify it as being from a specific locale just by examining the specimen. You will often see comments to this effect on specimens entered for judging at mineral shows. Figure 4-1 illustrates a typical card that might be used in a mineral collection.

PUBLIC COLLECTIONS

Museums and Exhibits

One method for collectors to learn more about the material they have collected or wish to collect is to visit a museum or other facility where rock, mineral, or fossil material is on display. Below is a list of some of the museums and exhibits with material of interest to collectors:

- Utah Museum of Natural History, University of Utah, Salt Lake City
- Earth Science Museum, Brigham Young University, Provo
- Natural Science Museum, Lind Lecture Hall, Weber State University, Ogden
- Science Museum, Southern Utah University, Cedar City
- Prehistoric Museum, College of Eastern Utah, Price
- Hutchings Museum, Lehi
- Natural Science Museum, Union Station, Ogden
- Utah Field House of Natural History State Park & Dinosaur Gardens, Vernal
- Cleveland-Lloyd Dinosaur Quarry, east of Cleveland

In most cases you will find members of the museum staff or volunteers who work in the museum available to help answer your questions with regard to the material on exhibit. Many will be glad to take time to assist you with identification of material that you have collected.

Collecting material from National Park Service land is prohibited, but visitor centers in the parks are sources of information and the more geologic oriented parks will often have a naturalist with formal geology training who may be able to assist you. The following National Parks and Monuments have exhibits in their visitor centers that explain some of the local geology:

```
NAME _____
FORMULA _____
LOCATION _____
DATE COLLECTED _____
         FROM THE COLLECTION OF
             JOHN & MARY DOE
```

Figure 4-1 *A typical card for use with a mineral specimen that has been added to your collection. Card for rocks and fossils would be similar.*

- Arches National Park
- Bryce Canyon National Park
- Capitol Reef National Park
- Dinosaur National Monument
- Great Basin National Park
- Natural Bridges National Monument
- Timpanogas Cave National Monument
- Zion Canyon National Park

Small exhibits of rock, mineral, and fossil material can be seen at the U. S. Geological Survey map sales office (2222 West 2300 South, Salt Lake City), and the Utah Geological Survey office (2363 South Foothill Drive, Salt Lake City). Geology departments at the state's colleges and universities often have exhibits in the halls and lobby of the building in which they are located. Additionally, many of Utah's towns with a history of mining in their past have established museums which emphasize the history of mining activity in the area.

CHAPTER 5
SUGGESTIONS FOR FURTHER READING

INTRODUCTION

As you become more involved with collecting natural materials such as rocks, minerals, and fossils, you will find that you need more information in order to properly label your specimens or in order to determine locations to search for new material. This chapter is an attempt to give you some guidance as to the range of publications available and their usefulness to the collector.

PUBLICATIONS

Periodicals

Periodicals fall into three categories: (1) those designed for lapidarists whose primary interests are in cutting, polishing, and faceting material, (2) those intended for collectors whose major interest is in learning about collecting sites and material that has been collected there, and (3) professional journals which are primarily an outlet for mineralogists and paleontologists to publish their findings.

The first category includes publications such as *Lapidary Journal* and *Rock and Gem* which may often have some field trip reports given describing collecting sites. These publications are commonly available on newstands where a copy may be purchased and inspected to see if it is of interest to you. Public libraries may carry copies of either of these and back issues may quite often be purchased cheaply at local mineral shows.

The second category includes publications that every serious mineral collector should consider acquiring through subscription. *Rocks and Minerals* is a publication that reports on a wide variety of collecting activities in the United States with a slight bias toward eastern localities. It is the official publication of both the Eastern Federation of Mineralogical and Lapidary Societies and the Midwest Federation of Mineralogical and Geological Societies. It is published bi-monthly by Heldref Publications, 4000 Albemarle St., N.W., Washington, D. C. 20016. It is available by subscription and larger newstands carry individual copies. Typical articles describe a well-known collecting site and recount the history and specimens produced there. Some issues feature a specific state and contain a series of articles about the minerals, fossils, rocks, and overall geology of that state.

Also within this category is the *Mineralogical Record*, a high quality, glossy magazine which has established a reputation for beautiful color pictures of minerals. This magazine is specifically mineral oriented and describes worldwide localities, although there is an emphasis on the western United States. The *Mineralogical Record* caters to both a professional audience as well as the collector; as a result, the articles are generally more technical and are often cited in professional journals. The photographs alone are sufficient reason for any serious mineral collector to subscribe. It is published by the Mineralogical Record Inc., P. O. Box 35565, Tucson, AZ 85715 and it is not available on newstands.

The Mineral News, a small newsletter with information about collecting localities and other happenings in the world of rock, mineral, and fossil collecting is published by Lanny Ream, P.O. Box 2043, Coeur d'Alene, ID 83816-2043.

The third category, professional publications, is of benefit to collectors primarily as a resource to be used when researching a particular topic, whether as a presentation to fellow club members, preparation of a newsletter article, or endeavoring to learn about new collecting localities and the minerals that occur there. The *American Mineralogist* is published by the Mineralogical Society of America and is available in all university libraries. Since the 1960s the articles have been extremely technical, often involving thermodynamics and detail of mineral structures, and therefore of little interest to the average collector. Early issues of this publication, particularly the 1930s through the 1950s, were filled with descriptions of new minerals and locations that had been recently discovered. Much has changed in the interim, but these descriptions often make useful reading.

The *Canadian Mineralogist* is a similar publication, but generally has more readable articles, even in recent issues. Its focus is primarily on Canada, but mineral occurrences are treated on a worldwide basis. It can be found at larger university libraries.

Brigham Young University *Geology Studies* is a serial publication that serves as an outlet for the results of faculty and student research. BYU has emphasized field mapping for many years and much of the material found in these volumes is a result of field work in Utah. This series can be consulted in university libraries and back issues, if still in print, can be purchased through the Department of Geology at BYU.

Publications of General Interest

An understanding of geology is essential to make the most use of the information presented in this book and to give you a better appreciation for the material that you collect. College-level textbooks on physical geology and Earth history are readily available at campus bookstores or older editions can be found at bargain prices at used book dealers. Another useful item is a geological dictionary. The most complete dictionary is the one published by the American Geological Institute, but a number of inexpensive paperback dictionaries are available; again, a campus bookstore is your best source.

Glossary of Geology, 3rd Ed., Robert L. Bates and Julia A. Jackson, eds. (1987) American Geological Institute, Falls Church, VA. 788 p.

This is the best available dictionary for geologists, but is relatively expensive. An abridged paperback version has been published.

Once you have done some introductory reading or if you have had a course in geology at some time, you may wish to acquire a book more specific to the geology of Utah. There are several of these books which are listed below.

Geologic History of Utah, Lehi F. Hintze (1988) Brigham Young University Geology Studies, Special Publication 7, Brigham Young University, Provo, UT 84602. 202 p.

Dr. Hintze has been responsible for much of the geologic mapping of western Utah and his work is cited many times in the location section of this guide. His book requires a basic knowledge of geology and is designed for the student or geology professional. It is extremely useful for the many stratigraphic sections he presents.

Geology of Utah, William Lee Stokes (1986) Utah Museum of Natural History and Utah Geological and Mineralogical Survey, Salt Lake City, UT. 280 p.

Dr. Stokes' book presents a typical Earth history textbook approach, but applied directly to Utah. It is written in an easily understood style (assuming you know something of geology) and has good pictures of features and excellent drawings of fossils found in Utah. Highly recommended.

Roadside Geology of Utah, Halka Chronic (1990) Mountain Press Publishing Co., Missoula, MT, 335 p. ($12.95)

One of a series of books covering the various states, it presents information on the geology that can be observed along the major highways of the state. It is useful as a book to have in the car so that travelers can appreciate features that may or may not be apparent to them as they pass, but the geology is relatively superficial and has been criticized as inaccurate in some reviews.

Field Guide Northern Colorado Plateau, J. Keith Rigby (1976) Kendall/Hunt Publishing Co., Dubuque, Iowa. 207 p.

One of a series of field guides published by Kendall/Hunt, this particular volume covers that part of the Colorado Plateau that falls in Utah. The book is a road guide for this particular geographic area with less explanation of the overall processes of geology than the previous book, but much more detail. Very worthwhile for southern Utah.

Mineralogy

Mineralogy books fall into several categories. First, and most important to a collector, are the various identification guides, which can take the form of small handbooks or college textbooks. You may want to consider such factors as price, pictures, amount of information about individual minerals, additional information presented, and sturdiness when you select a book for use as an identification guide. As mentioned before, a used college textbook can provide a lot of information at a low price. Even older editions from the 1940s and 1950s are still useful as very little information on minerals and crystals will have changed. Some of the older books are much easier to read than recent books which emphasize crystal structure and chemistry in contrast to field identification.

Additionally, there are a number of more detailed reference books on minerals that become more important as a collector either specializes in certain minerals or becomes more serious about trying to identify material that has been collected. Many of these are mentioned below.

Glossary of Mineral Species 1995, Michael Fleischer and Joseph A. Mandarino (1995) The Mineralogical Record Inc., P. O. Box 35565, Tucson, AZ 85740. 288 p. ($18).

This small paperback is a compilation of the names and chemical formulas of all known minerals and is thus an extremely important checklist and reference volume for collectors. For the lesser known minerals, a citation to the scientific literature (usually the *American Mineralogist*) is given so that more information can be obtained. This book should be owned by all mineral collectors.

Dana's Manual of Mineralogy, 18th Edition, Cornelius S. Hurlbut, Jr. (1971) John Wiley & Sons, Inc., New York. 579 p.

This is not the latest edition of this classic textbook, but any of the many recent editions is an excellent choice for a basic mineralogy reference book. Very early editions of this book are considered to be collectors items and command high prices. Slightly over half the book is mineral descriptions and identification keys. The remainder is a discussion of crystallography, optical mineralogy, and other topics.

A Textbook of Mineralogy, 4th Edition, William E. Ford (1932) John Wiley & Sons, Inc., New York. 851 p.

On the spine and in common practice this book is referred to as *Dana's Textbook of Mineralogy*. Some of the nomenclature in this book is greatly outdated, but it remains as an invaluable source of information on many of the less common minerals that are not mentioned in standard mineralogy books or reference guides. In spite of the early copyright date, it is still in print and can be found in the geology section of specialized bookstores. It can often be found in the used book section as well.

The System of Mineralogy, 7th Edition, Charles Palache, Harry Berman, and Clifford Frondel (1944, 1951) John Wiley & Sons, Inc., New York. 834p. 1124 p. (approximately $53.00 each for volumes I and II)

This three volume set is the culmination of the series of works by James D. Dana and Edward S. Dana. Volume I covers the elements, sulfides, sulfosalts, and oxides; volume II details the other minerals (except silicates). Volume III is a small volume that only discusses the forms of silica. Silicates are not treated in any of the volumes. This is an extremely good source of information on the non-silicate minerals, although some information is not up to date. This multi-volume series remains in print and can be purchased through any bookstore.

Rock Forming Minerals, 2nd Edition, Deer, Howie, and Zussman (1982) Longman-Wiley, New York.

This is a multi-volume work, periodically updated and revised, that deals exclusively with those minerals which make up the rocks of the Earth. For the most part, these are the silicate minerals, but one volume is devoted to rock-forming non-silicates. This is a highly technical and very complete, but expensive, source of information on these minerals. It can be consulted at university libraries. An abridged paperback version is available, also (see below).

An Introduction to the Rock-Forming Minerals, 2nd Edition, W. A. Deer, R. A. Howie, and J. Zussman (1992) Longman-Wiley, New York, 696 p. This is a paperback summary of the multi-volume set described above.

Encyclopedia of Minerals, 2nd Edition, Willard L. Roberts, Thomas J. Campbell, and George R. Rapp, Jr. (1990) Van Nostrand Reinhold Co., New York. 979 p. ($99.95)

An expensive book, but well worth the price for the extraordinary amount of information on approximately 3200 different mineral species. It is illustrated with 240 color photographs and 104 black and white photographs as well as 45 crystal drawings of rare species. This book gives crystal information, physical properties, mode of occurrence, and a reference for each of the entries. This book is a tremendous value for the serious mineral collector.

Handbook of Mineralogy, John W. Anthony, Richard A. Bideaux, Kenneth W. Bladh, and Monte C. Nichols (1990) Mineral Data Publishing, P.O. Box 37072, Tucson, AZ. 588 p. ($82.50).

Volume 1, all that is published thus far, is a compilation of data on elements, sulfides, and sulfosalts. Future volumes will cover the remaining mineral groups. This promises to be an important source of data for many of the less common minerals. It will be extremely useful as a reference set although the eventual total price of the full set may be more than individuals care to pay. It will be available in university libraries.

The Eyewitness Handbook of Rocks and Minerals, Chris Pellant (1992) Dorling Kindersley, New York, 256 p. ($17.95 pb, $29.95 hb).

This is similar to several handbook type volumes published by various companies, but this book has some of the best photographs to be found in this type of book. Photographs are by Harry Taylor of the Natural History Museum (British Museum), London.

Suggestions for Further Reading

Paleontology

In general, specific identification of fossils is more difficult than the identification of minerals and, therefore, popular guidebooks cannot be as accurate or as helpful as mineral guides. Popular guides are useful as far as helping you understand basic principles of paleontology and as a key to recognition of the various phyla. Even with a textbook of invertebrate paleontology, it may be quite difficult to identify an unknown fossil down to the genus level.

Invertebrate Fossils, Raymond C. Moore, Cecil G. Lalicker, and Alfred G. Fischer (1952) McGraw-Hill Book Co., New York. 766 p.

One of the standard college textbooks in this field, the book has a large number of drawings of fossils that are useful in attempting to make an identfication.

Principles of Invertebrate Paleontology, 2nd Edition, Robert R. Shrock and William H. Twenhofel (1953) McGraw-Hill Book Co., New York. 816 p.

Another one of the standard textbooks paleontology students have used for many years. This book is not as well illustrated as the previous one, but is still quite useful.

Treatise on Invertebrate Paleontology, R. C. Moore, ed. (various dates) Geological Society of America and University of Kansas Press.

With over 30 volumes this immense reference set has a description and discussion of all known invertebrate fossils. Updated volumes are periodically released to keep the series current. This set may be consulted at university libraries.

Index Fossils of North America, H. W. Shimer and R. R. Shrock (1944) John Wiley & Sons, Inc., New York. 837 p.

This book provides a short description and illustration of each of the thousands of common, widespread fossils of North America. Some changes of name and classification have occurred since it was first published, but it is still an invaluable source of information.

Fossils for Amateurs, Russell P. MacFall and Jay C. Wollin (1983) Van Nostrand Reinhold Co., New York. 374 p.

This paperback is designed as a general reference for the amateur collector, providing basic information about phyla, an explanation of typical collecting sites for fossils, and useful information about the cleaning of fossils. A very good book for the person just getting started with fossil collecting.

Trilobites, A Photographic Atlas, Richard Levi-Setti (1975) University of Chicago Press, Chicago. 213 p.

This book features large-scale photographs of many trilobites, including a number of species from Utah and Nevada.

Atlas of Invertebrate Macrofossils, John W. Murray, ed. (1985) Halsted Press, John Wiley & Sons, Inc., in association with The Palaeontological Society. 241 p.

This book has excellent small black and white photographs of all invertebrate fossils. It is designed to facilitate identification of fossils to the generic level. The text, keyed to each photograph, is a technical description of the fossil.

Fossils of the World, V. Turek, J. Marek, and J. Benes (1988) Paul Hamlyn Publishing, London. 495 p. ($32.00)

This is a companion book to Minerals of the World and, like that volume, originates in Czechoslovakia. The book features large color photographs of many fossil species, including some from U.S. locations. It is a relatively inexpensive book considering the quality of the pictures.

Fossil and Mineral Publications Specifically About Utah

The following section describes some books and serials that pertain directly to Utah and fossil or mineral ocurrences here. Several books are listed which are part of the series of bulletins published by the Utah Geological Survey as are publications that are part of the Professional Paper and Bulletin series of the U. S. Geological Survey. Some of these are out of print and may be difficult to find except in libraries or through used book dealers. Many USGS publications that are technically out of print can still be purchased over-the-counter at the Salt Lake office of the USGS, 2222 West 2300 South, Salt Lake City.

Minerals and Mineral Localities of Utah, Kenneth C. Bullock (1981) Utah Geological and Mineral Survey, Bulletin 117, Salt Lake City, UT. 177 p.

This is a listing by county, and within the county, by mining district, of all the known minerals to occur in Utah. As such, it is a useful guide to collectors who are visiting an old mining district by giving them some idea of what minerals have been found there in the past. It should be kept in mind, when using this book, that most of these mineral ocurrences were noted during active mining periods when fresh rock was available for study, and many of the minerals were determined by microscopic techniques, thus no collectable specimens were ever known. Many of the lists of minerals in this book come from old USGS publications, but since direct citations are not given, it is impossible to determine the source of the information in any specific case. This book should be used in connection with Fleischer's Glossary of Mineral Species since many of the names given in Bullock's book are discredited. There are also a large number of typos in the mineral names which can be misleading.

Fluorite Occurrences in Utah, Kenneth C. Bullock (1976) Utah Geological and Mineral Survey, Bulletin 110, Salt Lake City, UT. 87 p.

A useful listing of known fluorite occurrences that allows the collector to evaluate the type of material likely to be collected at any of the sites listed.

Geology and Mineral Resources of Box Elder County, Utah, Hellmut H. Doelling (1980) Utah Geological and Mineral Survey, Bulletin 115, Salt Lake City, UT. 251 p.

This is the best of a series of county publications that have been produced by the state. It serves as a detailed guide to the numerous abandoned mines of Box Elder County. Information can be found in many of the older county guides, but they are generally not nearly as complete or as useful as this one.

Geology, Ore Deposits, and History of the Big Cottonwood Mining District, Salt Lake County, Utah, Laurence P. James (1979) Utah Geological and Mineral Survey, Bulletin 114, Salt Lake City, UT. 98 p.

This is an interesting account of the history of mining in this popular hiking and ski area near Salt Lake City. Dumps of some of the mines in the canyon are still of interest to the collector as are some of the calc-silicate rocks associated with the igneous rocks. The collector can develop a number of possible locations for examination by studying this volume.

Gem Trails of Utah, Revised Edition, James R. Mitchell (1987) Gem Guides Book Co., Pico Rivera, CA. 111 p.

Suggestions for Further Reading

This book is available in most rock shops and book stores and gives relatively detailed directions and maps to 71 locations in Utah. About half of these locations are for agate and petrified wood, so the book is of limited usefulness to the mineral or fossil collector.

A Field Guide to Topaz and Associated Minerals of Topaz Mountain, Utah, John Holfert (1977) Privately published. 49 p.

An excellent small guidebook to this important Utah collecting area. It is difficult to find copies of this book, but a new edition is being prepared. Check with rock and mineral shops and club members.

Common Fossil Plants of Western North America, William D. Tidwell (1975) Brigham Young University Press, Provo, UT. 197 p.

An extremely useful and important book for collectors of plant fossils. Profusely illustrated with the amateur collector in mind, it is an essential book for Utah collectors.

Paleontology of the Green River Formation, with a Review of the Fish Fauna, Lance Grande (1984) Bulletin 63, The Geological Survey of Wyoming, Laramie, WY. 333 p. ($17.50)

This book describes the fossils of the Green River Formation in Wyoming, Utah, and Colorado. It is well illustrated with photographs and the text, although technical, is written such that the interested amateur can read it. Anyone who has been fascinated by the fish fossils so common to southwestern Wyoming should purchase and read this book.

The following USGS Professional Papers are all of relatively ancient vintage, but are still useful reading for the ardent mineral collector. They are long out of print and are fairly expensive to purchase from used book dealers, but all can be found at university libraries. In addition to the Professional Papers, there are many Bulletins and other publications of the USGS that pertain to Utah. There are indexes available to assist you in searching this literature.

USGS Professional Paper 38:	*Economic Geology of the Bingham Mining District, Utah.*
USGS Professional Paper 77:	*Geology and Ore Deposits of the Park City District, Utah.*
USGS Professional Paper 80:	*Geology and Ore Deposits of the San Francisco and adjacent districts, Utah.*
USGS Professional Paper 107:	*Geology and Ore Deposits of the Tintic Mining District, Utah.*
USGS Professional Paper 111:	*Ore Deposits of Utah*
USGS Professional Paper 173:	*Geology and Ore Deposits of the Fairfield and Stockton Quadrangles, Utah.*
USGS Professional Paper 177:	*The Gold Hill Mining District, Utah.*
USGS Professional Paper 201:	*Geology and Ore Deposits of the Cottonwood-American Fork Area, Utah.*
USGS Professional Paper 415:	*Geology and Mineral Deposits of the Thomas and Dugway Ranges, Juab and Tooele Counties, Utah.*

Maps

Both topographic maps and geologic maps are referred to extensively in this guide and by learning how to read maps you will be able to get more out of this guide as well as do more on your own. Topographic maps are those that show elevations through the use of contour lines and thereby create a two dimensional "picture" of the three-dimensional land surface. The ability to see this "picture" is based on training and experience; quite simply, once you know the basic map symbols, then the more you use maps while hiking or camping, the more you will see on the maps and recognize in the landscape around you. At the very least, you can use the topographic maps as you would use a road map, since roads and trails are shown in great detail.

Most topographic maps belong to one of several standard series which are based on latitude and longitude. The most common series currently available is the 7.5 minute series (7.5 minutes of latitude by 7.5 minutes of longitude) which now is available for the entire state of Utah. These maps are periodically updated and re-issued in a revised edition. Many older maps are still available in the 15 minute series. A new series of maps that is currently being issued cover an area of 30 x 60 minutes with contour lines in meters. This metric series is particularly useful as a detailed road map in backcountry areas.

Geologic maps are usually published on a topographic base, with geologic information in colors or patterns as an overprint. It is not necessary to be a geologist to make effective use of a geologic map. All you need to be able to do is to identify a particular geologic unit as being of interest and then use the geologic map to determine where this unit is exposed and where the best access is. This is especially important for fossil collectors who often need to know this type of information. Geologic maps are published as 7.5 minute maps most often, but special maps are sometimes available showing larger areas such as a particular mountain range or even the entire state.

The principal source for topographic maps and geologic maps is the U. S. Geological Survey which sells these maps by mail or over the counter at selected locations. Topographic maps of all the western states and most published geologic maps are available from the USGS Earth Science Information Center (ESIC) (call 1-800-USA-MAPS for the center near you), or the ESIC unit at 2222 West 2300 South, Salt Lake City. A group of knowledgeable people are there to assist you in locating what you need.

Another source of topographic maps for Utah and other geologic information is the Utah Geological Survey located at 2363 South Foothill Drive, Salt Lake City, UT 84109-1491. Maps and other publications are available in the front office where staff will assist you or you can write for a publication list.

Topographic maps are available in many sporting goods stores and outdoor equipment stores, although the selection is usually limited to the immediate area and popular recreation areas.

A few specific maps are listed below:

Geologic Map of Utah, Lehi F. Hintze, compiler (1980) Utah Geological and Mineral Survey, Salt Lake City, UT.

A useful wall or office map that depicts the overall geology of the state. This map is helfpul in planning trips or consulting after a trip to identify some of the geologic units that were seen.

Utah Geological Highway Map, Lehi F. Hintze, compiler (1975) Brigham Young University Geology Studies - Special Publication 3, Department of Geology, Brigham Young University, Provo, UT.

This map, in a folding road map format, is designed to be kept in your car where it will be available for consultation as you drive through Utah.

Geologic Map of the Tooele 1° x 2° Quadrangle, Utah, William J. Moore and Martin L. Sorensen (1979) Miscellaneous Investigations Series I-1132, U. S. Geological Survey.

This is an example of an intermediate series of geologic maps being compiled by the USGS. This is a very useful scale as it covers a relatively large area in sufficient detail so that the geology can readily be seen and understood.

Picture Books

This category refers to books which are of interest primarily because of the photography of mineral and fossil specimens. In general, these books are not useful as guides or identification keys, but make interesting reading.

Gem and Crystal Treasures, Peter Bancroft (1984) Western Enterprises and the Mineralogical Record, Tucson, Arizona. 488 p.

The author has compiled a short account of each of 100 classic mineral localities from around the world. Each location has several photographs, many in color, and a description of the human and mining history of each area. Probably the best book of this category that has been recently published. The author is often a speaker at major mineral shows.

Minerals of the World, Rudolf Duda and Lubos Rejl (1986) Hamlyn Publishing Group, Twickenham, Middlesex, England. 520 p.

This book, originally published in Czeckoslovakia, is self-described as a mineral encyclopedia, but the coverage is not comparable to the *Encyclopedia of Minerals* described earlier. Instead, this book is best appreciated for the color pictures, one for each mineral, and a selection that reflects the eastern European origin of the book. Since it is difficult to obtain English language information about eastern European and Asian locations, this book is valuable for that reason.

Some Dreams Die, Utah's Ghost Towns and Lost Treasures, George A. Thompson (1982) Dream Garden Press, Salt Lake City, UT. 194 p.

Strictly speaking, this book is not about rocks and minerals, but since many of Utah's ghost towns are old mining towns, there is an element of interest here for most mineral collectors. Most of the stories of lost mines and buried treasure are best regarded as tall tales.

CHAPTER 6
A GUIDE TO COLLECTING SITES

COLLECTING IN UTAH

The Occurrence of Rocks, Minerals, and Fossils

Most of the remainder of this book is a guide to locations where you can collect rocks, minerals, and fossils. It is by no means complete and each reader may know of other sites that might well have been included had the writer been aware of them. However, many people, especially when beginning to collect, may be uncertain of how to locate areas of potential interest, other than those that appear in guidebooks.

Knowledge of rocks and where these rocks occur is paramount in attempting to find new collecting areas. This is true, whether you are interested in minerals, fossils, or unusual rock types. The principal method of locating a specific type of rock is to consult a geologic map. Geologic maps show different rock units by colors or patterns and often have a brief explanatory text describing the individual rock units. The colors or patterns are so distinctive that you can use the geologic map to locate types of rock even though you may not understand all of the geologic symbols that may appear on the map. If you are interested in locating Mississippian crinoids, then a quick look at the state geologic map will give you immediate information as to where you can find Mississippian-age rocks. If you are interested in prospecting for topaz in rhyolite, then the map can guide you to occurrences of rhyolite lava flows.

Usually you would want to start with the state geologic map, and then proceed to more detailed regional maps to pinpoint locations. Geologic maps published by the U. S. Geological Survey (USGS) can be consulted at the map libraries of the state's universities or can be purchased at the Earth Science Information Center of the USGS in Salt Lake City.

Having located a particular type of rock that is of interest, you could travel to that area and examine the outcrop. You should mentally compare the rock to other areas where you have collected to try and judge how likely it is to contain the specimens of interest to you. Don't be too quick to dismiss a location as nonproductive. Often an hour or more of examination may be necessary before you can make a definitive judgement as to the quality of specimens that can be obtained at a given locality.

Even within a known productive area, there will be variation in quality of specimens from one location to another. Closely examine the rock in locations that you know have produced good specimens. Search the area for similar outcrops, even if there is no immediate indication of collectible material.

Utah Mining Districts

One of the most obvious starting points for mineral collecting is to visit one of the many mining districts in Utah. Many of the mines in Utah's mining districts have been long abandoned and collecting is usually possible on the mine dumps. You should keep in mind that the dump was generally for the purpose of disposing of waste rock and therefore you shouldn't expect to find exquisite specimens of ore minerals on the dump. Sometimes, however, sub-economic material was dumped which may contain interesting minerals to the collector and often the gangue minerals such as quartz, calcite, or pyrite may be present in well-formed crystals. Digging in the dump may reveal material that is less weathered than that exposed at the surface.

Not all of Utah's mining districts are abandoned. Some areas, such as the Bingham copper mine in the Oquirrh Mountains, have been in continuous operation since they were discovered. Others, such as the Mercur area, were mined and abandoned and then resurrected by new technology and/or new discoveries. Visits to working mines are usually strictly controlled because of safety and liability concerns, as well as the problem the busy mine personnel have in coping with a large number of visitors. The Bingham Pit has a view area that can be visited and the Mercur gold mine has a visitor center open in the summer months. Collecting trips to working mines are almost impossible for individuals and only rarely can be arranged for non-professional organized groups.

If you do have the opportunity to visit a working mine or quarry, be sure to pay close attention to all information you are given. Make sure you clearly understand what you are allowed to do and where you are allowed to go. Immediately obey any instructions from the person in charge of the group, particularly when asked to move away from an area. Loose rock on high headwalls and large equipment are major hazards in working mines and quarries.

Minerals in Utah Mining Districts

Upon consulting the literature (see the Suggested Readings chapter), you may be impressed with the tremendous variety of minerals that are listed as occurring in a particular district. When you actually search the dumps in that district, you may return home grumbling about having found only a few scraps of pyrite or quartz. Lists of minerals from mining districts are very misleading in some respects. These minerals were almost always identified during the time in which the mine was operating and abundant fresh material was available. Many of the mineral species were microscopic and were found only in thin sections of rock or polished sections of ore, examined and tested under the microscope. In more recent times, development of X-ray diffraction to identify mineral phases and the electron microprobe to analyze the constituents of minerals, has allowed many new minerals, identified from microscopic grains, to be added to occurrence lists.

The best use of mineral lists is to let them be a guide to the possibilities of a given mining district. They are often interesting because of the large variety of rare species that are sometimes found. This can lead to interesting research in some of the books listed in the Suggested Readings list as you attempt to learn more about these minerals. As examples, a few lists from some of the better known Utah mining districts are presented below. These are modified, based on personal knowledge and communications from mineral collectors, from the data presented in Bullock (1981).

The Bingham District

The major metal products of the Bingham District have been copper, molybdenum, gold, lead, and zinc. The deposit is an example of what are generally known as porphyry copper deposits, although molybdenite is quite common in this category of ore bodies. The term porphyry comes from the association with a granitic porphyritic igneous intrusion. At Bingham and many other similar deposits, the ore is zoned with molybdenite richest in the center of the intrusion, copper (as chalcopyrite and bornite) forming a broad zone throughout the intrusion, and a peripheral zone of lead-zinc mineralization. Bingham is remarkable for the wide variety of minerals that have been identified in its ores including the native elements gold, copper, bismuth, mercury, selenium, tellurium, platinum, and palladium, as well as a number of relatively rare phosphates. A new visitor center allows the public to view the mining operations but visits into the pit are generally restricted to professional groups of engineers and geologists because of the limited personnel available and danger from the steep highwalls.

Minerals of the Bingham Mining District

actinolite	faustite	platinum
allophane	foshagite	pyargyrite
anglesite	freibergite	pyrite
apophyllite	galena	pyrolusite
argentite	garnet	pyrrhotite
arsenopyrite	gold	quartz
azurite	goslarite	realgar
barite	gyrolite	rhodochrosite
bismuth	hematite	rutile
bismutite	illite	selenium
bornite	kaolinite	seligmannite
bournonite	limonite	sericite
calaverite	linarite	siderite
calcite	magnetite	siderotil
cerargyrite	malachite	silver
cerussite	mallardite	sphalerite
chalcanthite	marcasite	stilbite
chalcocite	massicot	talc
chalcopyrite	melanterite	tellurium
chlorite	mercury	tennantite
copper	molybdenite	tenorite
covellite	montmorillonite	tetrahedrite
cubanite	nontronite	thaumasite
cuprite	okenite	thomsonite
digenite	opal	torbermorite
dufrenoysite	orpiment	turquoise
enargite	palladium	vivianite
fluoroapatite		wavellite

A Guide to Collecting Sites

The Gold Hill District

Gold was the principal metal recovered in the early days of mining here, hence the name Gold Hill for this area. Since that time lead, silver, copper, tungsten, arsenic, and bismuth have been mined. During the 1940s large amounts of arsenic were produced from arsenopyrite and arsenates in the deposits. In more recent times, tungsten has been mined in small amounts, beryllium-bearing veins have been investigated, and gold is receiving renewed attention. Much of this area is open to collectors, although fluctuations in metal prices and economic conditions can bring quick changes to a district. The variety of metals and the oxidation of the deposits to produce a wide variety of arsenates have made this a popular area for collectors.

Minerals of the Gold Hill Mining District

adamite	chalcocite	hematite	rutile
adularia	chalcopyrite	hemimorphite	scapolite
aikinite	chenevixite	huebernite	scheelite
albite	chlorite	humite	scorodite
allanite	chrysocolla	ilmenite	sepiolite
anatase	clinoclase	jamesonite	siderite
andalusite	clinozoisite	jarosite	siderotil
anorthoclase	cobaltite	kaolinite	smithsonite
apatite	conichalcite	leucoxene	spadaite
arsenopyrite	cornwallite	limonite	sphalerite
arsenosiderite	covellite	magnetite	spinel
austinite	cuprite	malachite	stibnite
axinite	cuproadamite	mimetite	stolzite
azurite	cuprotungstite	molybdenite	talc
barite	danburite	monimolite	talmessite
beidellite	descloizite	muscovite	tennantite
bertrandite	diopside	natrojarosite	tetrahedrite
beudantite	dolomite	nontronite	titanite
biotite	enstatite	oligoclase	tourmaline
bismite	epidote	olivenite	tremolite
bismuth	ferberite	orthoclase	tyrolite
bismuthinite	ferrimolybdite	parisite	vesuvianite
bornite	ferrisymplesite	pharmacosiderite	wolframite
boulangerite	fluorite	plumbojarosite	wollastonite
calaverite	galena	powellite	wulfenite
calcite	garnet	pyrite	zircon
carminite	gold	pyromorphite	zoisite
cerussite	graphite	pyrrhotite	
chalcanthite	gypsum	quartz	

The Park City District

The Park City District has been mined since its discovery in 1869, with near surface bonanza deposits of high grade silver ore lending impetus to its early development. The mines of Park City are justly famous for producing some of the finest specimens of pyrite and tetrahedrite known to occur in the United States. Well-crystallized specimens of some of the more rare minerals, such as geocronite and bournonite have also been produced. Although no mining activity is occurring presently, most of the old mines and mine dumps are posted and collecting is not allowed.

Minerals of the Park City Mining District

anglesite	covellite	massicot
argentite	cuprite	metastibnite
azurite	enargite	mimetite
bayldonite	epidote	montmorillonite
barite	fluorite	olivenite
bindheimite	galena	pyrargyrite
bornite	garnet	pyrite
boulangerite	geocronite	pyrolusite
bournonite	gold	pyromorphite
brochantite	goslarite	quartz
calaverite	gypsum	rhodochrosite
calcite	halloysite	rhodonite
cerargyrite	hematite	sericite
cerussite	hemimorphite	serpentine
chabazite	jamesonite	silver
chalcanthite	limonite	sphalerite
chalcocite	linarite	spinel
chalcopyrite	magnesioferrite	stibnite
chlorite	magnetite	tetrahedrite
chrysocolla	malachite	thaumasite
		wulfenite

The Tintic District

The Tintic District, located at Eureka in Juab County, was discovered in 1869 and has been mined on an intermittently continuous basis to the present day. Much of the production of siliceous ore in the district has been utilized by smelters in Tooele and Salt Lake City to mix with the more iron-rich ores of Bingham. Tintic has produced gold, silver, lead, copper, and zinc as its major commodities. Morris (1968, p. 1063) states ... "The primary ores of the Tintic District consist chiefly of sulfides and sulfosalts of silver, lead, copper, iron, zinc, and bismuth in association with jasperoid (silicified carbonate rock), barite, aggregates of quartz crystals, calcite, dolomite, and ankerite. In addition, gold is locally abundant in some of the copper ores, in part as the native metal and in part as a telluride; primary native silver is also abundant in some late ore bodies in the Chief No. 1 Mine." The district continues to be active today with underground mining occurring at the Trixie Mine and a heap leach operation utilizing the dump material from the Mammoth Mine.

Minerals of the Tintic Mining District

adamite	chrysocolla	halloysite	pearceite
albite	cimolite	halotrichite	petzite
allophane	claudetite	hematite	pharmacosiderite
altaite	clinochlore	hemimorphite	phosgenite
alunite	clinoclasite	hetaerolite	pitticite
anatase	collophane	heulandite	plumbojarosite
anglesite	conichalcite	hisingerite	polybasite
ankerite	connellite	hollandite	potassium alum
antlerite	copiapite	huntite	proustite
aragonite	copper	hydrozincite	psilomelane
arduinite	coquimbite	jalpaite	pyrargyrite
argentite	cornwallite	jamesonite	pyrite
argentojarosite	coronadite	jarosite	pyrolusite
arseniosiderite	cotunnite	jasper	pyromorphite
arsenobismite	covellite	kaolinite	quenselite
arsenopyrite	crandallite	kieserite	rhodochrosite
atacamite	crednerite	kornelite	rhomboclase
aurichalcite	cryptomelane	krennerite	roemerite
azurite	cubanite	lanarkite	rutile
barite	cuprite	leadhillite	saponite
bayldonite	cuprogoslarite	leucoxene	scorodite
beaverite	daubreeite	limonite	sericite

beidellite	delvauxite	linarite	sickerlite
bilinite	diaspore	luzonite	siderotil
billingsleyite	dickite	malachite	silver
bindheimite	dolomite	manganite	smithsonite
birnessite	enargite	marcasite	spangolite
bismite	endellite	massicot	sphalerite
bismuth	epsomite	matildite	stephanite
bismuthinite	erinite	melaconite	stromeyerite
bismutite	famatinite	melanterite	sylvanite
boehmite	ferrogoslarite	metazeunerite	szomolnokite
bornite	freibergite	miagyrite	tennantite
brochantite	galena	mimetite	tenorite
calaverite	garnet	minium	tetradymite
calcite	gearksutite	mixite	tetrahedrite
carphosiderite	geocronite	montmorillonite	thompsonite
celadonite	gibbsite	mordenite	tyrolite
cerargyrite	goethite	nontronite	voltaite
cerussite	gold	nsutite	wurtzite
chalcanthite	goslarite	okenite	zeunerite
chalcocite	greenockite	olivenite	zoisite
chalcophyllite	gunningite	olivenite	zunyite
chenevixite	gypsum	pargasite	

THE GUIDEBOOK SECTION

Explanation of the County Location Information

The locations that follow in this guidebook are alphabetical by county. The information within each location site block is arranged as follows:

Location: This is a name given to the site. It is sometimes a well-known name used by collectors, but, in many cases, it is simply the name of a nearby geographic feature selected by this writer as a means of identifying the site.

Minerals/Rocks/Fossils: This gives the name of the materials that are most commonly found at that particular site. In almost all cases of mineral and fossil sites, there will be many additional mineral species or fossil species that can be found by the diligent and observant collector. Often the references given at the end of the section will provide more information about occurrences. The index to this book refers only to items named on this line of the location block.

Description: This section attempts to present some background information or more detailed information about the type of material to be found.

Directions: Where possible, very specific instructions are given to each site. In some cases, especially when the writer was unable to field check the information, the directions are more general to get you into the correct area, but may require some searching to find a specific site where the collectable material occurs. A few sites are given in terms of township, range, and section numbers, either as a backup to the descriptive directions or where there may be no roads leading to the site.

In the directions you will frequently see reference to HCV (high clearance vehicle) or 4WD (four wheel drive vehicle) being required. There may be many other sites in this book where such vehicles may be needed although not specifically mentioned in the directions. Use caution when driving in the areas mentioned in this guide. Be aware that a flash flood can change a good road into an impassable gully in a matter of minutes. It is best not to travel alone as car trouble can leave you stranded a long distance from help. Be particularly careful in spring or fall when sudden storms can bring cold temperatures. Carry plenty of water, food, and warm clothing regardless of the season of the year. A few people die from exposure every year in the backcountry of Utah.

Land Status: Many locations are on federal land that is open to the public for collecting (subject to guidelines described later). However, much of the mineralized land in Utah is held by individuals or corporations as mining claims. The claimholder cannot prevent you from reasonable use of the surface of the claim (hiking, for example), but, legally, you are prohibited from collecting any of the minerals. In the practical sense, most claimholders rarely object to recreational mineral collecting except in those cases where the claim is for the specific material being sought by collectors. In Utah such materials include topaz, red beryl, garnet, septarian nodules, picture stone, and petrified wood. It is always best to contact the claimholder before collecting or you may find yourself being prosecuted for theft of materials from the claim.

Other land in Utah may be state land which may be open to the public or there may be a mineral lease (similar to a federal claim) on the site. State leases on land occur in the Thomas Range for topaz and in the House Range for trilobites. There are some sites in this guide that are located on private land, in which case, the landowner should always be contacted for permission.

The land status has been determined from maps and some site visits and is intended only as a general guide. Land status as reported here may be incorrect, because small inholdings of private land occur within public land or mining claims may be staked at any time.

THE DESCRIPTION OF A SITE IN THIS GUIDE DOES NOT CONSTITUTE PERMISSION FOR YOU TO COLLECT ON THE SITE. IT IS YOUR RESPONSIBILITY TO DETERMINE THE ACTUAL STATUS OF THE LAND AND CONTACT THE APPROPRIATE PERSON OR AGENCY FOR PERMISSION. FOR SPECIAL REGULATIONS REGARDING FOSSIL MATERIAL, SEE BELOW.

Maps: This section lists the appropriate topographic maps for that particular site. In almost all cases, the 1:100,000 metric scale map is listed by name and designated by "m" in parentheses after the name. These maps are the best road maps to the various gravel roads and trails in the general area. More detailed maps of the 15 minute series and 7.5 minute series are listed for many sites. These are useful for pinpointing locations or decipering a confusion of trails in an area.

References: Here are listed sources of the information presented in the site description. Personal communications to the writer are presented with the name and city of the informant. The reference "Stowe (1979)" refers to an earlier guide published by the Utah Geological Survey. Almost all those locations have been incorporated into this guide. When that is the only reference listed, then the site has been described wholly on the basis of the previous guide. Other references are usually to professional geological publications which will give you considerable more detail about the site. Any location with the reference "Visited by this writer" can be assumed to have been checked to verify that the material to be collected there can be found as listed and the directions are reasonably accurate (subject to recent changes in road conditions or land status).

Legal Aspects of Rock, Mineral, and Fossil Collecting

The principal legal hurdle to the collecting of rocks and minerals is the status of the land and its mineral rights, as discussed above. There may also be a problem between what is perceived as hobby collecting and what is considered to be commercial collecting. This has led to conflicts with land managers of various agencies in some locations. Since policies are enforced at the local level, it is advisable to check with the local BLM or Forest Service office if you have questions about where you can collect, how much you can collect, and by what means you can collect.

Some land may be unencumbered by mining claims, but have special managerial status. Generally speaking, you are not allowed to collect in national parks, national monuments, national recreation areas, state parks, BLM recreation areas, locally administered recreation areas, tribal lands, and military reservations. Wilderness areas and wilderness study areas are particular problems. Although collecting is not prohibited in these areas, land managers are tending to strictly interpret the Wilderness Act to forbid any excavation while searching for specimens. This severely limits collecting in Wilderness areas.

The collecting of rocks, minerals, or fossils from private land requires the permission of the land owner. You may be asked to sign a waiver of liability and it is useful to carry copies of a waiver form with you so that you can fill one out if asked or volunteer one to convince a landowner of your sincerity when asking permission to collect.

A Guide to Collecting Sites

The legalities of fossil collecting are somewhat more complicated because of the scientific value of fossils. There is also the regrettable tendency of politicians and resource managers to lump together fossils and archaeological items which doesn't help in dispelling misconceptions the public may have about these objects. Suffice it to say that federal and state law prohibit the removal of artifacts from archaeological sites and any such artifacts encountered by collectors should be reported to the appropriate agency.

Much fossil material is found on BLM lands and, as of this writing, rules for collecting on BLM lands are in the process of being formalized. You should check with the state BLM office to obtain a copy of whatever rules are eventually developed.

Federal law makes it illegal to collect vertebrate fossils from public lands and the same holds true for Utah's state lands. These laws are aimed primarily at protecting mammal fossils and dinosaur fossils from disturbance until they can be studied by paleontologists. Unless the law is changed, it is not legal to collect locally abundant fossil vertebrates such as fish and traces of vertebrates such as shark teeth. Collecting of these materials is only legal on private land with the permission of the landowner.

Common invertebrate and plant fossils may be collected in small quantities on public land for personal use only.

A detailed explaination of laws and permit requirements is available from the office of the State Paleontologist. The following general guideline applies to most public lands in Utah: Collection of any fossils or petrified wood from certain lands is restricted, including national parks, national recreation areas, state parks, interpretive and recreation areas, and areas of critical environmental concern (ACEC) managed by the BLM, tribal lands, and military reservations.

Rockhounding permits for recreational collecting of non-vertebrate fossils, rocks, and minerals on state land are issued by the Utah School and Institutional Trust Lands Administration (355 West North Temple, 3 Triad Center, Suite 400, Salt Lake City, UT 84180-1204: 801-538-5508). Permit fees are $5.00 for an individual or family, and $200 for an association (i.e. gem and mineral clubs). The office of the Utah State Paleontologist (Utah Geological Survey, 2363 South Foothill Drive, Salt Lake City, UT 84109; 801-467-7970) acts as a clearing house for information on fossil localities in Utah and maintains an extensive data base. Collectors are encouraged to file information sheets with the State Paleontologist in order to allow that office to monitor the number of collectors and the sites that are being collected.

Planning for the Future

Anyone who wishes to contribute additional locations for future editions of this guide, or who has corrections and additions to locations contained herein, is urged to write to the following address:

Dr. James R. Wilson
Dept. of Geosciences
2507 University Circle
Weber State University
Ogden, UT 84408-2507

All contributions of information that are used in future editions of this volume will be acknowledged in the reference section of each location.

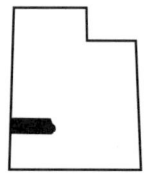

BEAVER COUNTY

Beaver County is one of the more mineral-rich counties in Utah. Rocks within the county are primarily igneous and include both intrusive and extrusive rocks. Relatively small areas of sedimentary rock have often been altered or metamorphosed by their proximity to the intrusives. Spectacular cliffs and pinnacles with the typical rounded edges common to granitic rocks occur in the Mineral Mountains. Numerous small mountain ranges have intrusives and associated mineral deposits that have been prospected and mined for many years. A number of interesting rock types can be found in the county, but the lack of extensive areas of unaltered sedimentary rock limits the possibilities for fossil collectors.

Location: **Highway 21 Quarry**

Minerals: **quartz, adularia, fluorite, chlorite, laumontite, epidote, sphene**

Description: This location is a small knob of igneous rock projecting above the sagebrush flat. The magma apparently engulfed large quantities of limestone which altered the composition of the magma by adding calcium and releasing carbon dioxide. The rock has numerous xenoliths and in places is strikingly rich in plagioclase phenocrysts (apparently a result of the assimilated limestone). The small quarry exposes fresh rock which has abundant miarolitic cavities in which the above listed minerals occur. These are all micro or occasionally thumbnail size specimens, but are quite attractive even with a small hand lens. Be forewarned that the rock is extremely tough; it requires a sledgehammer to break the rock. Some smaller specimens can be collected with lighter equipment. Be sure and wear eye and face protection as the rock "zings" when broken. The epidote at this location forms attractive sprays of acicular crystals. Adularia is a form of feldspar that occurs in crystals with apparent orthorhombic symmetry. The sphene forms lustrous brown crystals in the cavities and in the groundmass. Fluorite at this location is usually a red-purple color and is present as well-formed crystals which, unfortunately, may cleave as the rock is broken. Laumontite, a zeolite, is present as soft, almost chalky crystals, which may be mistaken for gypsum.

Directions: From the junction of Utah Highways 257 and 21 in Milford, go west on 21 for 4.9 miles and take an indistinct road to the right which goes toward a knob of rock about a 100 yards from the highway. Park near the wash and hike around the knob to the west to a small quarry.

Land Status: BLM public lands.

Maps: Wah Wah Mts. South (m), Milford (15), Milford (7.5).

References: Visited by this writer.

Location: **Bawana and Maria Pits, Old Hickory Mine**

Minerals: **chrysocolla, malachite, magnetite, bornite, chalcopyrite, grossular garnet, wollastonite, serpentine, clintonite, diopside**

Description: The Old Hickory Mine and other mines in this area were underground operations for copper during the early part of this century and some of these were later worked for scheelite during World War II. The Bawana and Maria are small open pit mines that were worked in the 1960s and early 70s. These are all skarn-type copper deposits in which the limestone of the Toroweap Formation has been altered and/or recrystallized. Large green garnets occur in masses of coarsely crystalline white calcite on some of the dumps, but fractures usually prevent them from being removed. The rare copper silicates whelanite and stringhamite were first described from these deposits, but are not distinguishable from chrysocolla in hand specimen. The mica found in these deposits is apparently clintonite, a calcium magnesium mica, one of the brittle micas.

 **Directions:** From the intersection of Highways 257 and 21 in Milford, go west on Highway 21 for 3.9 miles and turn right on a good gravel road that leads to the dumps. There are numerous haulage roads in the area, but the dumps are in sight at all times.

Land Status: Private lands. Keep away from the mill and tailings pond area. Obey any no trespassing signs. Recent activity may limit access to this area.

Maps: Wah Wah Mts. South (m), Milford (15), Milford (7.5).

References: Visited by this writer. Utah Geological Association (1973)

Location:	OK Mine
Minerals:	malachite, azurite, bornite, chalcopyrite, pyrite, cuprite, brochantite, molybdenite, chrysocolla

Description: The OK Mine is a small porphyry copper deposit that was mined in the late 60s. The quartz monzonite host rock is not extensively altered and has a core zone of quartz.

Directions: The mine is located northwest of the previously described Bawana, Maria, and Old Hickory Mines and is clearly visible from them. Several haulage roads lead across the valley to the Beaver Lake Mountains and the OK Mine.

Land Status: Private lands. Note: Recent exploration activity may limit access to this area.

Maps: Wah Wah Mts. South (m), Milford (15), Milford (7.5), Milford NW (7.5).

References: Visited by this writer. Utah Geological Association (1973).

Location:	West Spring
Minerals:	ludwigite, azurite, malachite, brochantite, chrysocolla, szaibelyite

Description: One of two places in Utah (the other is the Mountain Lake Mine, Salt Lake Co.) and only a few places in the world where the scarce borate ludwigite is found. Some of the ludwigite may be altered to cream-colored szaibelyite. Specimens of ludwigite are found as acicular sprays frozen in matrix on the dump of a mine at West Spring.

Directions: Take Utah Highway 21 west of Milford for 0.5 mile, turn right on a dirt road for 9 miles, and follow this road into the foothills at the north end of the Beaver Lake Mountains. Take a secondary road left (west) for 4.5 miles to West Spring.

Land Status: BLM public lands.

Maps: Wah Wah Mts. North (m), Beaver Lake Mts. (15), Lime Mountain (7.5), High Rock (7.5).

References: Stowe (1979).

Location:	Frisco
Minerals:	galena, calcite, wollastonite, magnesite, tremolite

Description: This area is one of the most famous historical mining districts in Utah. The district was organized in 1871, but did not become important until the discovery of the Horn Silver Mine in 1875. Most of the production from this mine occurred from 1875 to 1885, but it remained in production until the end of World War I and again in World War II. The dump of the Horn Silver Mine was reworked at one time, so little of interest can be collected there now. The mine collapsed in 1885 which hindered further development. Other mines in the area include the King David, Beaver Carbonate, Frisco Contact, and Lulu Mines. Some galena and calcite occur on the Beaver Carbonate dump. The calcite fluoresces bright red. Bullock (1981) reports magnesite and tremolite at Grampian Hill, behind the Horn Silver Mine.

On the west side of the San Francisco Mountains (across the ridge from the Horn Silver Mine), roads lead off the highway and go up Marble Gulch and Loeber Gulch. Up Loeber Gulch there is a small open cut about 50 feet in length exposing massive fibrous wollastonite.

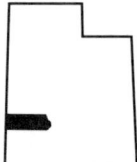
Directons: From the intersection of Utah Highways 21 and 257 in Milford, it is 15.1 miles west on Highway 21 to the roadside rest area at Frisco. From the highway at this point, the Horn Silver Mine and the King David are visible on the hill to the west. Just off the highway is the historic Frisco cemetery. Charcoal kilns (some visible from the highway) are scattered through the area. From this point it is 3.7 miles further west to one of the turnoffs that takes you up the west side of the San Francisco Mountains to the mines there.

Land Status: Private lands, claims, and BLM public lands.

Maps: Wah Wah Mts. South (m), Frisco (15), Frisco Peak (15), Frisco Special Map (this is an old map, 1909, part of a series on mining districts, and is shown on the cover of the 1973 UGA guide; it is useful for locating old mines). Frisco (7.5), Frisco Peak (7.5).

References: Visited by this writer. Butler, et al. (1920), Butler (1913), Utah Geological Association (1973).

Location:	Cactus Mine
Minerals:	pyrite, quartz, tourmaline, tourmalinated quartz, limonite after siderite, anhydrite, chalcopyrite, specular hematite

Description: The Cactus Mine represents an area where some interesting minerals can be collected with the possibility of very attractive specimens being found. Quartz crystals up to one inch, many with inclusions of hematite, can be found on the dump. Pyrite as pyritohedrons up to 2 inches have been found here, although pyrite is not abundant. Rhombohedral crystals of what was once siderite, now replaced by goethite or limonite, are relatively abundant and are commonly more than one inch in size. Anhydrite, some a delicate pink color, is abundant on the dump although the crystals tend to break easily.

Directions: From the intersection of Utah Highways 257 and 21 in Milford, go 20.1 miles west on Highway 21, through Squaw Springs Pass at Frisco and down to the valley. Turn right (north) on a gravel road, normally passable by car, but subject to washouts by flash floods. At the building foundations that mark the townsite of Newhouse, bear right toward the mountains. A dump is visible at the base of the mountains and some pyrite has been found here. Note: A gate was recently placed on the road to the Cactus Mine and access is currently restricted.

Land Status: Private land, mining claims, BLM public lands.

Maps: Frisco (7.5), Frisco (15), Wah Wah Mtns. South (m).

References: Visited by this writer.

Location:	South Creek Area
Rocks:	agate

Description: Agates are found in a large area centered along South Creek. Colors are blue, green, yellow, white and some mossy agate. Bullock (1981) reports black agate with blue bands in Blue Valley, southwest of South Creek, just off the interstate.

Directions: From the I-15 exit immediately south of Beaver several gravel roads branch to the southeast off the frontage road. These roads traverse the Kane Creek, Birch Creek, and South Creek drainages. Accessible by automobile, but hazardous when wet.

Land Status: BLM public lands.

Maps: Beaver (m), Greenville Bench (7.5).

References: Stowe (1979).

Location:	White Mountain Area
Minerals:	alunite, tremolite, kaolinite, chalcedony, opal, quartz, limonite, sulfur, and pyrite

A Guide to Collecting Sites

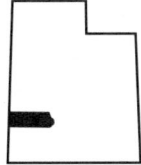

Description: This is an area of altered rock, hence the name White Mountain, as the original rocks have been leached and altered. Alunite, an aluminum sulfate, and kaolinite, a clay mineral, are fairly common in certain types of alteration.

Directions: Take Utah Highway 21 out of Milford to Frisco. After coming down from the pass at Frisco, turn south off Highway 21 on a gravel road to Antelope Springs (about 5 miles); then southwest (right) about 2.5 miles; then southeast (left) about 2.5 miles; then east (left) to the White Mountain area (about 2.5 miles).

Land Status: BLM public lands.

Maps: Wah Wah Mts. South (m), White Mountain (7.5).

References: Stowe (1979), Stringham (1964).

Location:	Indian Creek
Minerals:	alunite, amethyst, acanthite, calcite, cerargyrite, fluorite, limonite, pyrite, sericite, tellurides, and quartz

Description: The alunite, an alteration mineral, is found at the west base of the mountain on a hill some 350 feet above the alluvial slope. The other minerals mentioned above are associated with the gold mines in the area, the Sheeprock and Rob Roy mines. The Rob Roy mine is north of the alunite deposit; the Sheeprock mine is northeast.

Directions: From the I-15 interchange about 9 miles north of Beaver several gravel roads lead into the Indian Creek area and the various mines. Follow signs off Utah Highway 91 from Indian Creek Recreation Area into the canyon.

Land Status: National Forest lands.

Maps: Beaver (m), Pole Mountain (7.5).

References: Stowe (1979), Callaghan (1973).

Location:	Beaver Lake Mining District
Minerals:	chalcopyrite, quartz, chrysocolla, cuprite, azurite, calcite, diopside, garnet, hematite, malachite, magnetite, muscovite, pyrite, epidote, galena

Description: "The Beaver Lake Mining District includes several old mines. The Skylark Mine, located between West Spring and Fairview Springs, north-central Beaver Lake Mountains, is reached by unimproved road west of Fairview Springs, about 10 miles northwest of Milford. Mine shaft lies within a body of altered carbonate surrounded by quartz monzonite. The deposit is banded magnetite-epidote rock. Search along the dumps. Several other mines are in the area. The Copper Mountain mine on the eastern edge of the district produced azurite and malachite. Calcite and magnetite lens appear at the contact between altered carbonate and quartz monzonite in the central part of the north side of Bat Ridge. Galena specimens can be found in the Galena mine area about 1 mile west and slightly south of Bat Ridge." (Stowe, 1979, p. 2-3)

Directions: See above description.

Land Status: BLM public lands, private land, and claims.

Maps: Wah Wah Mts. North (m), Lime Mountain (7.5).

References: Barosh (1960), Welsh (1973), Stowe (1979).

Location:	Blawn Mountain area
Minerals:	fluorite, limonite, hematite, autunite, calcite, quartz, uranophane, and alunite

Directions: Do not attempt without map.

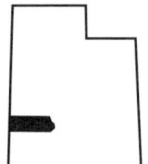

Land Status: BLM public lands and private claims.

Maps: Wah Wah Mts. South (m), The Tetons (7.5).

References: Whelan (1965).

Location: **Wah Wah Pass**

Minerals: **grossular garnet, pyrite**

Description: Wah Wah Pass is located along a zone of contact metamorphism adjacent to an intrusive body. Pyrite and contact metamorphic minerals can be found in this zone of contact metamorphism. The known occurrence of large green grossular garnet is of small extent and is under claim. No collecting is allowed on the claim.

Directions: Drive west of Milford on Utah Highway 21 and park about 0.6 mile past milepost 46. Look in roadcuts and the surrounding area.

Land Status: BLM public lands and private claims.

Maps: Wah Wah Mts. North (m), Wah Wah Summit (7.5).

References: Visited by this writer. Erickson (1966).

Location: **Star and North Star Districts, Star Range**

Minerals: **galena, wulfenite, barite**

Description: See the references for descriptions of individual mines.

Directions: The Star Range is immediately west-southwest of Milford. There are numerous mines in the range. The Harrington-Hickory Mine is located due west of Milford on the Windmill Road and is visible from town and from Utah Highway 21. The Wild Bill Mine is on the west side of the range and is accessible from a gravel road that turns off Highway 21 once past the end of the range.

Land Status: BLM public lands and private claims. Stay off posted property.

Maps: Wah Wah Mts. South (m), Milford (7.5), Milford NW (7.5).

References: Abou-Zied (1973), Baer (1973), Wray (1973).

Location: **Granite and North Granite Districts, Mineral Mountains**

Minerals: **scheelite**

Description: Scheelite occurs in garnet rock at the contact of limestones with the Mineral Mountains granitic intrusion. Scheelite is not easily recognized without an ultraviolet light. The mineral fluoresces blue-white in short-wave ultraviolet. Note that it does not fluoresce under long-wave ultraviolet.

Directions: Take Utah Highway 21 west from Beaver about 5 miles to the Pass Road, turn right onto the Pass Road for about 5 miles to another road turning right (north). Mines are located along this road at the foot of the Mineral Mountains.

Land Status: BLM public lands and private claims.

Maps: Beaver (m), Adamsville (7.5), Bearskin Mtn. (7.5).

References: Hobbs (1945), Crawford and Buranek (1945).

Location: **Lincoln District, Southern Mineral Mountains**

Minerals: **calcite, specular hematite, pyrite, epidote, and others**

Description: The two major mines here are the Lincoln and the Creole. The Lincoln Mine is said to be the

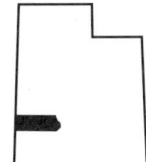 oldest mine in Utah as it was supposedly worked for lead for bullets at the instruction of Brigham Young in 1860 or earlier. The mines are near an intrusive body which itself has been altered.

Directions: The mines are located in the south end of the Mineral Mountains, about 5 miles by gravel road northeast of Minersville. The Creole Mine is visible as you approach the area whereas the Lincoln Mine is further up the valley.

Land Status: BLM public lands and private claims. Mines may be posted.

Maps: Beaver (m), Adamsville (15), Adamsville (7.5).

References: Visited by this writer. Crawford and Buranek (1945).

Location: **Antelope District, Mineral Mountains**

Minerals: **barite, calcite, galena, magnetite, malachite**

Directions: "Drive north of Milford on U-257 to milepost 4 (approximately 4 miles), continue 0.4 mile to a junction. Turn right on an improved gravel road and continue 2.6 miles to a junction. Turn left at the sign, *Antelope Point and US-91*. Continue north for 11.2 miles staying on the best road and ignoring side roads, to a junction. Take the road to the east and toward the mountains. At this point mines and prospects of the Antelope District can be seen on the mountain side. Several jeep trails lead to the individual mine workings." (Stowe, 1979, p. 10)

Land Status: BLM public lands and land under private ownership.

Maps: Beaver (m), Bearskin Mtn. (7.5).

References: Stowe (1979).

Location: **Beaumont Basin, Mineral Mountains**

Minerals: **wulfenite**

Description: Crystals occur in vuggy gossan material in a prospect at the head of Beaumont Basin. Crystals are less than 4 mm.

Directions: Take Utah Highway 21 from Beaver for 5 miles and turn right onto Pass Road. Follow it for 5 miles to where another gravel road turns right. Follow this road for 4 miles to a road that turns left, follow this for 1 mile until it becomes a 4WD road. From this point it is a steep hike up to the saddle where the prospect is located.

Land Status: BLM public lands.

Maps: Beaver (m), Adamsville (7.5), Bearskin Mtn. (7.5).

References: Stowe (1979).

Location: **Porcupine Ridge, Mineral Mountains**

Minerals: **beryl (aquamarine)**

Description: Beryl occurs in pegmatites within the granitic rocks of the Mineral Mountains in Sec. 17, 18, 19, and 20, T28S, R8W, and on up to the summit ridge. The beryl is often frozen in matrix in the pegmatite, but at some locations reported on the summit ridge, the beryl has grown into vugs.

Directions: See directions above for Beaumont Basin.

Land Status: Some private land, leave gates as they were found. BLM public lands.

Maps: Beaver (m), Adamsville (7.5), Bearskin Mtn. (7.5).

References: Visited by this writer. Stowe (1979). Crawford and Buranek (1945).

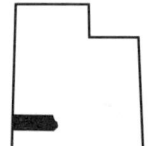

Location: Rock Corral, Mineral Mountains

Minerals: smoky quartz, feldspar

Description: This is a well-known collecting area that is justly famous for beautiful, large smoky quartz crystals as well as nice feldspar crystals. Crystals of quartz may exceed 12 inches and feldspar crystals often exhibit twinning. The crystals occur in vugs or pockets in the rock. Previously excavated pockets are everywhere and scraps of broken crystals and masses of feldspar are abundant around these excavations. Success requires walking, studying the rock, digging at likely locations, and a great deal of luck.

Directions: Go south out of Milford for 0.5 mile and take the Pass Road east about 6 miles. At the microwave towers turn left (north). About 1.5 miles down this road the right fork leads to the Rock Corral picnic area, straight ahead leads to the Big Rock picnic area and on north.

Land Status: BLM public lands.

Maps: Beaver (m), Adamsville (7.5), Bearskin Mtn. (7.5).

References: Visited by this writer. Stowe (1979).

Location: Star Range Area

Rock: Banded Sandstone

Description: Colorfully banded rock in outcrops of the Moenkopi Formation in Sec. 29, T28S, R11W.

Directions: Drive west-southwest out of Milford on the road paralleling the east front of the Star Range. Outcrops are in the foothills about 1 mile west of the road.

Land Status: BLM public lands and mining claims.

Maps: Wah Wah Mts. South (m), Milford Flat (7.5)

References: Baer(1962, 1973).

Location: Pine Grove District

Minerals: skarn

Directions: Drive west from Milford on Highway 21 to milepost 42 and 0.8 mile past the milepost. Take the Pine Valley Road toward Lund (south). Stay left at the intersection 4.8 miles from the highway and take the second gravel road to the left past this intersection. This road will lead into the Pine Grove area.

Land Status: BLM public lands and private claims.

Maps: Wah Wah Mts. South (m).

References: Visited by this writer.

BOX ELDER COUNTY

Box Elder County extends from the Wellsville Mountains of the Wasatch Front to the Grouse Creek Mountains of the northwest corner of the state. Most of the rocks exposed in the county are sedimentary rocks but there is a significant body of metamorphic rock in the Grouse Creek Mountains. There are scattered deposits of metallic minerals throughout the county although few have resulted in significant mining operations. The large areas of sedimentary rock provide opportunities for fossil collecting.

Location: Wellsville Mountains

Fossils: trilobites and other fossils

Description: The Spence Shale, named for its occurrence in Spence Gulch near Liberty, Idaho, is a fossiliferous unit of the Cambrian Langston Formation. It is located immediately above the steep, cliff-forming Brigham Quartzite, and is exposed in several canyons along the precipitous western slope of the Wellsville Mountains. Trilobites are plentiful in the Spence Shale and include species of the spiny trilobite *Zacanthoides*. Other trilobites found here are *Alokistocare*, *Ogygopsis*, *Kootenia*, *Kochina*, *Glossopleura*, *Dorypyge*, *Bathyuriscus*, *Athabaskia*, *Achlysopsis*, and the agnostid *Peronopsis*. Additionally, eocrinoids, hyolithids, sponges, jellyfish, echinoderms, phyllocarids, and worms occur in this unit.

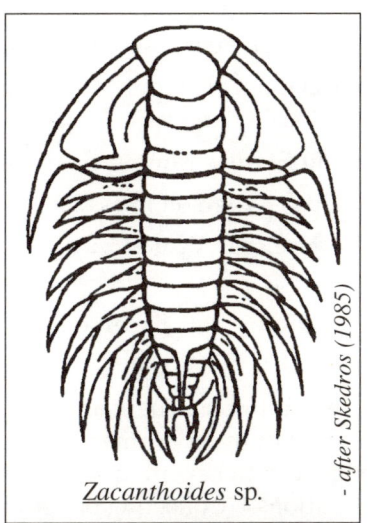

Zacanthoides sp. — after Skedros (1985)

Directions: The Spence Shale is exposed in Miners Hollow, Cataract Canyon, Dry Canyon, and the area from Antimony Canyon to Hansen Canyon. All of these locations necessitate a strenuous hike of over 1,000 feet elevation gain from the base of the mountain. Hike up the canyons and go to the top of the Brigham Quartzite (marked by cliffs) and look for exposures of the shale immediately above the quartzite.

Land Status: National Forest lands.

Maps: Brigham City (7.5), Tremonton (m).

References: Lloyd Gunther, Brigham City, UT. Gunther and Gunther (1981).

Location: Tecoma Hill

Minerals: wulfenite, aurichalcite, aragonite

Description: This small mining area along the Utah-Nevada border produced a large amount of wulfenite and the mineral can still be found on some of the mine dumps. It occurs in transparent yellow crystals with some of the smaller crystals being well formed. The larger crystals, up to 1 inch across, tend to form intergrown masses in the rock. Aragonite commonly occurs with the wulfenite. Some pockets of aurichalcite were found in the mines and may be seen on the dumps. The wulfenite occurs in a crumbly, goethite gossan where veins in the limestone have been altered from the original sulfide mineralization.

Zacanthoides idahoensis Walcott. Trilobite common in Spence Shale of the Wellsville Mountains; about 2 inches long. Photo: Val Gunther

Directions: This location is reached from Montello, Nevada. A short distance north of Montello a dirt road heads southeast across the valley. Follow this for several miles and take a road to the left (north) to head toward the mines which are on a low hill at the foot of the range. The open pit mine at Copper

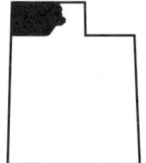

Mountain, above Tecoma Hill, may be visible to guide you. There are many small roads out in the valley, but your destination is usually in view.

Land Status: Most of this area is held by mining claims.

Maps: Patterson Pass (7.5).

References: Visited by this writer.

Location: **Copper Mountain**

Minerals: **chrysocolla, copper-bearing clays, cuprite, native copper**

Description: This is an inactive open pit mine on the summit of the mountain which contains numerous bright blue boulders largely composed of chrysocolla and clay. With close examination, it is usually possible to find nodules with a core of cuprite within which are wires of native copper. The native copper can usually be detected by lightly brushing your fingers across the cuprite. Wire copper makes it prickly.

Directions: Copper Mountain is at the head of the canyon that begins at Tecoma Hill. See directions to the locality above.

Land Status: Mining claim. At times in the past the access road has been posted.

Maps: Patterson Pass (7.5).

References: Visited by this writer.

Location: **Sardine Summit**

Fossils: **fish**

Descriptions: There are several areas in Utah where the Devonian Water Canyon Formation occurs and fish have been reported from this unit. They are usually difficult to find. (See also Cache County locations.) Collecting of vertebrates is restricted by federal and state law. Check with the national forest office or the office of the State Paleontologist to see if permits are available.

Directions: This locality is along the west side of the road at Sardine Summit near the Highway Department maintenance shed on U.S. 89-91 from Brigham City to Logan.

Land Status: Highway right-of-way and national forest lands.

Maps: Mt. Pisgah (7.5), Logan (m).

References: Stowe (1979).

Gogia sp. An eocrinoid found in Spence Shale of the Wellsville Mountains. Photo: Val Gunther.

Location: **Rozel Point**

Minerals: **gypsum**

Description: Large, well-formed crystals of gypsum occur in the mud at Rozel Point, but can be located only when the lake level is low. Crystals were quite abundant here before the railroad causeway was filled. There are some reports that crystals are not as plentiful as before.

Directions: Rozel Point is located on the headland west of Promontory Point. It is reached by driving to the Golden Spike National Historical Site at Promontory and following secondary roads southwest and south.

Directions: Refer to the topographic map. Inquiry at Golden Spike Monument may provide information about the status of local roads and land access.

Land Status: BLM public lands and private lands.

Maps: Rozel Point (7.5).

References: Otto Reiter, Salt Lake City, UT.

A Guide to Collecting Sites

Location: Deweyville
Fossils: brachiopods, corals

Description: The Mississippian Great Blue Limestone crops out on the middle slopes of the Wellsville Mountains east and southeast of Deweyville. Material can be collected in place and from talus on the lower slopes.

Directions: Access is through private property and across the irrigation canal east of Deweyville.

Land Status: National Forest lands, but access through private property.

Maps: Tremonton (m), Honeyville (7.5).

References: Dr. Richard W. Moyle, Dept. of Geology, Weber State University.

Location: Dove Creek Pass
Minerals: garnet, staurolite

Description: Metamorphic rocks are exposed thoughout a wide area of the Grouse Creek Mountains and the Raft River Range. This location lies in the Dove Creek Mountains, a small range between the Grouse Creek Mountains and the Raft River Range.

Directions: Dove Creek Pass lies on the road from Rosette to Lynn, west of Utah Highway 30 in the extreme northwest part of the state. Garnet and staurolite occur in road cuts through the pass.

Land Status: Highway right-of-way and private land.

Maps: Grouse Creek (m), Lynn Reservoir (7.5).

References: Dave Miller, USGS, Menlo Park, CA.

Location: Ingham Pass
Minerals: kyanite

Description: Kyanite is a high-grade metamorphic mineral which occurs here in close proximity to some Tertiary intrusives.

Directions: The location is in the vicinity of Ingham Pass in the central Grouse Creek Mountains. Secondary roads from Utah Highway 30 on the east and from Grouse Creek Valley to the west lead up to the pass.

Land Status: BLM and private lands.

Maps: Grouse Creek (m), Ingham Canyon (7.5), Potters Creek (7.5).

References: Dave Miller, USGS, Menlo Park, CA.

Zacanthoides idahoensis Walcott. A large trilobite common in the Spence Shale of the Wellville Mountains. Specimen is about 2.5 inches long. Photo: Val Gunther.

Location: Pilot Range
Mineral: andalusite (variety chiastolite)

Description: Andalusite is an aluminum silicate that results from metamorphism. The variety chiastolite has carbonaceous inclusions creating a cruciform pattern.

Directions: The occurrence is in metamorphosed rocks on the east side of the Pilot Range. A road leads south from Lucin along this side of the range.

Land Status: BLM lands.

Maps: Newfoundland Mountains (m).

References: Dave Miller, USGS, Menlo Park, CA.

CACHE COUNTY

Cache County extends from the crest of the Wellsville Mountains on the west, across Cache Valley, and includes the Bear River Range on the east. Rocks in the county are all sedimentary and, as a result, there are opportunities for fossil collecting in many of the formations. There are scattered small deposits of lead-zinc ore where galena, sphalerite, and quartz may be collected.

Location: Water Canyon Formation

Fossils: fish

Description: The Water Canyon Formation is a silty, white- and buff-weathering dolomite and dolomitic sandstone, named for its type occurrence in a tributary of Green Canyon northeast of Logan. There are a number of localities where this unit is exposed and may be searched for fish fossils. These fossils are generally difficult to find and require considerable persistence. Collecting of vertebrates is restricted by federal and state law. Check with the national forest office or the office of the State Paleontologist to see if permits are available.

Directions: Localities and general directions are listed below:

(1) The type locality is in Water Canyon, a tributary of Green Canyon.

(2) Also exposed where Green Canyon turns north, several miles below the type locality.

(3) Crosses Logan Canyon in the vicinity of the hydro electric plant.

(4) Also crosses Logan Canyon between Card Campground and Brown's Roll Off.

Land Status: National Forest lands.

Maps: Mt. Elmer (7.5), Logan (m).

References: Williams (1958), Stowe (1979).

Eocrinoids. Echinoderms found in the Spence Shale of the Wellsville Mountains and thought by some to be the ancestors of other, more common, echinoderms such as crinoids and blastoids. Specimens are about 2 inches long. Photo: Val Gunther.

Location: High Creek

Fossils: trilobites, eocrinoids, and others

Description: The Spence Shale, host to a varied trilobite fauna, occurs in this area. The spiny trilobite *Zacanthoides* is found here. See the Box Elder County listing for a more complete description of the species that occur here.

Directions: The turnoff to High Creek Canyon is about 1.5 miles north of Richmond and is marked by a Forest Service sign, "Campground 6 miles, Trailhead 8 miles." Follow the road to the trailhead at the wilderness boundary. The Spence Shale crops out in a band that crosses the ridge between the South Fork Trail and the North Fork Trail. The diggings are most easily accessed by taking the South Fork Trail, crossing the wooden bridge, and turning up the slope shortly past the sign "trail" where the old jeep road rejoins the trail. Head up toward the open areas glimpsed through the brush and up the nose of the ridge. Shale is abundant on the slope when you reach the area of outcrop. The diggings are in the upper part of

THOMAS RANGE

Doubly terminated topaz from the Thomas Range. Most topaz are attached to the rock matrix on one end, so doubly terminated crystals are much less common. Specimen is about 1 inch in length. Specimen: David Richerson. Photo: David Richerson.

"Sandy" topaz (overall size 0.9 inch x 0.7 inch). Topaz in the Thomas Range is sometimes found with numerous inclusions giving the crystal a sandy appearance. Crystal form can be well preserved. Specimen: Hugh and Fay Burnside Collection. Photo: David Richerson.

Cluster of topaz crystals from the Thomas Range. Doubly terminated crystal is approximately 1 inch. Specimen: John Holfert and Steve Allred. Photo: John R. Shupe.

Etched topaz crystal (1.25 inches). Etched crystals are often found in association with red beryl. The fluids that deposited the red beryl apparently attacks the topaz creating the etched surface. Specimen: John Holfert and Steve Allred. Photo: David Richerson.

Doubly terminated topaz crystal (1.7 inches) with inclusions of hematite. Thomas Range. Specimen: Jim and Paula Wilson. Photo: John R. Shupe.

THOMAS RANGE

Red beryl on topaz from the Thomas Range. Overall specimen is about 1 inch. Specimen: John Holfert and Steve Allred. Photo: John R. Shupe.

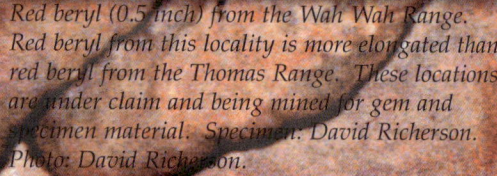

Red beryl (0.5 inch) from the Wah Wah Range. Red beryl from this locality is more elongated than red beryl from the Thomas Range. These locations are under claim and being mined for gem and specimen material. Specimen: David Richerson. Photo: David Richerson.

Red beryl on topaz (about 1 inch) from the Thomas Range. When beryl occurs with topaz, the topaz may show evidence of etching from the fluids that deposited the beryl. Specimens: John Holfert and Steve Allred. Photo: John R. Shupe.

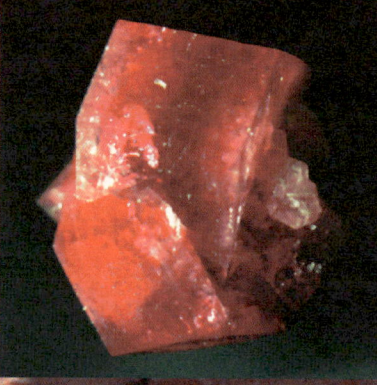

Red beryl from the Thomas Range. Large crystal is about 0.25 inch in diameter. Specimen: David Richerson. Photo: David Richerson.

Red beryl from the Thomas Range. Largest crystal is about 0.5 inch. Specimens: John Holfert and Steve Allred. Photo: John R. Shupe.

Bixbyite on the rhyolite matrix as it occurs in many locations in the Thomas Range. Crystal is about 0.25 inch and exhibits trisoctahedral faces on the corners of the cube. Specimen: Jim and Paula Wilson. Photo: John R. Shupe.

Bixbyite crystals on topaz from the Thomas Range. Topaz crystal is about 0.75 inch long. Specimen: David Richerson. Photo: David Richerson.

Bixbyite crystals on crystals of altered garnet that grew in a pocket in the rhyolite. Thomas Range. Specimen: Joe Marty. Photo: Joe Marty.

Bixbyite on topaz from the Thomas Range. Specimen: Jim and Paula Wilson. Photo: John R. Shupe.

Bixbyite with minor topaz and rhyolite. Largest bixbyite is about 0.2 inch. Thomas Range. Specimen: David Richerson. Photo: David Richerson.

THOMAS RANGE

Garnets, partially altered to hematite, about 0.5 inch in diameter. Thomas Range. Specimens: Jim and Paul A. Wilson. Photo: John R. Shupe.

Durangite, a rare arsenate, is known from only one locality in the Thomas Range, but may be more widespread. This stacked group of crystals is about 0.4 inch across. Specimen: John Holfert and Steve Allred. Photo: David Richerson.

A radiating spray of durangite crystals, about 0.4 inch across. Specimen: David Richerson. Photo: David Richerson.

Tridymite, an aggregate of crystals on amethyst. Overall specimen is about 1 inch. Thomas Range. Specimen: John Holfert and Steve Allred. Photo: David Richerson.

Pseudobrookite from the Thomas Range. These delicate needles occur on cavities in the rhyolite and also attached to topaz crystals. Longest crystals are about 0.5 inch. Specimen: Hugh and Fay Burnside Collection. Photo: David Richerson.

BINGHAM

The Bingham open pit copper mine has produced a wide variety of mineral specimens. A viewing area is maintained on the rim of the pit where the public may watch the mining operation. Photo: Jim Wilson.

Stibiconite pseudomorphous after stibnite from the Mercur gold mine. Specimen is about 1.3 inches in height. Specimen: Hugh and Fay Burnside Collection. Photo: David Richerson.

Dendritic growth of native copper on a fracture surface of a rock. Specimen measures 2 inches by 3 inches. Specimen: Jim and Paula Wilson. Photo: John R. Shupe.

Quartz (about 1.5 inches) on pyrite from the Lark Mine, an underground mine (now closed) adjacent to the Bingham pit. Specimen: Hugh and Fay Burnside Collection. Photo: David Richerson.

PARK CITY

Pyrite from the Silver King Mine, Park City. Largest crystal is about 1 inch. Specimen: Utah Museum of Natural History (MC2162). Photo: John R. Shupe.

Quartz on sphalerite and pyrite from Park City. Largest quartz crystal is 4.25 inches. Specimen: Utah Museum of Natural History (MC2471). Photo: John R. Shupe.

Pyrite from the Silver King Mine, Park City. Largest crystal is about 1.6 inches. Specimen: Utah Museum of Natural History (MC2175). Photo: John R. Shupe.

ALTA

View looking down Little Cottonwood Canyon from the vicinity of Grizzly Gulch above Alta. This old mining district has numerous mine dumps as well as exposures of contact metamorphic minerals. Photo: Jim Wilson

Clintonite, a calcium-magnesium mica, can be found in the skarns of the Alta and Solitude areas. This relatively rare mica is also found near Milford. This specimen is 0.5 inch in diameter. Specimen: David Richerson. Photo: David Richerson.

Cerussite, the lead carbonate, was a common ore mineral in some of the mines of the Alta area. This specimen is about 2 x 4 inches. Specimen: Utah Museum of Natural History (MC2493). Photo: John R. Shupe.

Pyromorphite, a lead phosphate mineral, occurs at scattered locations in the Alta area, such as Cardiff Fork and American Fork Canyon. Crystals are about 0.1 inch. Specimen: David Richerson. Photo: David Richerson.

Hemimorphite sometimes occurs in a botryoidal habit as seen here in this specimen from the Emma Mine at Alta. The specimen is 1.5 inches across. Specimen: Hugh and Fay Burnside Collection. Photo: David Richerson.

Photomicrograph of wulfenite (yellow) in hemimorphite (clear) from the Grizzly Gulch area at Alta. Wulfenite is lead molybdate and hemimorphite is a zinc silicate. Both are common as small crystals on some of the mine dumps. Specimen: Joe Marty. Photo: Joe Marty.

OPHIR

The waste rock on old mine dumps provides the collector with material to search for specimens. Photo: Jim Wilson.

Photomicrograph of spheres of rosasite, a copper-zinc carbonate, and clear crystals of hemimorphite, a zinc silicate, from the Ophir area. Specimen: Jim and Paula Wilson. Photo: Jim Wilson.

Aurichalcite, a zinc-copper carbonate, and hemimorphite from the Ophir area. Specimen: Jim and Paula Wilson. Photo: John R. Shupe.

Photomicrograph of rosasite spheres on hemimorphite. Specimen: Joe Marty. Photo: Joe Marty.

Tufts of blue aurichalcite and white crystals of calcite. Specimen: Joe Marty. Photo: Joe Marty.

GOLD HILL

Sphere of cuprian adamite, a zinc arsenate, on limonite from Gold Hill. Sphere is about 0.75 inch across. Specimen: Jim and Paula Wilson. Photo: John R. Shupe.

Photomicrograph of connellite, a copper chlorosulfate, one of many rare species found at Gold Hill. Specimen: Joe Marty. Photo: Joe Marty.

Photomicrograph of conichalcite, a calcium-copper arsenate, from Gold Hill. Specimen: Joe Marty. Photo: Joe Marty.

Photomicrograph of philipsburgite from Gold Hill. This is only the second known occurrence of this mineral in the world. Specimen: Joe Marty. Photo: Joe Marty.

Photomicrograph of conichalcite, a calcium-copper arsenate, from Gold Hill. Specimen: Joe Marty. Photo: Joe Marty.

Photomicrograph of conichalcite spheres on quartz crystals from Gold Hill. Specimen: Joe Marty. Photo: Joe Marty.

Photomicrograph of blue tuft of mixite, a bismuth-copper arsenate, from Gold Hill. Specimen: Joe Marty. Photo: Joe Marty.

DUGWAY RANGE AREA

Sceptered quartz crystals from the interior of a geode from the Dugway geode beds. The cluster of crystals is about 0.6 inch across. Part of this area is maintained as a collecting area by the BLM. Private claims also exist in the vicinity. Specimen: Hugh and Fay Burnside Collection. Photo: David Richerson.

Purple fluorite on crystal blades of white barite from the Dugway Range. Overall height of the specimen is about 4 inches. Specimen: Jim and Paula Wilson. Photo: John R. Shupe.

Cut and polished slab of banded fluorite from the Dugway Range. Crystals of fluorite occur, but much of the material from here is massive. This specimen measures 3 x 6 inches. Specimen: Utah Museum of Natural History (MC0174R). Photo: John Shupe.

Distorted pyritohedral pyrite crystal (1.0 inch) from the Dugway Range. Specimen: Jim and Paula Wilson. Photo: John R. Shupe.

Pyrite crystal (1.25 inches) showing pyritohedron modified by cube faces. Dugway Range. Specimen: Jim and Paula Wilson. Photo: John R. Shupe.

Hollow quartz crystals from the Dugway Range. Specimen is 0.5 inch across. Specimen: Hugh and Fay Burnside. Photo: David Richerson.

MILFORD AREA

The Mineral Range which lies between Milford and Beaver provides the opportunity to collect quartz and feldspar crystals. Photo: Jim Wilson.

Twinned orthoclase feldspar from a miarolitic cavity in the Mineral Range. Specimen: Jim and Paula Wilson. Photo: John R. Shupe.

Group of smoky quartz crystals from a cavity in the Mineral Range. Specimen: Jim and Paula Wilson. Photo: John R. Shupe.

Photomicrograph of brochantite, a copper sulfate, found on mine dumps near Milford. Specimen: Joe Marty. Photo: Joe Marty.

TINTIC MINING DISTRICT

Photomicrograph of mixite and azurite from the Carissa Mine, Tintic District. Specimen: Joe Marty. Photo: Joe Marty.

Native copper and cuprite from the Tintic District. This specimen is 3 x 4 inches. Specimen: Utah Museum of Natural History (MC2282). Photo: John R. Shupe.

Native copper from the Burgin Mine, Tintic District. This specimen is 2 inches in length. Specimen: Jim and Paula Wilson. Photo: John R. Shupe.

Stalactitic malachite from the Mammoth Mine, Tintic District. This specimen is 3 x 3 inches. Specimen: Utah Museum of Natural History (MC2301). Photo: John R. Shupe.

Photomicrograph of mixite from the Northern Spy Mine, Tintic District. Specimen: Joe Marty. Photo: Joe Marty.

Photomicrograph of crystals of cornwallite, a copper arsenate, from the Centennial Eureka Mine, Tintic District. Specimen: Joe Marty. Photo: Joe Marty.

Azurite and malachite replacing selenite gypsum from the Bullion-Beck Mine, Tintic District. Specimen is 3 x 6 inches. Specimen: Utah Museum of Natural History (MC2491). Photo: John R. Shupe.

Malachite from the Mammoth Mine, Tintic District. This specimen is 3 x 6 inches. Specimen: Utah Museum of Natural History (MC2168). Photo: John R. Shupe.

VARIOUS LOCATIONS

Azurite nodule from the La Sal area, San Juan County. Nodule is about 3 inches in diameter. Specimen: Jim and Paula Wilson. Photo: John R. Shupe.

Two-inch high crystals of halite from the Great Salt Lake. Specimen: Utah Museum of Natural History (MC2795). Photo: John R. Shupe.

Sawn slab of crandallite and variscite, rare aluminum phosphates, from the Fairfield area, Utah County. Specimen is 2 x 6 inches. Note the small faults that offset the layers. Specimen: Utah Museum of Natural History (MC2685). Photo: John R. Shupe.

Sawn block of variscite from the Fairfield area, Utah County. Specimen is 4 x 5 inches. Specimen: Utah Museum of Natural History (MC2485). Photo: John R. Shupe.

Gypsum crystals from the Great Salt Lake. Overall specimen is 1.0 inch x 0.6 inch. Specimen: Hugh and Fay Burnside Collection. Photo: David Richerson.

Halite crystals on a stick from the Great Salt Lake. Specimen: Utah Museum of Natural History (MC2343). Photo: John R. Shupe.

SAN RAFAEL SWELL

Gypsum crystals from the Temple Mountain area. Rosettes such as this are often referred to as ram's horn gypsum or gypsum flowers. The rosette is about 0.75 inch in diameter. Specimen: Hugh and Fay Burnside Collection. Photo: David Richerson.

Close-up view of celestite crystal (about 1 inch) from geode. Specimen: Hugh and Fay Burnside Collection. Photo: David Richerson.

Celestite and calcite in a geode from the San Rafael Swell. Overall height of the specimen is about 5 inches. Specimen: Jim and Paula Wilson. Photo: John R. Shupe.

Celestite, strontium sulfate, from the San Rafael Swell. This specimen measures 12 x 8 inches. Specimen: Utah Museum of Natural History (MC2327). Photo: John R. Shupe.

Group of celestite crystals from a geode. The cluster of crystals is 2 inches x 1.5 inches. Specimen: Hugh and Fay Burnside Collection. Photo: David Richerson.

Relatively large celestite crystals from the San Rafael Swell. This specimen measures 4 x 6 inches. Specimen: Utah Museum of Natural History (MC2297). Photo: John R. Shupe.

Polished slab of jasper from the San Rafael Swell. This specimen is about 3 x 4 inches. Specimen: Utah Museum of Natural History (MC2197). Photo: John R. Shupe.

VARIOUS LOCATIONS

Aurichalcite on limonite from Tecoma Hill, Box Elder County. Specimen: Jim and Paula Wilson. Photo: John R. Shupe.

Azurite cabochon from the Dixie Apex Mine, Washington County, Utah. Specimen is 1.5 x 2 inches. Specimen: Utah Museum of Natural History (MC2215). Photo: John R. Shupe.

Azurite and malachite from the Dixie Apex Mine, Washington County, Utah. Specimen measures about 7 x 7 inches. Dumps of this mine were removed in recent years and the mine operated as a source of gallium and germanium. Specimen: Utah Museum of Natural History (MC2254). Photo: John R. Shupe.

Photomicrograph of fluorite crystals from near Mountain Springs, Wah Wah Range, Iron County. Specimen: Jim and Paula Wilson. Photo: Joe Marty.

Photomicrograph of wulfenite crystals from Tecoma Hill, Box Elder County. Specimen: Joe Marty. Photo: Joe Marty.

VARIOUS LOCATIONS

Fluorite crystals from the Deer Trail Mine near Marysvale, Utah. When found these crystals were covered with fine-grained quartz. This specimen measures about 4 x 6 inches. Specimen: Utah Museum of Natural History (MC3073). Photo: John R. Shupe.

Limonite pseudomorphs after pyrite crystals, Lake Mountains, Utah County. This grouping of crystals measures 6 x 9 inches. Specimen: Utah Museum of Natural History (MC3151). Photo: John R. Shupe.

Curved mass of stibnite crystals from near Antimony, Garfield County. The specimen measures about 2.75 inches high. Specimen: Utah Museum of Natural History (MC2822). Photo: John R. Shupe.

Sulfur crystals from Sulphurdale, Utah. This specimen measures about 4 x 6 inches. Specimen: Utah Museum of Natural History (MC2238). Photo: John R. Shupe.

Spray of stibnite crystals from near Antimony, Garfield County. The specimen measures about 6 inches high. Specimen: Utah Museum of Natural History (MC0409R). Photo: John R. Shupe.

Curved mass of stibnite from near Antimony, Garfield County. The specimen measures about 6 x 9 inches. Specimen: Utah Museum of Natural History (MC2484). Photo: John R. Shupe.

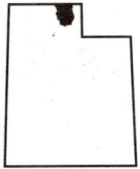the shale near its contact with the overlying limestone. Eight or more small pits can be found along the strike of the bed. Note: Strict interpretation of the Wilderness Act can be used to prohibit digging in Wilderness Areas established by the Federal government. A spokesperson for the Forest Service has indicated that while you may collect material exposed at the surface, digging would be viewed as a violation. Since few minerals or fossils are found exposed at the surface, this, in effect, prohibits collecting in Wilderness Areas.

Land Status: National Forest lands.

Map: Naomi Peak (7.5), Logan (m).

References: Visited by this writer. Lloyd Gunther, Brigham City, UT.

Location:	Spring Hollow area
Fossils:	brachiopods

Description: Brachiopods occur in the Leatham Formation in Spring Hollow in Logan Canyon between the elevations of 5,600 and 6,000 feet. The brachiopod *Schizophoria williamsi* (a species named for the late Dr. J. S. Williams of Utah State) is found encased in stromatolitic algal nodules and in the sediments between the nodules. Other brachiopods found here include *Rhipidomella*, *Syringothyris*, *Spirifer*, *Composita*, *Beecheria*, and *Tylothyris*.

Directions: Go up Logan Canyon about 6 miles to the reservoir and campground at Spring Hollow. Go up Spring Hollow to the approximate elevation given above and search in rocks on both sides of the hollow in this vicinity.

Land Status: National Forest lands.

Maps: Mt. Elmer (7.5), Logan (m).

References: Lloyd Gunther, Brigham City, UT. Rodriguez and Gutschick (1978).

Athabaskia bithus (Walcott). A trilobite from the Spence Shale of the Wellsville Mountians. Specimen is about 2.6 inches long. Photo: Val Gunther.

Location:	Lodgepole Limestone
Fossils:	crinoids, brachiopods, corals, bryozoans

Description: The Mississippian Lodgepole Limestone is an extremely fossiliferous unit and fossils can be found at almost any outcrop.

Directions: Some of the more accessible locations at which the Lodgepole Limestone crops out are listed below:

(1) The Lodgepole occurs about 0.5 miles up Spring Hollow, Mill Hollow, and Beirdneau Hollow in the lower part of Logan Canyon.

(2) It crops out about 0.75 mile up Leatham Hollow off the Left Fork of Blacksmith Fork.

(3) It occurs in the steep slopes at the head of Wood Camp Hollow.

(4) It is found in Millville Canyon about 1.5 miles from the canyon mouth.

(5) The Lodgepole Limestone occurs in Providence Canyon about 1.75 miles from the mouth of the canyon.

(6) It is found in Dry Canyon, east of Logan, about 2 miles from the canyon mouth.

(7) The higher cliffs on both sides of Blacksmith Fork, beginning about 1 mile up the canyon, are Lodgepole Limestone.

Land Status: National Forest lands.

Maps: Logan (m), Logan (7.5), Logan Peak (7.5), Mt. Elmer (7.5).

References: Williams (1958).

Location:	**Lucky Star Mine area**
Minerals:	**quartz, limonite after pyrite, dolomite, malachite, azurite, galena**

Description: There are a number of small mines and prospects in Cache County most of which had very little production. This particular mine has a dump that extends well down the hill from the mine and, in fact, the dump looks much like any of the many taluses that occur on the canyon sides. Quartz crystals, up to 1 inch in length, occur in the dump material along with pyritohedrons of pyrite that have been replaced by limonite creating pseudomorphs. Aggregates of curved rhombohedral dolomite crystals are common on the dump. Malachite and azurite, while not abundant, can easily be found. Small masses of oxidized galena, up to 2 inches in diameter, are scattered through the material and can be recognized by the high specific gravity when you heft a specimen.

Directions: From Hyrum, take Utah Highway 101 up Blacksmith Fork toward Hardware Ranch. Near milepost 13 turn left onto the gravel road going up the Left Hand Fork. At about 5.6 miles is a major intersection with the road to the left going up Cowley Canyon. Stay to the right and 0.8 mile further you will pass Gray Cliff Spring. The Forest Service sign here has been vandalized, but the sign post remains and the spring is large and obvious, coming from the cliff on the left hand side of the road. The mine dump is located about 2.1 miles beyond this spring. If you reach another large spring, Lime Spring, coming down the hill on the left, then you have gone too far. Because of the steep slope and narrow canyon, the dump is not visible from the road while driving. It is marked by a few small debris piles, containing quartz crystals, on the roadside where material has washed down from above. The slope on which the mine dump is located has several flat-sided spires of rock projecting from the hill. Passenger cars can reach the intersection to Cowley Canyon, but an HCV is recommended beyond that point.

Land Status: National Forest lands.

Maps: Logan (m), Boulder Mtn. (7.5).

References: Visited by this writer.

Location:	**Dry Lake area**
Fossils:	**horn coral, brachiopods**

Description: The Mississippian Great Blue Limestone is exposed in large roadcuts along each side of U.S. 89-91 north of Mantua, Utah. Horn corals and brachiopods, some showing pyritization, can be found here. A few quartz crystals up to 2 inches in length were found along fault zones exposed during recent construction work.

Directions: This location is north of Sardine Summit overlooking the Dry Lake area, just before Milepost 11. Off-road parking is available at the south end of the eastern road cut and in a large pull-out at the north end of the western road cut. Road construction (July 1995) may provide other collecting opportunities in some of the new exposures created along this highway.

Land Status: Highway right-of-way. Private land past fences.

Maps: Mt. Pisgah (7.5), Logan (m).

References: Visited by this writer.

Glossopleura gigantea Resser. A very large trilobite found in the Spence Shale of the wellsville Mountains. Specimen is about 5 inches long. Photo: Val Gunther.

CARBON COUNTY

Carbon County includes part of the Wasatch Plateau (and its coal deposits) and the lowland area at the north end of the San Rafael Swell. The rocks are all sedimentary and most are Cretaceous in age. Excellent fossils can be found at many localities in the shale beds.

Location: Ford Creek

Fossils: plants, coal

Description: Thin beds of coal occur south of Ford Creek in the North Horn Formation. Shale beds near the coal seams contain plant fossils.

Directions: This site is located 1.5 miles south of the Utah County - Carbon County line where U.S. 6 crosses Ford Creek.

Land Status: BLM public lands.

Maps: Price (m), Kyune (7.5).

References: Rigby, et al. (1974).

Location: Mounds Reef

Fossils: pelecypods, cephalopods

Descriptions: Sandstone concretions within one of the horizons forming the caprock of the Mounds Reef contain abundant remains of pelecypods and cephalopods. Some coiled specimens up to 6 inches have been found in this area.

Directions: This site is located along the Emery-Carbon County line. From Wellington, proceed east on U.S. 6 and turn south on a good gravel road just past milepost 253. This road crosses to the Reef and travels along its crest before descending through the Reef to the railroad. As a starting point, search along the middle bench area where the road descends through the Reef. By taking a left after descending from the Reef, the road can be followed back to U.S. 6 at milepost 259. (If coming from that direction, take a right after leaving the highway.)

Land Status: BLM public lands.

Maps: Huntingdon (m), Mounds (7.5).

References: Visited by this writer.

DAGGETT COUNTY

Daggett County is a small county on the north slope of the Uinta Mountains and is best known for Flaming Gorge Reservoir. There are sedimentary rocks on the north slope so fossil collecting is possible. Interesting metamorphic minerals occur in the Red Creek Canyon area.

Location: Red Creek Canyon area

Minerals: garnet, staurolite, kyanite, tourmaline, anthophyllite, beryl

Description: The Red Creek Quartzite occurs in this area and, in addition to the dominant quartzite lithology, there are abundant layers of mica schist which has garnet and staurolite as accessory minerals. Garnets are up to 2 inches in diameter, although most are much smaller. Staurolite crystals are up to 1.5 inches in length and contain abundant inclusions of quartz. Kyanite, from 1 to 2 inches in length, occurs in some horizons and may be associated with black tourmaline. Kyanite also occurs in the Mountain Home Draw area. Anthophyllite occurs in the first large ravine east of Mountain Home Draw in the SW ¼, NE ¼, Sec. 11, T2N, R24E. It constitutes about a third of the rock and consists of minute prismatic grains less than 0.25 inch. Beryl has been reported from a pegmatite in the area. Most of the pegmatites are found in Sec. 11 and 12 and are generally of very simple mineralogy.

Directions: This remote area is accessible by gravel roads leading south from Rock Springs, Wyoming, and by gravel roads from north of Dutch John. Consult detailed maps and inquire locally about road conditions.

Land Status: National Forest lands.

Maps: Dutch John (m), Clay Basin (7.5).

References: Hansen (1957).

DAVIS COUNTY

Davis County is a small county which includes that part of the Wasatch Front from Weber Canyon south to Bountiful. The mountains in this area are formed from the Farmington Canyon Complex, a diverse mixture of regionally metamorphosed rocks and small igneous bodies. The county also includes Antelope Island in the Great Salt Lake.

Location: Farmington Canyon area

Rock: migmatite, pegmatite, gneiss

Description: The Farmington Canyon Complex is a suite of Precambrian metamorphic and igneous rocks that extend from Ogden to Bountiful and are well exposed in the vicinity of Farmington Canyon. The gneiss often shows folding that creates interesting banded patterns suitable for slabbing. Also found here are migmatites, rocks that were partially melted during metamorphism such that stringers of quartz-feldspar run through the gneiss. Sometimes these exhibit ptygmatic folding, somewhat like a contorted ribbon of toothpaste, indicating the rock was probably quite plastic at the time it occurred. Pegmatites are found throughout the Farmington Canyon Complex, but are best developed in the Farmington Canyon area. Since these pegmatites are the result of intense metamorphism, rather than igneous processes, they are mineralogically uninteresting except for the coarse intergrown quartz and feldspar. Sometimes large books of mica can be found in association with the pegmatites. Quartz crystals and garnet crystals can sometimes be found in the metamorphic rocks of this area, although they are usually of inferior quality.

Directions: Access is available at any number of locations along the Wasatch Front from the Ogden area to Bountiful. An interesting drive that takes you into the heart of the complex can be made by taking the road up Farmington Canyon from the north end of 100 East Street in Farmington and coming down at Bountiful.

Land Status: National Forest lands.

Maps: Ogden (7.5), Kaysville (7.5), Peterson (7.5), Bountiful Peak (7.5).

References: Visited by this writer. Bryant (1988).

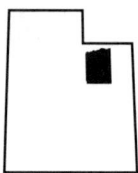

DUCHESNE COUNTY

Duchesne County extends from the crest of the Uinta Mountains southward across the Uinta Basin. Rocks vary in age from Precambrian in the Uintas, through narrow outcrops of Paleozoic and Mesozoic rocks on the south slope, to extensive areas of Tertiary rocks in the basin. Fossils will be found in many of the sedimentary units thoughout the county.

Location: Near Starvation Reservoir

Fossils: gar fish

Directions: Fish fossils are reported to occur in a large road cut along U.S. 40 immediately west of Starvation Reservoir. Collecting of vertebrates is restricted by federal and state law. Check with the national forest office or the office of the State Paleontologist to see if permits are available.

Land Status: Highway right-of-way.

Maps: Duchesne (m), Rabbit Gulch (7.5), Duchesne (7.5)>

References: Bob Randolph, Salt Lake City, UT.

 # EMERY COUNTY

Emery County encompasses the eastern edge of the Wasatch Plateau, where coal and plant fossils occur in the Cretaceous rocks exposed there, and includes the entire San Rafael Swell. A variety of fossils including ammonites and oysters are found in the broad valleys formed in the Mancos Shale around the margin of the Swell. Agates are abundant in certain rock units and a variety of interesting minerals can be found here as well.

Location: Willow Springs

Rock: agate

Description: Agate in the form of loose chips and fragments.

Directions: From the intersection of Utah Highway 10 and I-70 south of Emery, take the graded dirt road (on the south side of the interchange) east about 1.5 miles and then go south about 9 miles. Coming up from the valley floor, you will see a pond on the right side which may be dry during the summer. Agate chips are found in this vicinity. Larger pieces can be found in the washes nearby.

Land Status: BLM public lands.

Maps: Salina (m), Willow Springs (7.5).

Reference: Stowe (1979).

Location: West of Green River

Rock: grape agate

Description: Agate in this area is referred to as grape agate because of the botryoidal habit.

Directions: Go west from Green River to the junction of I-70 and Utah Highway 24. In the immediate area of the junction, west of Highway 24, agate can be found. About 4.2 miles south of the junction (about 0.5 mile before the San Rafael River bridge) a road to the east leads about 1 mile to another agate area.

Land Status: BLM public lands.

Maps: San Rafael Desert (m), Jessie's Twist (7.5).

Reference: Stowe (1979).

Location: Summerville Wash area

Rock: agate

Fossils: petrified wood

Description: Red agate and petrified wood are found in the hills south of the Summerville Wash.

Directions: From Woodside, on U.S. 6-50 south of Price, go about 5 miles south and take a gravel road west under the railroad. Travel about 3 miles into the hills and search in that area.

Land Status: BLM public lands.

Maps: Huntingdon (m), Dry Mesa (7.5).

Reference: Stowe (1979).

Location: Grassy Wash area

Fossils: pelecypods

Description: Fragments of the pelecypods *Ostrea* and *Inoceramus* are common in the Mancos Shale throughout this area.

Directions: Located 0.4 miles south of Grassy Wash, 11.2 miles south of the Carbon-Emery County line, and 5.6 miles north of Woodside on U.S. 6-50. Search the road cuts on both sides of the road.

Land Status: BLM public lands and highway right-of-way.

Maps: Huntingdon (m).

References: Rigby, et al. (1974).

Location: Head of Buckhorn Wash

Fossils: pelecypods

Description: The pelecypod *Inoceramus* occurs in outcrops of the Cretaceous rocks alongside the road into Buckhorn Wash.

Directions: The Buckhorn Wash Road leaves Utah Highway 10 about 8 miles south of Huntingdon. Turn east on the road and follow it across Castle Valley (about 15 miles) until it starts to descend Buckhorn Wash to the campground on the San Rafael River. Search on the left side of the road at the head of the wash.

Land Status: BLM public lands.

Maps: Huntingdon (m),

References: Bob Randolph, Salt Lake City, UT.

Location: South of Castle Dale

Fossils: ammonites

Rock: jasper, agate

Description: The ammonoid cephalopod *Scaphites* is common throughout a broad outcrop area of the Mancos Shale in the Emery-Castle Dale-Price-Woodside area, forming a broad arc around the north end of the San Rafael Swell. The fossils commonly occur in silicified nodules that weather out of the shale and are marked by a rusty brown color compared to the gray shale. Some of the higher hills in this area are capped by a veneer of stream gravels which include abundant clasts of jasper and agate.

Directions: These fossils occur in a broad area. Examine the area south and east of Castle Dale behind the power plant and under the power lines running from the plant. One such area occurs in Sec. 34, T19S, R8E and can be reached by taking the gravel road due east out of Clawson, going straight at the intersection marked by the yield signs, down the hill and past the power lines to the shaly outcrops along the road (total distance about 4.6 miles). (Alternatively, turn south off the highway south of the overpass at the power plant and follow that road past the coal loading area of the plant until you reach the intersection marked with the yield signs and there turn left for 1.4 miles.)

Land Status: BLM public lands.

Maps: Manti (m), Huntingdon (m)

References: Visited by this writer. Steve Robison, Ogden, UT. Cobban (1976).

Location: Straight Canyon

Fossils: leaves

Description: Plant material is abundant in the Cretaceous Blackhawk Formation of Emery and Sevier Counties. Parker (1976, p.100-101) reports that of 7,400 specimens collected in Straight Canyon and Salina

A Guide to Collecting Sites

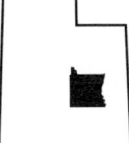

Canyon, there were "about 115 species ... (including) one thalloid liverwort, one club moss-like plant (*Lycopsida*), 14 ferns (*Filicopsida*), 2 cycad-like plants (*Cyadopsida*), and 12 coniferous plants (*Coniferopsida*), and 86 flowering plants (*Angiospermopsida*)."

Directions: Proceed west from the Orangeville-Castle Dale area on U-29 toward Joes Valley Reservoir. The Blackhawk Formation forms the walls of Straight Canyon beginning about one mile past the turnoff to Cottonwood Creek. Plant fossils can be found at the abandoned Black Diamond Coal Mine, about midway between milepost 8 and 9; at the gully north of the road near milepost 8; and at Cox Swale, a small canyon on the south side of the canyon about 0.4 mile past milepost 8.

Land Status: National Forest lands.

Maps: Manti (m), Mahogany Point (7.5).

References: Parker (1976), Cross, et al. (1975).

Location:	**The Squeeze**
Minerals:	**celestite, quartz, calcite**
Rock:	**jasper, geodes**

Description: Certain horizons within the Curtis Formation contain nodules of jasper. Some of the jasper nodules are hollow, forming geodes, which may contain crystals of quartz, calcite, or celestite. Other nodules are solid containing bands of the same minerals.

Directions: This location is reached from the westbound lane of I-70 about 2.5 miles west of the interchange with U-24 to Hanksville. The turnoff is a gravel road passing through a gate in the interstate fence, located between the "Rest Area, 1 Mile" sign and the rest area itself. As of this writing, blue ribbon on the highway reflector marks the turn. If you miss this turn it is many miles to an interchange. Once through the gate, you may pass under the interstate to outcrops of the Curtis south of I-70, or you may take the fork to the right (rather than crossing the wash) and drive about 0.3 mile to the bluff near the north side of the interstate. Walk along the base of the bluffs and in areas below the outcrop horizon of the nodules. They will be found scattered abundantly on the ground.

Land Status: BLM public lands.

Maps: San Rafael Desert (m), Tidwell Bottoms (15).

References: Visited by this writer.

Location:	**Tidwell Draw**
Rock:	**jasper**

Description: Jasper is abundant in the Curtis Formation in this vicinity.

Directions: Turn west off U.S. 6 about 4 miles north of the intersection with I-70 on a BLM road marked by signs indicating Tidwell Draw and Buckmaster Reservoir. Follow the signs toward Tidwell Draw and pass under the power line and through a gate in the fence. About 0.25 mile past the gate, park and search the sandstone ledges below the red shaly unit.

Land Status: BLM public land.

Maps: Huntingdon (m), San Rafael Desert (m), Jessies Twist (7.5), Spotted Wolf Canyon (7.5).

References: Visited by the author.

Location:	**Greasewood Draw**
Mineral:	**quartz, celestite**
Rock:	**jasper**

Description: Jasper is abundant in the Curtis and Summerville Formations that crop out along Greasewood Draw south of Hatt Ranch. Some of the jasper nodules are geodes containing pink, white, or blue celestite. A few of the geodes contain quartz crystals.

Directions: Proceed south from I-70 on U-24 toward Hanksville. After crossing the San Rafael River, about 5 miles south of the interstate, turn west on a gravel road just south of milepost 156. Greasewood Draw is the broad wash leading west to the San Rafael Reef.

Land Status: BLM public land.

Maps: San Rafael Desert (m), Tidwell Bottoms (15).

References: Visited by this writer.

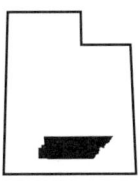

GARFIELD COUNTY

This county is located in the extreme south-central part of the state. Rocks in this county include the volcanic rocks of the high plateaus such as the Markagunt Plateau, Sevier Plateau, Aquarius Plateau, and Boulder Mountain in the western part of the county. In the eastern half of the county are the Henry Mountains with their distinctive intrusive igneous rocks. Sedimentary rocks of the Mesozoic Era are found from Tropic eastward across the county. Metallic minerals are found in a few locations, but the widespread sedimentary rocks produce good specimens of agate, gypsum, petrified wood, and fossils.

Location: Hansen Creek

Fossils: petrified wood

Directions: Drive south from Hanksville on Utah Highways 95 and 276 toward Ticaboo and Bullfrog. Continue 0.8 mile beyond milepost 19 to a junction with a sign "Starr Springs Recreation Area". Go north 5 miles to a junction and turn west toward Clay Point. At 6.4 miles is another junction. Stay to the right and continue for approximately 2 miles to the next drainage which is Hansen Creek. Go down the drainage and collect in this area. HCV and/or 4WD recommended.

Land Status: BLM public lands.

Maps: Hite Crossing (m), Mt. Hillers (15).

References: Stowe (1979).

Location: Casto Canyon

Rock: agate

Description: Red, white, and some blue agate scattered over the surface of Agate Hill.

Directions: Go about 4.5 miles south of Panguitch, turn east and cross a wooden bridge leading to Casto Canyon. Proceed 3 miles, passing through a gate, and into a valley. A hill on the south side of the road is known as Agate Hill.

Land Status: BLM public lands and private lands.

Maps: Panguitch (m), Casto Canyon (7.5).

References: Stowe (1979).

Location: Spencer Flat

Rock: concretions

Description: Concretions occur in a wide variety of shapes although spherical concretions are most common. These are rust-colored, iron-impregnated sandstone known locally as "Navajo Cherries", "Kayenta Berries", "Entrada Berries", or "Moqui Marbles." Sizes range from 0.25 inch up to 4 inches in diameter.

Directions: From the east edge of Escalante drive 10 miles on Utah Highway 12 and watch for the scenic overlook of the Escalante River. A half mile past the overlook take the dirt road to the right with a sign indicating "Spencer Flat." Take this road to Spencer Flat (5 miles) and drive out onto the flat for 1.5 miles to where the main road makes a right angle turn and heads toward the cliffs on the south edge of the flat. Concretions appear along the road in this area.

Land Status: BLM public lands.

Maps: Escalante (m), Tenmile Flat (7.5), Red Breaks (7.5).

References: Stowe (1979).

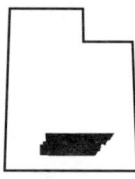

Location: Antimony Creek

Minerals: stibnite, gypsum

Description: Stibnite and gypsum can be found in the dumps and bulldozer cuts associated with the various mines in this area. The Emma Mine was the largest producer of antimony ore in the area.

Directions: Drive south from Antimony for 1.75 miles and turn left at the sign marked "Antimony Creek." Three miles from the junction you will enter Dixie National Forest. Continue up Antimony Creek for 1.75 miles to an unimproved 4WD road taking off to the right. Go up the road to the second branch to the right (about 0.5 mile), turn right and follow the trail 0.5 mile to the Emma Mine. Other mines are in the Antimony Creek area and may be located by consulting the topographic map.

Land Status: Mining claims and National Forest lands.

Maps: Loa (m), Antimony (7.5).

References: Stowe (1979).

Location: Coal Bed Canyon

Rock: clinkers

Description: Clinkers represent the rocks associated with coal beds that have burned. They are red, dark grey, or black in color.

Directions: Turn south at the Moqui Motel in Escalante and drive 4.6 miles along an improved gravel road to the mouth of Coal Bed Canyon which is on the right. Walk up the canyon and clinkers can be found in the gravel bars.

Land Status: BLM public lands.

Maps: Escalante (m), Canaan Creek (7.5).

References: Stowe (1979).

Location: Tenmile Wash

Mineral: gypsum

Description: Gypsum is exposed in road cuts in the Tenmile Wash area.

Directions: Drive east out of Escalante on Utah Highway 12 for 4.3 miles to the junction marked with the "Hole in the Rock" sign. Turn south at the junction and go 5 miles to the headwaters of Harris Wash (Tenmile Spring area). After crossing the wash, look for exposures of gypsum in the road cuts to the left.

Land Status: BLM public lands.

Maps: Escalante (m), Dave Canyon (7.5), Tenmile Flat (7.5).

References: Stowe (1979)

Location: South Creek

Mineral: hornblende

Description: Boulders in South Creek contain large, well-formed hornblende crystals. You can continue up the creek to trace the boulders to their outcrop.

Directions: From Caineville go west on Utah Highway 12 for 5 miles to Notom junction. Turn south to Notom, stay to the left and continue south for approximately 10 miles to a junction, stay left and continue 4.5 miles to another junction, stay left and continue another 4.5 miles to the South Creek drainage.

A Guide to Collecting Sites

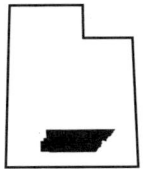

Land Status: BLM public lands.

Maps: Hanksville (m), Notom (15), Mt. Ellen (15).

References: Stowe (1979).

Location: **Horse Canyon Wash**

Fossils: **petrified wood**

Description: Wood is found associated with the red- and blue-colored Chinle Formation.

Directions: Take the Burr Trail from Boulder for 6.5 miles to Deer Creek. Continue for 4 miles to Long Canyon and up the canyon to the Long Canyon overlook. Two miles past the overlook turn right at a junction which says "Petrified wood 12, Burr Trail 34." Continue for 4.5 miles to Horse Canyon Wash which enters from the right. Drive up Horse Canyon Wash about 1 mile to the base of the cliffs. A 4WD is recommended for the drive up the wash.

Land Status: BLM public lands.

Maps: Escalante (m), Wagon Box Mesa (15).

References: Stowe (1979).

Location: **Blue Spruce Campground**

Rocks: **agate and jasper**

Description: Agate is widespread throughout the area.

Directions: Go north out of Escalante and across the Escalante River. Agates are found near the right side of the fence and cattle guard. Go north for 19 miles to the Blue Spruce campground. Jasper can be found in the gullies about 0.5 mile north of the campground. From the campground you can drive about 6.5 miles north to a ranch road turnoff. Agates are located along the road about 1 mile before reaching the ranch road. Other agate locations can be found along this road as you continue toward Utah Highway 12 west of Boulder.

Land Status: National Forest lands.

Maps: Escalante (m), Escalante (7.5).

References: Stowe (1979).

Location: **East of Tenmile Flat**

Mineral: **sand calcite crystals**

Description: Sand calcite crystals are crystals of calcite that have incorporated sand grains within the sandstone unit in which they form. These particular crystals occur within the Jurassic Morrison Formation and analysis has shown them to be 31.6% calcite (Sargent and Zeller, 1984, p. 2). The crystals are in the form of scalenohedrons with rounded terminations, believed to be the result of rhombohedral faces.

Directions: The location is reached by going south on the Hole in the Rock Road, after leaving Escalante, for about 3 miles and taking a road to the right (south), crossing the wash, and continuing about 3.5 miles. The site is on a ridge about 0.9 mile southeast of this point. The outcrop area is less than an acre and may be difficult to locate.

Land Status: BLM public lands.

Maps: Escalante (m), Dave Canyon (7.5), Tenmile Flat (7.5).

References: Sargent and Zeller (1984).

Location:	Henrieville area
Fossils:	pelecypods, gastropods, cephalopods
Mineral:	gypsum
Rock:	septarian nodules

Description: An abundant fauna of gastropods, cephalopods, and pelecypods occur within a concretionary zone of the Tropic Shale, a widespread unit in southern Utah that commonly forms steel-gray hills and badlands. In the area of Henrieville, the concretionary zone lies within a gray, bench-forming unit above white sandstone bluffs and a ledgey brown sandstone unit. Within the brown sandstone ledges is a 3-foot-thick oyster shell bed, which weathers to produce abundant shells on the slopes. The concretions are septarian nodules, but seldom hollow, and fragments of them can be found on the slopes below the outcrop zone. The concretions contain a number of different molluscs and may include the pelecypods *Camptonectes, Corbula, Exogyra, Gryphaea, Inoceramus, Lima, Liopistha, Lucina*, and *Unio*; the gastropods *Anchura, Aporrhais, Lunatia, Sigaretus, Tritonium*, and *Turritella*; and the cephalopods *Allocrioceras, Baculites, Eucalyoceras, Kanabiceras, Metoicoceras*, and *Scaphites*.

Gypsum is fairly abundant in the carbonaceous shales and coaly beds of the Tropic Shale. Irregular pieces of gypsum are common and occasional well-formed monoclinic crystals up to 1.5 inches are found.

Directions: The Tropic Shale is best exposed in the area from the base of the Bryce Canyon escarpment west of Tropic to several miles east of Henrieville. The shale is well exposed in the mesa along the east side of U-12 immediately east and north of Henrieville. The west and north slopes are accessible from U-12; a road leading south and east out of Henrieville goes around the south end of the mesa and offers access into that area. Other exposures of the Tropic Shale can be determined from a geologic map.

Land Status: BLM public lands.

Maps: Panguitch (m), Escalante (m), Henrieville (7.5), Pine Lake (7.5), Tropic Canyon (7.5).

References: Visited by this writer. Swenson (1962).

GRAND COUNTY

Grand County is located along the Utah-Colorado border and extends from the Book Cliffs on the north to Moab and the La Sal Mountains in the south. It is bordered on the west by the Green River and encloses Arches National Park. Rocks in the county are primarily Mesozoic sedimentary rocks, but Precambrian rocks are exposed in Westwater Canyon and in the Big Triangle area southeast of Westwater. Intrusive rocks are found in the La Sal Mountains.

Location: Little Valley

Rock: agate and petrified wood

Description: Agate and petrified wood occur throughout the Little Valley area. (Secs. 17, 20, 21, 27, 28, 34, T23S, R20E).

Directions: Drive north 5.5 miles from the junction of U.S. 191 and Utah Highway 313 (the road to Dead Horse Point) to a junction with a dirt road leading to the east (right) with the sign "Burro Seep Spring 1.5 miles." Follow this road about 3 miles to a junction. Turn left at the junction and go north passing through a gate. Search gullies east and west of the road.

Land Status: BLM public lands.

Maps: Moab (m), Moab (7.5), Thompson (7.5).

References: Stowe (1979).

Location: Poison Strip area

Rocks: agate and petrified wood

Description: The Poison Strip represents an area of uranium mineralization along with the selenium that often accompanies it. Selenium is a poisonous substance, resulting in poisonous springs, and is also taken up by locoweed.

Directions: Drive east from Crescent Junction on I-70 for 11.5 miles and exit at the "Ranch Exit." Drive south for 8.1 miles to a junction, turn left (east) and continue into the Poison Strip area.

Land Status: BLM public lands, mining claims.

Maps: Moab (m), Thompson (7.5).

References: Stowe (1979).

Location: Hotel Mesa area

Rock: agate

Description: Agate is abundant in this area.

Directions: Take Utah Highway 128 east from Moab. Cross the Colorado River and proceed 3 miles until you see some buildings on the right side of the road. The mountain on the west (left) side of the road has several areas where agate occurs.

Land Status: BLM public lands.

Maps: Moab (m), Cisco (7.5).

References: Stowe (1979).

Location: South of Floy Station

Rock: agate

Description: Deep red agate (pigeon blood agate) occurs in this area, as well as petrified wood.

Directions: Go 12 miles east of Green River on U.S. 6-50 and turn south on a graded dirt road marked by a sign for "Ruby Ranch." Continue south 6.2 miles to a fenced area. Turn east and go south about a mile to a series of ridges.

Land Status: BLM public lands.

Maps: Moab (m), Crescent Junction (7.5).

References: Stowe (1979).

Location: Thompson area

Rock: agate, agate pseudomorphs after barite

Description: Agate is mainly red, blue, and white. Approximately 0.25 mile to the east of this site, agate replacing barite can be found.

Directions: Starting at Crescent Junction, go south on U.S. 191 for about 4 miles to a dirt road that leads east toward Thompson. Take this road for 1.3 miles to a bridge, cross the bridge and go 300 feet and turn right. Go 1.5 miles to a junction, turn left and continue for 200 yards. With 4WD you can continue over the ridge into the next valley where the agate is found. Location is in Secs. 28, 29, T22S, R20E.

Land Status: BLM public lands.

Maps: Moab (m), Thompson (7.5), Crescent Junction (7.5).

References: Stowe (1979).

Location: Owl Draw area

Rock: agate

Directions: From the Cisco exit on I-70 drive east on U.S. 6-50 for about 2.5 miles to Utah Highway 128. Take Highway 128 south 6 miles to a bridge over a wash and turn west 100 yards past the bridge on an unimproved 4WD road. Continue for 0.5 mile to a junction, take the right fork and continue northwest for a few miles to where the road turns west and heads up Owl Draw. Continue for a couple of miles up and out of the draw past two cabins constructed of narrow guage railroad ties. About 0.75 mile past the cabins agate will be found along the road and can be traced to the southwest.

Land Status: BLM public lands.

Maps: Moab (m), Cisco (7.5).

References: Stowe (1979).

Location: Dubinky Well area, Hell Roaring Canyon, and Mineral Canyon

Rock: agate, petrified wood

Description: These areas are along the Green River just north of Canyonlands National Park.

Directions: Take Utah Highway 313 (the road to Dead Horse Point) for about 8.5 miles to the road to Dubinky Well. Turn right on this road and continue for 1.3 miles (staying right at the junction with Spring Canyon trail) to an unimproved 4WD trail to the right. Follow the trail 1.3 miles to where the trail climbs up on a low flat area. The limestone capping the flat area has blood red agate. Return to the Dubinky Well road and continue north about 3.7 miles until you cross a fenceline. Look for white agate along the road in this area. It can be traced several miles northeasterly from this point. An unimproved 4WD trail takes off to the right about 50 yards past the fence. This is the Bartlett Rim Trail and makes a circle of several miles before coming back to the Dubinky Well road. About 1 mile along the trail are a series of bluffs

on the right side that continue for several miles. Search along these bluffs for agate.

To reach Hell Roaring and Mineral Canyon take Utah Highway 313 for 10.5 miles (2 miles past the road to Dubinky Well) to a dirt road leading to the right. This junction is 2 miles from the junction of Highway 313 and the road to Island in the Sky. Take this road about 13 miles across the flats to a spectacular view of the Green River and then continue down the switchbacks to the bottom and a junction. Turn right (sign says "Boat Ramp and dead end road") and continue up the Green River for 0.5 mile to the mouth of Mineral Canyon. Hell Roaring Canyon is 2 miles further along this road. Search for agate in the loose gravels in the canyon bottoms. The road is passable to HCVs to the canyon mouths, 4WD is necessary to drive up the canyons.

Land Status: BLM public lands.

Maps: Moab (m), The Knoll (7.5), Upheaval Dome (7.5).

References: Stowe (1979).

Location:	**Dead Horse Point Road Junction**
Rock:	**petrified wood**

Description: The wood occurs in the greenish-gray beds of the Chinle Formation which can be traced along the cliffs for several miles north and south of this point.

Directions: At the junction of Utah Highway 313 (the road to Dead Horse Point) and U.S. 191 north of Moab, drive 1.5 miles on Highway 313 to a dirt road to the left. Take this dirt road across the wash and up the side canyon about 0.5 mile.

Land Status: BLM public lands.

Maps: Moab (m), Moab (7.5).

References: Stowe (1979).

Location:	**Monitor and Merrimac Buttes**
Rock:	**agate**

Description: Heavy sand in this area requires 4WD.

Directions: Starting at the Colorado River bridge in Moab, drive north on U.S. 191 for 13.2 miles to Courthouse Wash. An unimproved 4WD road turns off to the left on the south side of Courthouse Wash and crosses the railroad tracks and a cattle guard. Stay to the left at the first two junctions and to the right at the third junction. There are many side roads in the area, but work your way over to the two prominent buttes. Look for pieces of agate in the red sand.

Land Status: BLM public lands.

Maps: Moab (m), Moab (7.5).

References: Stowe (1979).

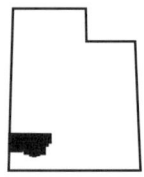

IRON COUNTY

Iron County is named for the renowned occurrence of magnetite that occurs associated with intrusive rocks in the Iron Springs area west of Cedar City. The western portion of the county includes the southern extensions of the Indian Peak Range (Needle Range in older publications) and the Wah Wah Mountains where there are extensive outcrops of rhyolitic rocks. The central section of the county is the Escalante Desert where few rocks are exposed. Mesozoic sedimentary rocks are found in the Hurricane Cliffs east of Cedar City, and the higher parts of the plateau are capped by recent volcanic rocks.

Location: **Western Hurricane Cliffs**

Rock: agate

Description: Agates occur on gradual slopes leading up to the foothills in many colors and pieces weighing up to several pounds. There is a graded gravel road just south of Summit and agate can be found within a 100 yards of the road.

Directions: Turn east off the "Summit" off ramp of I-15, 11 miles north of Cedar City and south of Parowan. Turn south on the frontage road along the east side of the highway. At the second, third, and/or fourth gate turn east. (Be sure to close all gates that you open.)

Land Status: BLM public lands.

Maps: Panguitch (m), Summit (7.5).

References: Stowe (1979).

Location: **Brian Head-Cedar Breaks Area**

Rock: agate

Description: Colorful agate can be found in the mountain meadows south of Cedar Breaks National Monument and also in the vicinity of the Brian Head ski area.

Directions: Located along Utah Highway 143 south of Parowan, or take Utah Highway 14 southeast from Cedar City to Highway 143. Well-marked on highway maps.

Land Status: National Forest lands. No collecting in Cedar Breaks National Monument.

Maps: Panguitch (m), Brian Head (7.5), Navajo Lake (7.5).

References: Stowe (1979).

Location: **Fiddlers Canyon**

Rock: agate

Description: Red and blue agate occur in this area. A major home development is being created at the mouth of Fiddler Canyon which may affect access to this area.

Directions: At the intersection of I-15 and Utah Highway 130 about 2 miles north of Cedar City, a gravel road leads east into Fiddlers Canyon.

Land Status: BLM public lands and private ownership. Seek permission at the development office before trespassing on private land.

Maps: Cedar City (m), Cedar City (7.5).

References: Stowe (1979)

A Guide to Collecting Sites   87

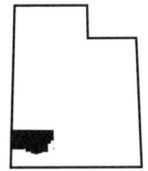

Location: Lund area

Minerals: topaz

Description: Abundant topaz is reported occurring in the rocks in an area approximately 3.5 miles northwest of Lund. This material is not expected to be as high quality as material from the Topaz Mountain area and is much harder to access.

Directions: Lund is 32 miles northwest of Cedar City. The location is in the NE ¼, Sec. 12, T32S, R15W. No roads to this location. Strenuous hike required.

Land Status: BLM public lands.

Maps: Wah Wah Mts. South (m), Lund (7.5).

References: Duttweiler and Griffitts (1988).

Location: Mountain Spring Peak

Minerals: topaz, quartz, fluorite

Description: Topaz with individual crystals up to 0.5 inch are reported to occur here.

Directions: Drive west from Lund on the Pine Valley Road for about 10 miles to Mountain Spring Peak. About a mile past Mountain Spring Peak, park and walk 0.5 mile north of the road to a prominent north-south ridge. Exact location is SW ¼, NE ¼, SW ¼, Sec. 2, T32S, R16W.

Land Status: BLM public lands.

Maps: Wah Wah Mts. South (m), Mountain Springs Peak (7.5).

References: Stowe (1979).

Location: Meadow Spring area

Minerals: topaz, quartz, chalcedony, hematite, fluorite

Description: Micro-sized topaz occurs along the roadside in an area about 0.5 mile north of Meadow Spring. Crystals less than 0.15 inch occur in lithophysae with micro-quartz and associated hematite. Chalcedony, that fluoresces bright green in short wave UV, is abundant on the hillslope above the road. Some seams in the gray rhyolite along the road have small purple fluorite cubes, modified by dodecahedrons, perched on chalcedony.

Directions: From Mountain Spring Peak (see previous location) drive about 3.5 miles north along the Pine Valley Road to Meadow Spring. Topaz occurs along the road north of there. Search the area where light gray rhyolite occurs at road level on a steep hillslope adjacent to the road.

Land Status: BLM public lands.

Maps: Wah Wah Mts. South (m), Bible Spring (7.5).

References: Visited by this writer. Stowe (1979).

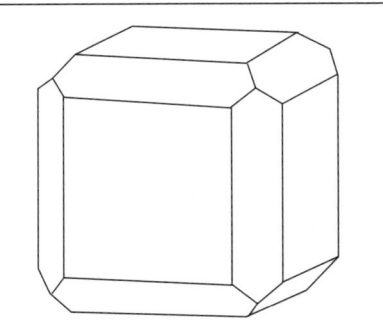

An example of the combination of cube and dodecahedral form exhibited by some of the fluorite crystals at the Mountain Spring area location. Actual size about 0.25 inch.

Location: Modena Draw

Minerals: topaz, quartz, chalcedony

Description: Topaz crystals to 0.5 inch on micro-quartz are reported from this locality.

Directions: From Modena drive 5.5 miles north. Topaz occurs on a ridge east of the road. Chalcedony is

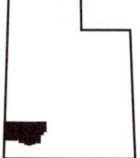

reported to occur in the area 2.5 to 3 miles north of Modena. A side road goes to the west in this vicinity.

Land Status: BLM public lands.

Maps: Cedar City (m), Modena (7.5).

References: Stowe (1979).

Location:	**Iron Springs District**
Minerals:	**magnetite, siderite, calcite, apatite, amethyst**

Description: The Iron Springs District is a famous mining district in which magnetite occurs as replacement of limestone. In addition to the replacement bodies, there are fissures in which the magnetite along with accessory pyroxene, apatite, calcite, and hematite was deposited. The magnetite is derived from three laccolithic intrusions of quartz monzonite composition. Most of the mines are no longer active, but there are still some operating mines in the area, and many of the closed mines are posted. Some mined areas are not posted and, in many locations, abundant nodules of magnetite and octahedral crystals of magnetite can be found on slopes and in stream beds where they have washed down from the mining areas. The better crystals will be found in thin veins and fractures in the rock and not in the large open pits where massive ore was mined.

Directions: Take Utah Highway 56 west out of Cedar City. The dumps of the iron mines are clearly visible along Highway 56 and side roads that lead to Iron Springs and Desert Mound. Washes along the road to Desert Mound contain abundant magnetite crystals and nodules. Search in areas that are not posted or seek permission before entering posted areas.

Land Status: Private lands and BLM public land.

Maps: Cedar City (m), Cedar City NW (7.5), The Three Peaks (7.5), Desert Mound (7.5).

References: Visited by this writer. Stowe (1979), Mackin (1954, 1968).

Location:	**Cedar Canyon**
Fossils:	**pelecypods (oysters)**

Description: A 10 to 15-foot-thick bed of gray limestone with abundant oyster shells occurs in Cedar Canyon alongside the road.

Directions: Take Utah Highway 14 east out of Cedar City and up Cedar Canyon. The outcrop is located along the road, about 0.6 mile past milepost 10, after emerging from the narrowest part of the canyon. A side road on the right, about 100 feet past the outcrop gives a place to park.

Land Status: Highway right-of-way.

Maps: Panguitch (m), Flannigan Arch (7.5).

References: Visited by this writer. Dr. Richard Kennedy, Southern Utah University, Cedar City.

JUAB COUNTY

Juab County is best known as the location of Topaz Mountain at the south end of the Thomas Range. Spectacular topaz and associated minerals have long been collected here. Juab also encloses part of the Tintic mining district which has produced a number of interesting minerals throughout its history.

Location: **East Tintic Mountains**
Rock: agate
Description: Agate is abundant in this area.
Directions: Search in the foothills of the East Tintic Mountains east of Jericho on U.S. 6-50.
Land Status: BLM public lands.
Maps: Lynndyl (m), McIntyre (7.5).
References: Stowe (1979).

Location: **Southwest of Levan**
Rock: black agate
Directions: Approximately 13 miles south of Levan on U-28, a dirt road turns east toward the San Pitch Mountains. Drive east on this road about 0.75 mile and search in this area.
Land Status: Mixture of BLM public lands and private lands.
Maps: Nephi (m), Chriss Canyon (7.5), Hells Kitchen Canyon SE(7.5).
References: Stowe (1979).

Location: **Dugway Geode Beds**
Rock: geodes
Description: This area has been set aside by the BLM for use by rockhounds and mineral collectors, using hand tools only. There are some mining claims on portions of the geode area so seek permission before collecting there. Report use of heavy equipment, off legitimate mining claims, to the BLM. The geodes weather out of a spherulitic, green volcanic glass which crops out in a number of isolated spots in the north end of the Thomas Range and the south end of the Dugway Range. Wave action by Lake Bonneville scattered the geodes over a wide area, but many years of collecting has resulted in very few geodes available on the land surface. Most specimens require digging to locate the proper horizon. Be careful when digging to maintain terraced slopes to your hole. Never undermine the walls of the hole. You are digging in soft, unconsolidated material and it will cave in on you. Even with help immediately available at the site, people can die from suffocation before they can be extracted from a cave in. The typical geode is 3 to 4 inches in diameter with an outer layer of translucent agate. The center is usually hollow and may be lined with quartz crystals. The quartz may be amethystine and it is not unusual to find sceptered quartz crystals.
Directions: Consult the West Desert Area map (p. 104). Take the Pony Express Road off Utah Highway 36 near Vernon and continue over Lookout Pass, past Simpson Springs, and across Dugway Pass. Six miles beyond the pass is the turnoff to the geode beds and it is marked by a BLM sign.

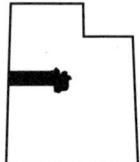

Land Status: BLM public lands.

Maps: Fish Springs (m), Dugway Range (15), Dugway Pass (7.5).

References: Stowe (1979).

Location: **Nebo Scenic Loop**

Mineral: **calcite**

Description: Massive banded calcite occurs in a quarry here.

Directions: Drive east on Utah Highway 132 out of Nephi for 6 miles to a junction that has a sign indicating Mt. Nebo Scenic Loop. Turn north at the sign and continue for 3.3 miles to an intersection with a dirt road going right. At the junction is a sign "Payson Lake 21, Payson 34." Continue past the junction for 0.2 mile at which point an unimproved dirt road goes to the left (HCV or 4WD required), crosses the creek, and winds up at the quarry.

Land Status: National Forest lands.

Maps: Nephi (m), Santaquin (15), Nephi (15).

References: Stowe (1979).

Location: **Silver City area**

Mineral: **pyrite, enargite**

Description: This area is at the south edge of the Tintic Mining District and there are many mine dumps in the area. A heap leaching gold operation has closed off access to some of this area, but it may be possible to reach some of the dumps on various secondary roads. Pyrite occurs as cubes, octahedrons, and pyritohedrons, usually of relatively small size. A gray-black mineral that occurs with pyrite in some of these dumps is enargite. Rattlesnakes are abundant in this area.

Directions: Take Utah Highway 67 south from Eureka and watch for the sign for Mammoth and then Silver City.

Land Status: Almost all of the Tintic District is held either by mining claim or as private land. Avoid posted land and seek permission from any active operations in the area.

Maps: Lynndyl (m), Tintic Junction (7.5), Eureka (7.5).

References: Visited by this writer. Stowe (1979).

Location: **Southeast of Trout Creek**

Mineral: **aragonite**

Description: Aragonite and calcite are polymorphs, i.e., chemically identical, but with different crystal structures.

Directions: Several deposits occur here as follows:

White Quee	NE ¼, Sec. 17, T14S, R16W
White Cloud	NE ¼, Sec. 8, T14S, R16W
White Dragon	NW ¼, Sec. 33, T13S, R16W
Onyx Queen	SE ¼, Sec. 9, T14S, R16W

Land Status: Mining claims, patented land, BLM public lands.

Maps: Fish Springs (m), Granite Mountain (15), Granite Mountain (7.5), Hole in the Wall Reservoir (7.5).

References: Stowe (1979).

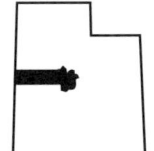

Location: Topaz Mountain area

Minerals: topaz, red beryl, bixbyite, pseudobrookite, hematite, garnet, chalcedony, amethyst, ilmenite, fluorite, calcite, cassiterite, durangite

Description: Topaz Mountain is the southern extremity of the Thomas Range, a range composed of rhyolitic lava and volcanic ash. Several eruptive centers in the area contributed to building the pile of volcanic materials. Later, gases bubbling up through the cooling lava and ash formed cavities known as lithophysae which create the remarkable honeycombed appearance of some of the rhyolite layers. Within these cavities and along fissures in the rock, gases and fluids deposited topaz and other minerals.

The primary area for collectors of topaz is Topaz Valley (or Topaz Cove). A major part of the valley has been set aside by the BLM for collectors using hand tools only. There has been some conflict with mining claims that were allegedly established before the BLM withdrawal occurred, but, regardless, this area has produced the largest, best-colored, topaz of any locality in the Thomas Range.

Topaz can be found throughout the Thomas Range although only a few areas, such as Topaz Valley, produce large, clear, well-formed crystals. The topaz is sherry-colored (orange-brown) when removed from the rock. Exposure to the sun or to strong lights in a mineral cabinet causes the color to fade. Crystals that have weathered out of the rock and have been on the land surface for many years are completely clear and colorless.

Countless collectors, over the years, have gathered up most of the clear crystals that once littered the ground in the Topaz Valley area. There are still clear crystals to be found by searching gravel areas and pockets of sand among the ledges of rhyolite, but most collectors want to find colored crystals and to do so requires hard work. Since the colored crystals occur within rock where they have not been exposed to the sun, rock must be broken and moved to locate pockets and fissures with crystals.

Useful tools include a large pry bar to move blocks of rock, a sledge hammer or heavy maul to break the large rocks, a rock hammer with pick end for digging or breaking small rocks, chisels for splitting rock, knife or screwdriver for extracting crystals from cavities, and shovel and screen if you plan to sieve sand and gravel.

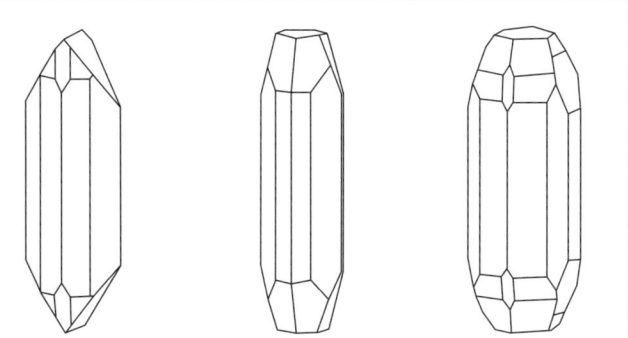

Common forms that are seen on topaz crystals from the Thomas Range. The greater the number of forms, the more rounded the termination appears, as in the crystal on the right. Most topaz crystals from the Thomas Range will only have one termination because they were attached to the rock at the other end, but "floaters" with double termination, as shown above, do occur.

If this list of equipment sounds daunting, you should be aware that there are many people who stepped out of their car and found a nice crystal within 30 minutes using only a light hammer. Likewise, there are many people who have spent an entire day breaking rock with heavy tools and found nothing worth keeping. Luck plays a role, but you can also learn to read the rock.

The gases and fluids that deposited the minerals did so as they moved through the rock. If the rock is massive without lithophysae or veins, then relatively little fluid could have moved through the rock and topaz and other minerals are unlikely to be found. The first step, then, is to look for rock that appears to have had sufficient permeability for fluids to migrate through it. Much of the rock (but not all of it) in Topaz Valley is of this type. Secondly, the fluids may have left some sign of their presence, even if topaz is not immediately evident. The rocks are often altered to produce seams and pockets of clay; there may be calcite and fluorite visible; and often the rock is speckled with flakes of hematite. Each of these is a promising sign and should encourage you to continue digging along the vein or layer in which you find them. Sometimes crystals seem to form where two or more veins, fissures, or layers intersect. Try to

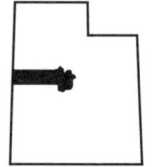

watch for structural features of this type. They also mark zones of weakness in the rock that you can exploit as you try to break or move the rock.

The most highly prized topaz has a deep sherry color, is clear, and has well-formed crystal faces. Many topaz crystals will have inclusions of sand (usually quartz) which will lessen their attractiveness and value. At a few locations, crystals can be found that are totally impregnated with sand, but still have well developed crystal terminations. Topaz from Topaz Valley and most other locations in the Thomas Range has well developed orthorhombic crystal forms that will give the crystals sharp, angular terminations. Some topaz from the Garnet Basin area has a series of forms that give a more rounded appearance to the termination. In the central and northern parts of the Thomas Range, pink topaz occurs, usually in small crystals less than 0.5 inch. The pink color is permanent and does not fade when exposed to the sun.

Red beryl is a rare variety that is almost unique to Utah. The best red beryl comes from a private claim in the Wah Wah Mountains, but it was first found in the Thomas Range. Red beryl occurs in Topaz Valley, primarily along the west wall, and is typically in the form of small flat discs seldom more than 0.25 inch in diameter. Other occurrences are known in the Thomas Range, but are under claim.

Bixbyite is a relatively rare iron-manganese oxide, that is common in the Thomas Range and is named for noted Utah mineralogist Maynard Bixby. It commonly occurs as shiny black cubes with the corners often truncated by the faces of a trisoctahedron. At some locations the bixbyite has a more tabular habit.

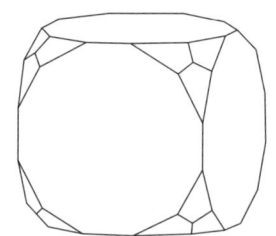

Typical bixbyite crystal, exhibiting a strongly developed cubic habit with the corners of the cube modified by the faces of a trisoctahedron.

Pseudobrookite occurs as delicate, hair-like needles in small lithophysae or perched on topaz and bixbyite. Needles up to 1 inch are known, but their fragility makes collecting them extremely difficult. Some collectors reattach the needles to the matrix after getting them home. Specimens of this type should always be labeled as "repaired."

Hematite is often found as lustrous metallic flakes on, in, and around topaz, and in the rock itself. The hematite can be quite attractive when it occurs as sheaves of large flakes, but this is rare in the Thomas Range.

Chalcedony is common in the rocks of Topaz Cove and elsewhere in the Thomas Range. This rather nondescript material is brightly fluorescent in colors of vivid green. The green color may be due to the inclusion of uranium atoms in the chalcedony.

Quartz in the form of amethyst occurs at a few localities in the Thomas Range. At the north end of the range, amethyst occurs in a belt leading to the southern Dugway Range and the geode beds. Amethyst also occurs in Garnet Basin, usually as a druse of small crystals on rock surfaces, but sometimes crystals are 0.3 inch in diameter. Tridymite and cristobalite, polymorphs of quartz, occur in the rhyolite at some localities.

Fluorite and calcite are found in association with altered rock as mentioned earlier. They are seldom of any significant size, although the fluorite can be attractive under the microscope.

Garnets occur at many locations in the Thomas Range, often as well-formed trapezohedral crystals. Garnet Basin, on the west side of the range, has been the location traditionally associated with garnet. At one time, they could be found in abundance where they had weathered out of the rock. Today, loose garnets are uncommon in Garnet Basin, but they still can be found in the rock. Another, easier-to-reach location is at the north end of Antelope Ridge, just outside of Topaz Valley. A few garnets can be found loose in this area, but most must be extracted from the rocks. Garnets occur sparingly in the rocks of Topaz Valley and have been reported to occur in the ridges directly across the paved road south of Topaz Valley. Most of the garnets found in the Thomas Range have been partially or totally replaced by hematite and thus lack the bright luster usually associated with garnets. At some locations, bixbyite occurs as crystals perched on balls of hematite formed from altered garnets.

A Guide to Collecting Sites

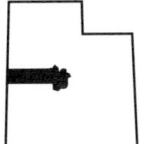

Ilmenite, cassiterite, and durangite are relatively uncommon or unrecognized minerals in the Thomas Range. Ilmenite is probably confused with hematite and seldom identified. Cassiterite is relatively common as a minor constituent of rhyolitic rocks and it is not surprising that it is reported to occur here. Again, identification may be difficult for most collectors. Durangite is a rare sodium aluminum arsenate fluoride which is known from one location in the Thomas Range. This location is under claim and collecting is not allowed, but collectors should be aware of the mineral as it may occur elsewhere. It occurs as orange-red, opaque, monoclinic crystals.

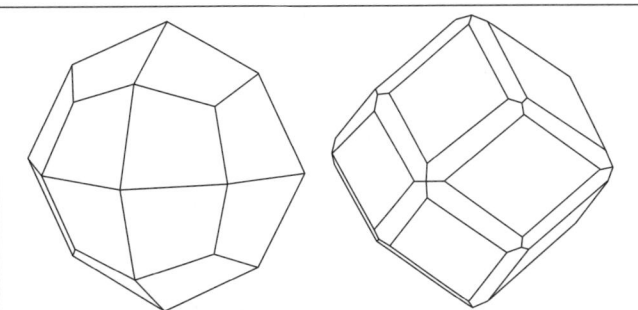

Garnet crystals from many locations commonly exhibit both the dodecahedron and the trapezohedron, as does the crystal on the right. Some garnets have only the trapezohedron faces as shown by the crystal on the left. Both types can be found in the Thomas Range.

Directions: Consult the West Desert Area map and the Topaz Mountain map in this section.

Land Status: BLM public lands and mining claims with an area set aside for mineral collectors in Topaz Valley. You should recognize that claims in the Thomas Range are for the purpose of obtaining topaz, bixbyite, etc., and as such you cannot collect on any of these claims or leases without the permission of the claimholder. Mineral clubs in Salt Lake City, Ogden, or Tooele usually are aware of the current claimholders and can tell you about existing collecting opportunities.

Maps: Fish Springs (m), Topaz Mountain (15), Topaz Mountain East (7.5), Topaz Mountain West (7.5), Dugway Pass (7.5).

References: Visited by this writer. Holfert (1977).

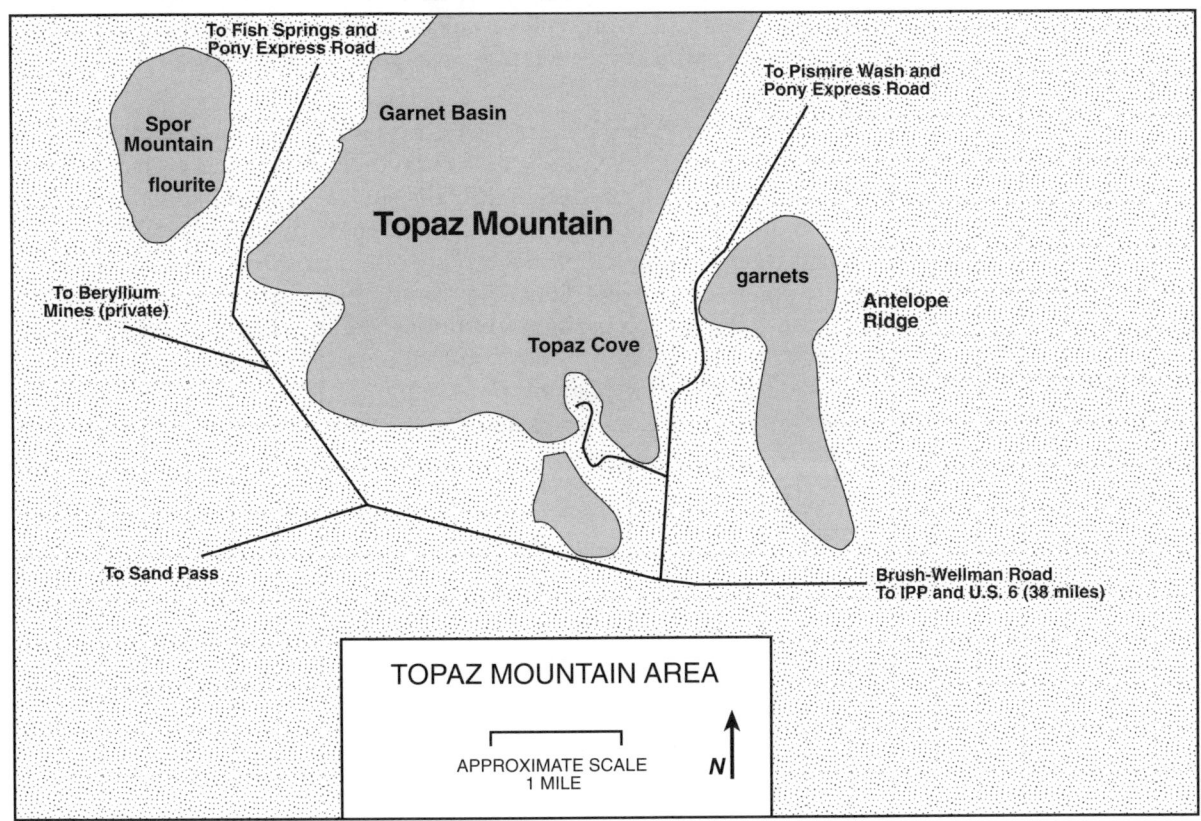

KANE COUNTY

Kane County lies along the Utah-Arizona border. The rocks that occur here are almost all Mesozoic sedimentary rocks and are likely to yield fossils, agate, and petrified wood. Kane County is best known to collectors for the occurrence of septarian nodules which are hollow and lined with calcite crystals.

Location: **Seaman Wash - Petrified Hollow Wash**

Rocks: **petrified wood, agate, jasper**

Description: Abundant material is found here along the flanks of the Vermilion Cliffs.

Directions: Approximately 15.7 miles east of Kanab on U.S. 89 is a light-duty gravel road leading north into Seaman Wash and on to Petrified Hollow.

Land Status: BLM public lands and some mining claims for petrified wood in the area. Collect on unclaimed land or seek permission from claimholders.

Maps: Kanab (m), Buckskin Gulch (7.5).

Location: **Muddy Creek area**

Rock: **septarian nodules**

Description: This Utah locality is famous for the thousands of septarian nodules which have been mined and sold to the public, primarily through shops and wholesalers in Orderville. These nodules are very attractive because they are often hollow with pleasing yellow calcite crystals contrasting with the gray limestone. The skeleton of a plesiosaur, an extinct marine reptile, was recently unearthed during the digging operations here.

Directions: These areas are all under claim by Wiley Berry of Tetla Septarians and Joe's Rock Shop, both in Orderville. Both claimholders are willing to let the public collect on their claims and no fee is currently charged, but because the nodules must be dug from deep below the surface, it is unlikely that anything other than scraps of nodules left from the digging operations can be recovered by the collector. As a courtesy, and to obtain maps and current road conditions, please contact either of the above claimholders at their businesses in Orderville before entering the area. Stay away from all equipment and highwalls left at the diggings. Pack all your litter out. Continuing problems with litter left by collectors could close this area to the public. Contact Joe's Rock Shop, Box 149, U.S. 89, Orderville, UT 84758. Telephone (801)-648-2425. Wiley Berry of Tetla Septarians is at 195 South Center, Orderville, UT 84758. Telephone (801)-648-2310. Tetla Septarians is wholesale only. Joe's Rock Shop and several others are open to the public in Orderville.

Land Status: Mining claims.

Maps: Kanab (m), Mt. Carmel (7.5), Orderville (7.5).

References: Visited by this writer.

Location: **Straight Cliffs**

Rock: **petrified wood and agate**

Description: A widespread occurrence of material along the foothills of the Straight Cliffs.

Directions: Drive east out of Escalante on Utah Highway 12 just over 4 miles to the Hole in the Rock

A Guide to Collecting Sites

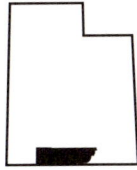
Road. Turn right on this road and follow it for 17 miles to the Garfield-Kane County line. Any of the roads leading to the right after this point will probably get you over into the hills where the material can be collected. Look in the ledges near the tops of hills as well as in the washes. The Hole in the Rock Road is passable to a passenger car in good weather, but 4WD is necessary to drive up to the outcrop areas.

Land Status: BLM public lands.

Maps: Escalante (m).

References: Stowe (1979).

Location:	**Grosvenor's Arch area**
Rock:	**petrified wood**
Fossils:	**pelecypods**

Description: Petrified wood and fossils are found in the area back of the arch and on past the arch on the right side of the road. Further south in the Cottonwood Canyon area, red agatized wood can be found. The fossils occur in a 4-foot-thick bed which crosses the road in the vicinity of the dam located 0.25 mile east of the arch. It can be followed up the hills south of the road.

Directions: The road to Kodachrome Basin State Park and Grosvenor Arch leaves U-12 in Cannonville, east of Bryce Canyon National Park.

Land Status: BLM public lands.

Maps: Butler Valley (7.5), Horse Flat (7.5).

References: Stowe (1979).

Location:	**Mt. Carmel Junction**
Fossils:	**crinoid**

Description: The star-shaped crinoid *Pentacrinus* occurs in a limestone outcrop located at Mt. Carmel Junction.

Directions: Mt. Carmel Junction is the junction of U-9 out of Zion National Park with U.S. 89.

Land Status: Mixture of BLM public land and private land.

Maps: Kanab (m), Mt. Carmel (7.5).

References: Various rockhounds.

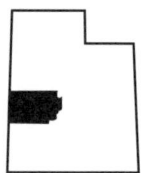

MILLARD COUNTY

Millard County is located in west-central Utah and extends to the Nevada border. There are a number of interesting mineral occurrences in the county, but it is best known for the abundant trilobites found as fossils in the Cambrian shales and limestones and the extremely fossiliferous Ordovician strata.

Road Log: Antelope Springs-Wheeler Amphitheater-House Range Area

(This is intended as a means of giving directions to the large number of collecting sites in the Antelope Springs and House Range area. The traveler should note that all odometers are slightly different and therefore your mileage may differ from what is given. Whenever possible, signs and landmarks are noted to indicate that you are on the correct route. Consult the West Desert Area Map (p. 104) for a regional overview.)

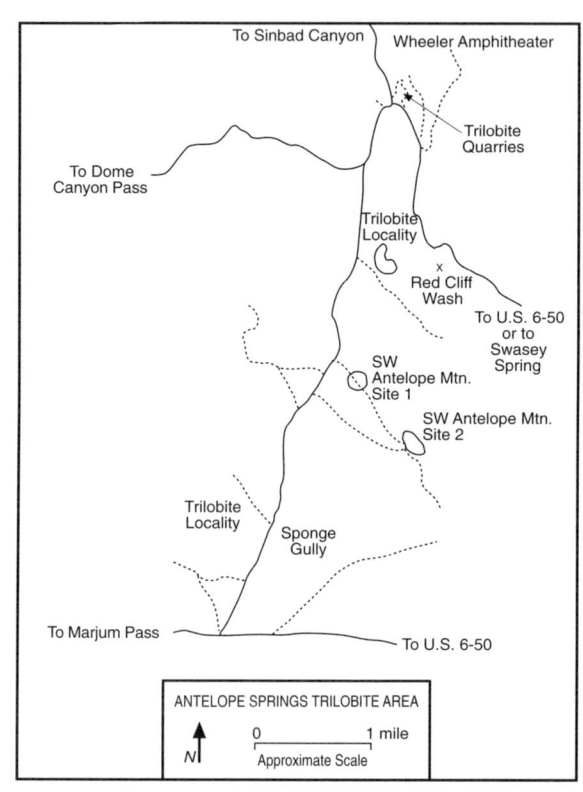

In the road log below, the first number indicates the mileage between sucessive points whereas the second number is the cumulative mileage.

Leave Delta on U.S. Highway 6-50 traveling west toward Ely, Nevada. Shortly past milepost 58 (Sevier Lake is visible ahead and to your left), approximately 32 miles out of Delta, turn right on a graded gravel road where a sign indicates Long Ridge Reservoir.

0.0	0.0	Jct. U.S. 6-50 and graded road to Long Ridge Reservoir.
6.4	6.4	Road curves around Long Ridge Reservoir. Be careful of the curve and stay on the main road and proceed northward.
3.9	10.3	Intersection with a major east-west graded road. West leads to Marjum Pass. A side road (3.9 miles west of this intersection) leads through North Canyon to Amasa Valley in the House Range. Proceed north.
4.7	15.0	Intersection. Lower Antelope Spring standpipe and pond are near this point. Road to the right (east) leads around Swasey Mountain to Swasey Spring (Sign indicates "Swasey Spring 12." Proceed northward.
1.9	16.9	Road to the left leads to the Red Cliffs Wash site. (To reach this collecting location, follow the side road to a wash. Go up the wash to the Red Cliffs location.) Continue north on the main road toward Antelope Springs.
1.3	18.2	Continue straight. Road at the right leads into the Wheeler Amphitheater. Ridges and slopes in the amphitheater can be searched for trilobites that have weathered out of the shale.

A Guide to Collecting Sites

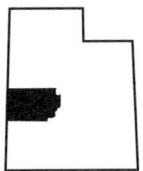

Elrathia kingi x1
- after Skedros (1985)
from Walcott 1886.

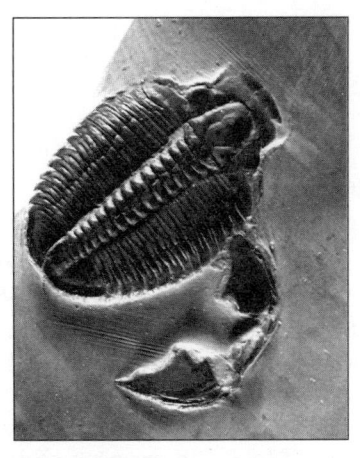

Elrathia kingi (Meek). This medium-sized trilobite is the most common in the Wheeler Shale of the House Range. It is the Utah state invertebrate fossil and thousands have been mined for sale to universitioes and museums. Specimen is about 1 inch long and may have been molting. Photo: Val Gunther.

0.6	18.8	Agnostid trilobites can be found on the slope east of the road. Roads to the right lead to the trilobite quarries.
0.1	18.9	Road junction (Sign "Sinbad 4, Death Canyon"). The Death Canyon (Dome Canyon Pass) road leads to the west. The right fork leads north toward Sinbad Canyon. About 0.1 mile up the right fork is a road that leads to the trilobite quarries which are located a short walk to the east. To continue the road log to other sites, take the road heading toward Death Canyon.
0.9	19.8	Intersection. The right fork leads west to Death Canyon. Take the left fork to the south.
1.1	20.9	Intersection. The road that forks to the left leads down the wash to several collecting sites on the slopes of Hill 6468 and adjacent areas. (See Wheeler Amphitheater Map in this section.) Continue on the main road.
1.7	22.6	Jeep trail on the left leads southeastward down the wash to sites on Antelope Mountain for trilobite collecting.
2.6	25.2	Road approaches a wash. A faint road leads approximately 0.5 miles along the wash to the Sponge Gully site. (See description below.) In the wash area above the main road trilobites can be found in the Wheeler Shale that crops out there. Continue on main road.
1.5	26.7	Intersection with the major east-west graded road. Turn west (right) toward Marjum Pass.
2.0	28.7	Head of Marjum Canyon (Marjum Pass sign). Trilobites occur in the Wheeler Shale here, but they are more difficult to extract from the rock. The Wheeler Shale forms the lower slopes and the higher ledges are the Marjum Formation.
6.7	35.4	Road intersection (Sign "Cowboy Pass 18, Highway 50-6 15, Tule Valley Road 7"). Turn south along the west face of the House Range. From this road, especially in late afternoon as the sun sets, there is a scenic view of the granite intrusion that makes up this part of the House Range. At 4.9 miles along this road there is an intersection at a water tank. (1) The road to the east leads to Painter Spring at the base of the House Range.

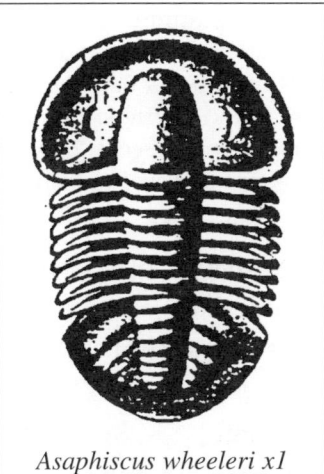

Asaphiscus wheeleri x1
- after Skedros (1985)
from Walcott 1886.

Asaphiscus wheeleri Meek. This trilobite is fairly common in the Wheeler Formation and lower Marjum Formation of the House Range. Specimen is about 2 inches long. Photo: Val Gunther.

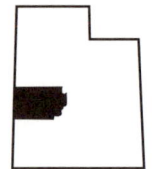

(2) Continuing about 10 miles south leads to U.S. 50-6. (3) Turning west at this intersection takes you across Tule Valley to the Confusion Range.

Location: **Wheeler Amphitheater (Antelope Springs)**

Fossils: **trilobites**

Description: This area is a world famous location for the occurrence of trilobites. It is generally referred to as Antelope Springs although the springs are some distance away from the actual collecting localities. There are a number of commercial trilobite quarries in the Wheeler Amphitheater and these are shown as "mines" on the Marjum Pass topographic map. These commercial collectors usually allow people to collect in the piles of loose rock that they have already pulled from the quarry. You are not allowed to collect from the rock face of the quarry unless you have specific permission from the person who leases the site. There is a large area here where you can dig or search on the land surface. The trilobites often weather out of the rock and can be found loose on exposed slopes especially in the spring after winter storms or after summer thunderstorms. The two most common large trilobites at this location are *Asaphiscus wheeleri* (2 inches) and *Elrathia kingi* (1.6 inches). *Asaphiscus* is characterized by its large pygidium (tail section) and is usually found as fragments. The most common agnostid trilobites are *Peronopsis interstricta* and *Hypagnostus parvifrons*, each about 0.3 inch in length. Other trilobites found in this area include *Bathyuriscus elegans*, *Bathyuriscus fimbriatus*, *Bolaspidella housensis*, *Elrathia marjumi*, *Marjumia typa*, *Modocia brevispina*, *Olenoides majumensis*, *Olenoides superbus*, and *Utaspis majumensis*.

Directions: See maps and road log.

Land Status: BLM lands, state lands, private leases.

Maps: Tule Valley (m), Marjum Pass (7.5).

References: Visited by this writer. Gunther and Gunther (1981); Robison (1964).

Location: **Sponge Gully**

Fossils: **sponges, trilobites**

Description: As the name implies, this location is an important paleontological site for sponges. It was excavated by geologists from BYU whose published reports are cited below. Agnostid trilobites are abundant. Non-agnostid trilobite species include *Bolaspidella* sp. and *Modocia typicalis*.

Directions: See preceding road log and maps.

Land Status: BLM public lands.

Maps: Tule Valley (m), Marjum Pass (7.5).

References: Visited by this writer. Hintze (1982); Rigby (1983); Rogers (1984); Lloyd Gunther, Brigham City, UT.

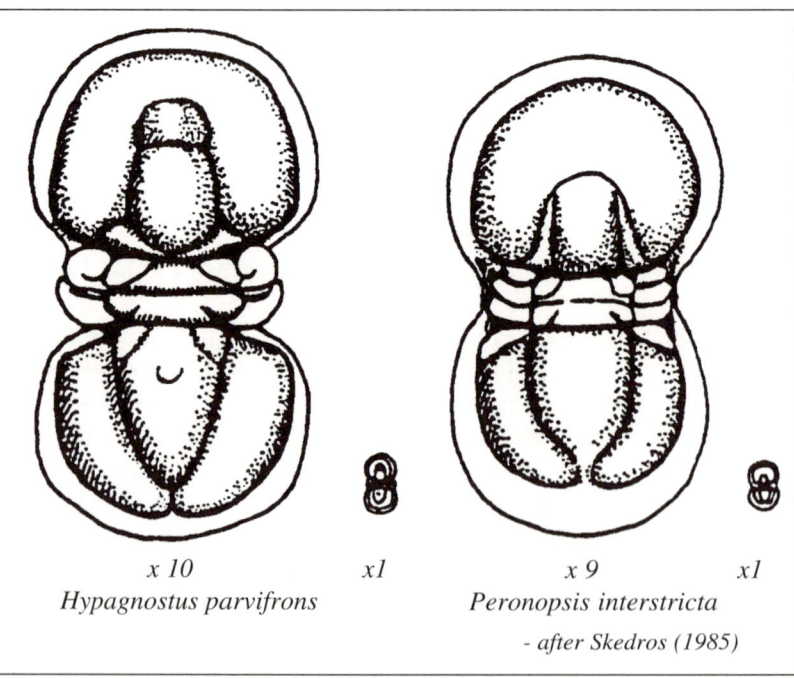

x 10 *x1*   *x 9* *x1*
Hypagnostus parvifrons   *Peronopsis interstricta*
- after Skedros (1985)

Location: Swasey Spring

Fossils: trilobites

Description: This is another quarry site developed by BYU. Agnostid trilobites occur here as well as the larger trilobites *Brachyaspidion microps*, *Jenkinsonia varga*, and *Elrathia*.

Directions: See preceding road log and map.

Land Status: BLM public lands.

Maps: Swasey Peak (7.5), Tule Valley (m)

References: Rogers (1984); Lloyd Gunther, Brigham City, UT.

Location: Conger Springs

Fossils: crinoids, brachiopods, corals

Description: The Mississippian Chainman Shale occurs at Conger Spring and crinoid stems and brachiopods can be found weathered out of the shale in the dirt pile at the spring. To the right of the spring in the wash, recent digging has exposed the weathered shale and a large number of crinoid stem pieces. Search around the hill to the west for additional material. The brachiopods *Composita*, *Eumetria*, *Spiriferina*, *Spirifer*, *Punctospirifer*, *Marginifera*, and *Hustedia* occur here, as well as the rugose coral *Amplexizaphrentis*.

Directions: At milepost 16 on U.S. 50-6 (about 77 miles west of Delta) turn north on a gravel road toward Little Valley. Proceed straight at any unmarked intersections; most intersections indicate direction and distance to Conger Spring, which is about 8.7 miles from the highway.

Land Status: BLM public lands.

Maps: Tule Valley (m), Conger Mtn. (7.5).

References: Visited by this writer. Hintze (1973); Sadlick (1965).

Location: Skull Rock Pass

Fossils: graptolites

Description: Graptolites were marine organisms that lived in free-floating colonies made up of many individuals arranged on branches. Graptolites existed from Middle Cambrian time to Mississippian and reached their greatest abundance in the Ordovician and Silurian periods. As a result of their floating lifestyle, rapid evolution, and worldwide occurrence, graptolites are among the most important index fossils; fossils that identify and date the strata in which they are found and allow its correlation with other units elsewhere. As fossils, graptolites commonly occur as flattened carbon films on surfaces of shales. Road cuts from the summit of Skull Rock Pass to the intersection with the Ibex Road (elev. 4,922 on map) are in the Fillmore Formation which is described by Hintze (1987, p. 263) as a unit "... whose most conspicuous rock type is intraformational flat-pebble conglomerate made up of silty or fine quartzose sandy limestone containing fragments of trilobites, brachiopods, echinoderms, and occasionally other organisms. Interbedded with these ledge-forming beds are less resis-

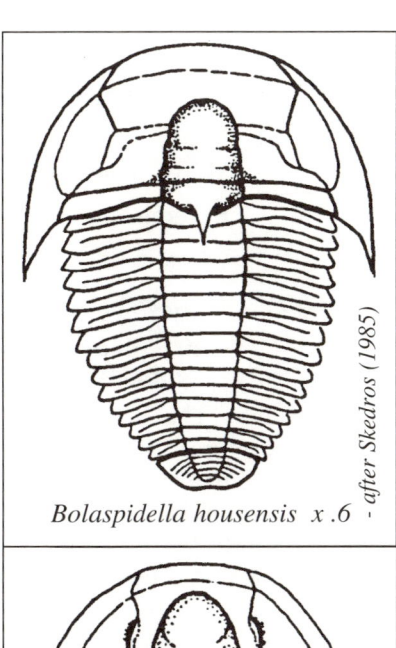

Bolaspidella housensis x .6 — after Skedros (1985)

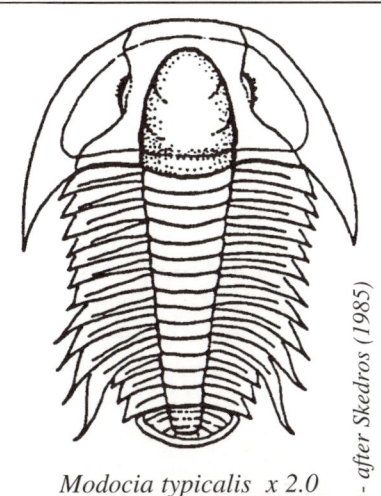

Modocia typicalis x 2.0 — after Skedros (1985)

Modocia typicalis (Resser). This medium-sized trilobite is found in the Marjum Formation in the vicinity of the House Range. Specimen is about 2.5 inches long. Photo: Val Gunther.

tant, light-olive-gray shales that contain graptolites."

Directions: Located on U.S. 6-50 approximately 47 miles west of Delta.

Land Status: BLM public lands.

Maps: Tule Valley (m), Notch Peak (15).

References: Hintze (1987), Braithwaite (1976)

Location:	Ibex - Fossil Mountain area
Fossils:	**brachiopods, trilobites, echinoderms, cephalopods**

Description: The exceptionally fossiliferous rocks of the Lower Ordovician Pogonip Group that occur here have been studied by Hintze and his co-workers for many years and they have used this area to establish fossil zones for rocks of this age that are used by paleontologists throughout the world. However, as noted by Hintze (1987, p. 262) most of the fossils that occur here are fragmented as a result of their having accumulated in a high energy, wave-dominated, shoreline environment. It is very difficult to find a complete, unbroken, trilobite, echinoderm, or brachiopod.

Directions: At the west end of Skull Rock Pass (on U.S. Highway 6-50, near milepost 39, approximately 54 miles west of Delta) turn southwest on the Ibex Well road. This will require an HCV; the road is washed and sandy in spots. Follow the main graded road southward along the margin of the playa. Continue south past the Ibex Well at the south end of the playa for 1.2 miles and then leave the main graded road to take a less prominent road to the southwest. At 2.7 miles you round an orange-weathering hill with fossiliferous material on its slopes. Continuing westward another 3.5 miles takes you to the end of Warm Point where the road divides. Fossil Mountain is the near summit, about 1.5 miles northwest of this point. The east-facing slopes north and south of this junction can be examined for fossiliferous material. The road leading south can be taken to the Black Rock - Garrison road.

Land Status: BLM public lands.

Maps: Tule Valley (m), Wah Wah Mountains North (m), The Barn (15), The Barn (7.5).

References: Visited by this writer. Hintze (1974d, 1987).

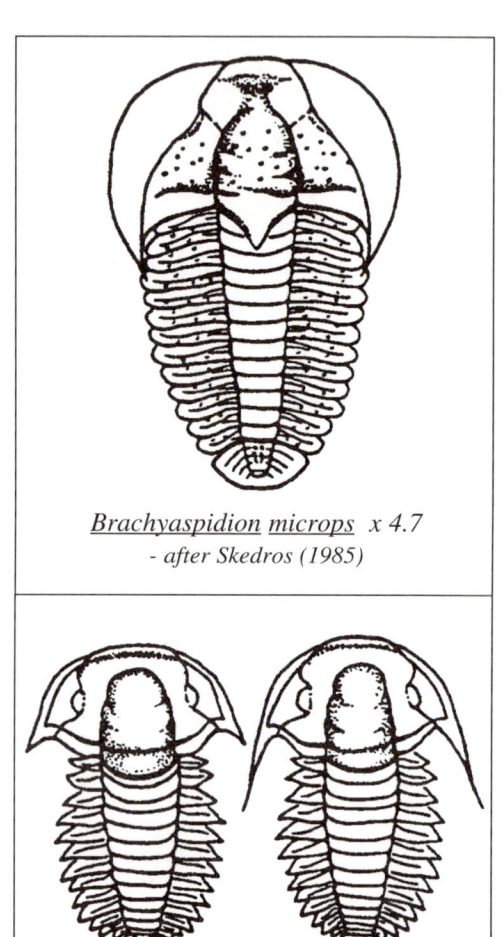

Brachyaspidion microps x 4.7
- after Skedros (1985)

Jenkinsonia varga x 10
- after Skedros (1985)

Location:	Foote Range and Indian Pass area
Fossils:	**corals, blastoids, brachiopods, ammonites**

Description: In the Indian Pass area of Chevron Ridge a slope-forming, argillaceous limestone unit about 5 feet thick occurs that contains *Barbouria* sp. corals in great abundance. They weather out of the rock and litter the slope. The corals are up to 5 inches in length and 0.5 inch in diameter.

Directions: The Foote Range is a small ridge located 9 miles east of Gandy and about 16 miles north of Conger Spring. The area can be reached by taking U.S. 6-50 west from Delta to near the Utah-Nevada line, then north about 31 miles to Gandy and east out of Gandy to the range. If coming from the Antelope

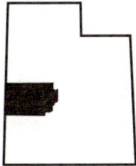 Springs trilobite area, take the road through Marjum Pass and continue straight on this road across Tule Valley and through Cowboy Pass in the Confusion Range. After you emerge from the Range, a major fork in the road appears with the left fork going south to Eskdale and the right fork going north to Gandy. Take the right fork about 11.3 miles to a point where a side road leads over to the Foote Range. Collect on the north and east sides of the Range.

Land Status: BLM public lands.

Maps: Tule Valley (m), Foote Range (7.5).

References: Lloyd Gunther, Brigham City, UT; Hose and Repenning (1959).

Location:	Cowboy Pass
Fossils:	ammonites

Description: Ammonites (*Meekoceras* sp.) occur in the Triassic Thaynes Formation at the northeast end of Cowboy Pass in the Confusion Range.

Directions: Take the road leading south at the east end of Cowboy Pass. Travel about 1.2 miles and walk to the right of the road across a wash.

Land Status: BLM public lands.

Maps: Tule Valley (m), Cowboy Pass (7.5).

References: Hose and Repenning (1959).

Location:	Sunstone Knoll
Mineral:	sunstone (yellow labradorite), aragonite

Description: Sunstone Knoll is a small basaltic hill in which transparent, yellow labradorite occurs as phenocrysts. Labradorite is the name given to one of the intermediate varieties of plagioclase feldspar. Plagioclase feldspar is distinguished from orthoclase feldspar by the occurrence of very fine lines or striations on certain surfaces. Careful examination of a handful of fragments from this locality will usually reveal a few with the tell-tale striations. Large, fractured grains can be seen in the rock, but it is very easy to gather a cup of small fragments by searching the flats surrounding the knoll. They are very easily seen on sunny days as they resemble fragments of glass. Aragonite occurs as white opaque material in vugs in the basalt. There is a private claim on part of this area, but individual collectors are welcome and invited to sign a register maintained at the turnoff into the area.

Directions: Drive west of Delta about 4.5 miles to the junction with Utah Highway 257. Drive south on Highway 257 approximately 13 miles and turn east off the road and cross the railroad tracks to the small black hill. The road circles around the hill and many crystal fragments can be found on the flats extending eastward behind the hill.

Land Status: Mining claim and BLM public lands.

Maps: Delta (m), Sunstone Knoll (7.5).

References: Visited by this writer. Stowe (1979).

Location:	Black Springs area
Rock:	obsidian

Description: Many different varieties of the volcanic glass obsidian can be found in an area extending about 2 miles south and 6 miles north of Black Springs. There are some private claims here, but the material is very abundant throughout the area and collectors will have no difficulty finding all that they need. Digging is seldom necessary.

Directions: From the intersection of U.S. 6-50 and Utah Highway 257 west of Delta, drive south on Highway 257 about 44 miles and turn east across the railroad track on a dirt road that leads to the Black Spring watering trough. Do not camp close to the watering trough as it is used by wild horses and they will not approach if campers are near. From the spring, the road leading north has several branches that lead into different areas to search for material.

Land Status: Mining claims and BLM public lands.

Maps: Richfield (m), Cruz (7.5).

References: Stowe (1979).

Location:	**Painter Spring area**
Minerals:	quartz, garnet, diopside, vesuvianite, chalcopyrite, molybdenite

Description: Painter Spring is a beautiful desert spring that attracts many birds and animals. It is under consideration for special manangement status by the BLM. Be careful with litter and try not to damage the trees or mar the rocks in the immediate area of the spring. The spring is located at the edge of the granitic intrusion that makes up the central part of the range. The pink granitic rock of the intrusion is cut by quartz veins some of which have cavities containing large quartz crystals. The low hills north and south of Painter Springs are garnet-bearing rocks created by contact metamorphism of the original limestone. Garnet, diopside, and vesuvianite may be found here, although not necessarily as crystals. Chalcopyrite and molybdenite occur in the intrusive a short distance up the North Fork.

Directions: From Delta, proceed west on U.S. 6-50 about 60 miles and take the gravel road to the right near milepost 33. It should be marked with a sign indicating "Painter Springs, 10 miles." At 9.4 miles an intersection with a water tank is reached. Turn east toward the mountain for 1.8 miles to Painter Spring. A 4WD or HCV may be necessary to cross the wash just below Painter Springs. (If coming to Painter Spring from the trilobite collecting areas at Antelope Springs, see the road log earlier in this section for directions.)

Land Status: BLM public lands. Some mining claims in the area.

Maps: Tule Valley (m), Notch Peak (15), Notch Peak (7.5).

References: Visited by this writer. Stowe (1979).

Location:	**Amasa Valley**
Minerals:	quartz (smoky, amethystine), albite, garnet, scheelite

Description: Amasa Valley is a high hidden valley at the top of Sawtooth Mountain in the House Range. The valley is the site of placer gold claims which have been worked on an intermittent basis. Do not disturb any buildings or equipment in the area. In addition to the placer gold claims, there are also some areas around the high rim of the valley to the north and west where contact metamorphosed rock containing garnet and scheelite has been mined. Smoky quartz, associated with elaborately twinned albite, has been found on the low knob east of the placer mining operation and a vein of amethystine quartz has been found near the tungsten mines on Pine Peak. From the summit of Pine Peak there is a tremendous view across the west desert.

Directions: See the road log and maps. A 4WD or HCV will be necessary on the steep rocky road up North Canyon to Amasa Valley.

Land Status: Mining claims and BLM public lands.

Maps: Tule Valley (m), Notch Peak (15), Notch Peak (7.5).

References: Visited by this writer.

A Guide to Collecting Sites

Location: North Canyon

Fossils: trilobites

Description: The Cambrian Weeks Limestone is exposed on the north side of North Canyon. Trilobites found here include the agnostid *Lejopyge*, and other trilobites such as *Tricrepicephalus coria*, *Deiracephalus multisegmentus*, and *Cedaria minor*.

Directions: This is the road to Amasa Valley. See preceding description and maps and road log.

Land Status: BLM public lands.

Maps: Tule Valley (m), Notch Peak (15), Miller Cove (7.5).

References: Hintze (1974c); Lloyd Gunther, Brigham City, UT.

Location: Crystal Peak

Fossils: brachiopods, trilobites, and others

Minerals: quartz

Description: Extremely small (< 0.25 inch) doubly terminated quartz crystals occur at Crystal Peak and in the related Tunnel Springs Tuff unit. Outcrops of fossiliferous Kanosh Shale, a member of the Ordovician Pogonip Group, form the lower slopes north of the road at Crystal Peak.

Directions: Crystal Peak is a prominent landmark appearing on most maps and lies along the Garrison-Black Rock Road in Sec. 24, T23S, R16W. This road begins at Black Rock on U-257 south of Delta. Other access is from U.S. 50-6 west of Delta.

Land Status: BLM public lands and mining claims.

Maps: Wah Wah Mtns. North (m), Crystal Peak (15), Crystal Peak (7.5).

References: Visited by this writer. Hintze (1974b).

Location: West side of Tule Valley

Fossils: brachiopods, trilobites, ostracods

Description: This location is at the contact of the fossiliferous upper Pogonip Group and the overlying quartzites.

Directions: Turn north off U.S. 50-6 near milepost 30 and travel north and northeast about 3.5 miles to an intersection. Turn left and continue northwest about 4 miles. The outcrops are the ledgey slopes below the quartzite cliffs. The location is on the east side of the ridge south of the road junction at elevation point 5,231 (1,594 m) in Sec. 18, T19S, R15W. As an alternate approach if coming from Painter Spring: From the Painter Spring water tank, travel west across Tule Valley for 5.9 miles then turn left (south) for 2.5 miles.

Land Status: BLM public lands.

Maps: Tule Valley (m), Conger Mtn. (15), Bullgrass Knoll (7.5), Dowdell Canyon (7.5).

References: Visited by this writer. Hintze (1974a), IAPG (1951).

Hemirhodon amplipyge Robison. This large trilobite occurs in the Marjum Formation of the House Range. Specimen is about 4 inches long. Photo: Val Gunther.

Acrothele sp. This small brachiopod is relatively common in the Cambrian rocks of the House Range, occuring with trilobites in the Wheeler Amphitheater area. This specimen is about 0.5 inch. Photo: Val Gunther.

WEST DESERT AREA MAP
Tooele-Juab-Millard
0 6
Miles
paved roads
unpaved roads
N
TO WENDOVER
GOLDHILL
TO TOOELE
DUGWAY
VERNON
X SIMPSON SPRINGS
DUGWAY RANGE
CALLAO
TOOELE COUNTY
JUAB COUNTY
FISH SPRINGS RANGE
THOMAS RANGE
TROUT CREEK
PARTOUN
TOPAZ MTN
JUAB COUNTY
MILLARD COUNTY
CONFUSION
DRUM MTNS.
GANDY
FOOTE RANGE
UTAH
NEVADA
HOUSE
WHEELER AMPHETHEATER
U.S. 6
DELTA
HINCKLEY
U.S. 50
DESERET
RANGE
CONGER SPRING
RANGE
PAINTER SPRING
U.S. 6-50
X SUNSTONE KNOLL
CLEAR LAKE
SKULL ROCK PASS
TO IBEX (FOSSIL MTN)
TO MILFORD

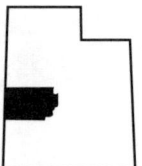

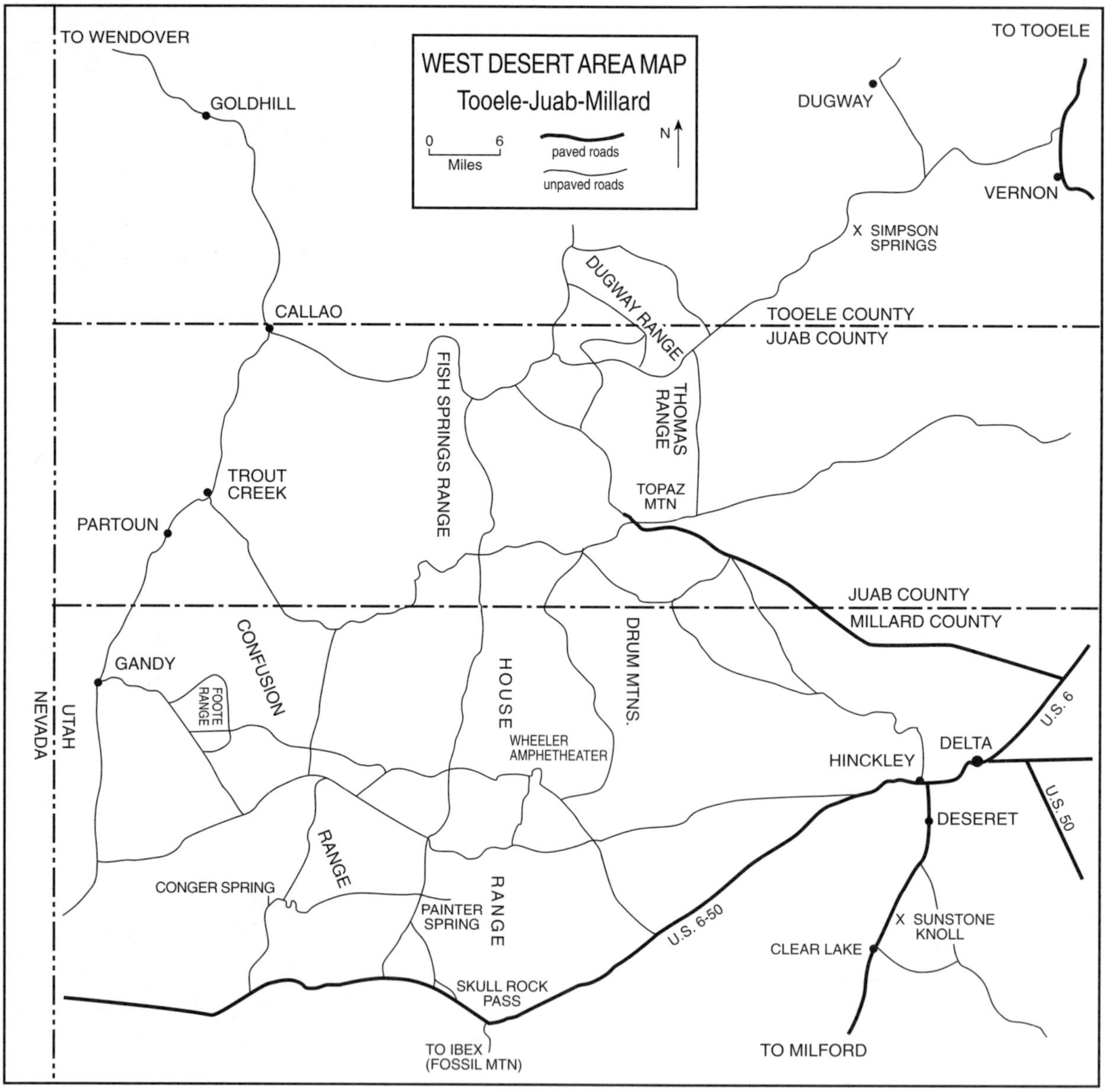

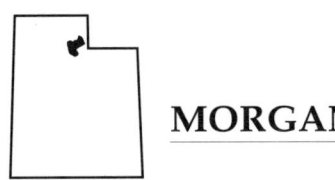

MORGAN COUNTY

Morgan County is a relatively small county in north-central Utah, located on the east side of the Wasatch Range. At its extreme western end it incorporates some of the Precambrian gneisses and schists of the Farmington Canyon Complex. Most of the county is covered by Tertiary rocks, some sedimentary and some volcanic in origin. A section of Paleozoic rocks is exposed from Morgan to the Devil's Slide area and fossils can be found there.

Location: **Argenta District**

Minerals: **pyrite**

Description: This is an old mining district that produced only a very small amount of ore.

Directions: This area is accessed by taking the road up Cottonwood Canyon from the town of Mountain Green. The mines are on the south side of Cottonwood Canyon and are reached by way of a series of steep switchbacks near the top of Miller Gulch.

Land Status: BLM public lands.

Maps: Ogden (m), Morgan (7.5).

References: Stowe (1979).

Location: **Devil's Slide area**

Rocks: **ripple marks, geodes**

Minerals: **calcite**

Description: Ripple marks, indicating either wave or current action, occur in red Triassic rocks in Upper Weber Canyon, west of Devil's Slide. Small hollow concretions with well-developed calcite crystals can be found in the river bed where they have weathered out of the rock on the hillsides.

Directions: Exit I-84 at the Taggarts exit between Morgan and Devil's Slide and take the old road east along the north side of the canyon.

Land Status: Highway right-of-way.

Maps: Ogden (m), Morgan (7.5), Devils Slide (7.5).

References: Dr. Richard W. Moyle, Geology Department, Weber State University, Ogden, UT.

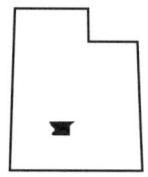

PIUTE COUNTY

Piute County is a small county is central Utah and is almost completely underlain by volcanic rocks. A major part of the Tushar Mountains are included in the county as well as part of the Sevier Plateau. Marysvale is the site of an important mining district, principally for uranium, but alunite, lead, zinc, and gold have been mined in this area.

Location: Alunite townsite

Mineral: alunite

Description: Alunite is a basic potassium aluminum sulfate which is a common potassic alteration product accompanying some mineral deposits. In Piute County it occurs in sufficient quantity that, at one time, it was mined for use by the aluminum industry. Quantities were stockpiled around the old mill.

Directions: Beginning at the south city limits of Marysvale, drive south about 3 miles to milepost 116 and continue past it for 0.5 mile to a dirt road going west. Turn west and continue on this road for 1.1 miles to the old townsite of Alunite. The old mill is on the north side of the power substation.

Land Status: private.

Maps: Beaver (m), Marysvale (7.5).

References: Stowe (1979).

Location: Deer Trail Mine

Minerals: sphalerite, fluorite

Description: The Deer Trail Mine was operated during the 1960s and 1970s primarily for sphalerite. During that time it produced some pale-green, dodecahedral (or cubo-octahedral) crystals of fluorite which are attractive to mineral collectors. Broken crystals can be found on the dump along with specimens of sphalerite. When found, the fluorite is coated with white quartz which can only be removed with hydrofluoric acid. This should not be attempted without access to a fume hood and appropriate safety equipment.

A number of unusual minerals were produced from the mines of this area earlier in this century, including tiemannite (mercury selenide) and onofrite (mercury sulfide selenide).

Directions: The dirt road that leads to the mine is located almost exactly 2 miles south of the Marysvale south city limit, about 3.5 miles south of the center of town. The mine is on the lower slopes of the mountain and is clearly visible from the highway.

Land Status: Private land. Collectors can usually collect on the dump, but stay away from mine buildings and equipment. There may be mining activity occurring here in the future, if so, stay off posted property and seek permission for access to the dump.

Maps: Beaver (m), Marysvale (7.5), Mt. Brigham (7.5).

References: Visited by the author. Butler (1920).

Location: Durkee Creek area

Minerals: chabazite, stilbite, heulandite, mordenite, scolecite, calcite, quartz

Description: Several areas within the volcanic rocks of the Marysvale area have undergone zeolitic alter-

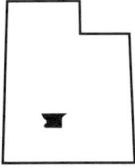ation resulting in a variety of zeolite minerals. These minerals usually occur along fracture surfaces, form veins, or fill vugs in the volcanic rock. At most locations stilbite and heulandite are the most common zeolites to form crystals. Mordenite is often present as fibrous material filling veins and occasionally as fine fibers forming tufts in cavities. Rhombohedral crystals of chabazite are not uncommon, usually in vugs. Quartz lines some openings, both as chalcedony and as drusy crystals. Calcite crystals are sometimes found perched on the zeolites.

Directions: There are two locations in the Durkee Creek area, both relatively close together. They are reached by taking a street east in downtown Marysvale and crossing the Sevier River. This road then turns north paralleling the river. Stay to the right as the road rounds the north end of the mountain and heads southeast. At the road fork, just before the power line crosses the road, take the left fork curving east along the north side of Durkee Creek. Go about 1 mile and park and walk across the creek to the small hill on the other side. Zeolites are particularly abundant on the north side and the top of the hill. The second area is across the valley and about midway up the slopes of the wash visible about 0.5 mile southeast of the first location.

Land Status: BLM public lands.

Maps: Beaver (m), Marysvale (7.5).

References: Visited by the author. Kerr, et al. (1957).

Location:	**Elbow Ranch area**
Minerals:	**chabazite, stilbite, heulandite, mordenite, scolecite, calcite, quartz**

Description: This is a relatively large zeolitized area similar in mineralogy to the Durkee Creek areas described above, but with larger vugs and better crystallized material.

Directions: From Marysvale drive south 2 miles from the city limit (about 3.5 miles from downtown Marysvale) and turn left on a paved road paralleling the highway. After 0.25 mile turn left on a dirt road and follow this across the Sevier River, across the ridge on the other side, and continue to the abandoned Elbow Ranch. Continue on the main dirt road south from Elbow Ranch. The zeolite location is the first canyon north of Dry Canyon, where the road enters the mountains. A dim track left by deer hunters and mineral collectors leads from the road, across the sagebrush, to a parking area at the mouth of the canyon. Zeolites occur in the cliff- and ledge-forming rocks of the north wall of the canyon near its head. It is a strenuous hike to reach the collecting areas and there is no shade for collectors on the south-facing canyon wall. Map location of the canyon is the S ½, Sec. 15, T28S, R2½W.

Land Status: BLM public lands and mining claims. Claims in this area are owned by Keith Berben who lives in the house on the hill 0.25 mile west of Elbow Ranch. He can give directions, if necessary, and it is a courtesy to let him know that you are collecting here.

Maps: Beaver (m), Marysvale (7.5), Malmsten Peak (7.5).

References: Visited by the author.

Location:	**Blackbird Mine**
Minerals:	**psilomelane and other manganese minerals**

Description: Psilomelane is the hard botryoidal form of various manganese oxides. It may occur with pyrolusite (soft, sooty) and manganite (silvery, metallic).

Directions: Follow the directions to Elbow Ranch given above. At Elbow Ranch, either of the two roads that lead north (left) from the main gravel road can be followed up the creek beds of the foothills to the Blackbird Mine which is located just below the steep front of the Sevier Plateau, about 3.5 miles from Elbow Ranch.

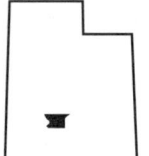

Land Status: National Forest lands and mining claims.

Maps: Beaver (m), Marysvale (7.5), Marysvale Peak (7.5).

References: Dr. Richard Kennedy, Geology Dept., Southern Utah University, Cedar City, UT.

Location:	**Pine Creek area**
Minerals:	**corundum, spinel, nepheline**

Description: An unusual mineral occurrence has been noted in the headwater areas of Pine Creek on the east side of the Sevier Plateau. Loose blocks of a dark colored rock consisting predominantly of corundum, spinel, and nepheline, but also hibonite, diaspore, forsterite, clinohumite, sillimanite, and orthoclase, occur in this area. The unusual mineralogy is attributed to a deep source for this material which was brought to the surface during the volcanic eruptions that built the Sevier Plateau. The corundum is a pale blue color, sapphire, but is extremely small, less than 1/16 inch.

Directions: Since the blocks occur as float, there is no specific location, and there is no road directly into the area, although there is a road that goes part way up Pine Creek Canyon. The general location is Sec. 22, T28S, R2W.

Land Status: Mining claims and National Forest lands.

Maps: Beaver (m), Malmsten Peak (7.5).

References: Callaghan (1973); Dr. Richard Kennedy, Geology Dept., Southern Utah University, Cedar City, UT.

Location:	**north of Marysvale**
Rock:	**gray banded rhyolite**
Mineral:	**amethystine quartz**

Description: A distinctly flow-banded, gray rhyolite occurs in this area and within the rhyolite are pockets of small quartz crystals, some with an amethystine color.

Directions: Located up the hill from U.S. 89, about 0.5 mile north of the Black Rock alongside the road, north of Marysvale.

Land Status: BLM public land.

Maps: Beaver (m), Marysvale (7.5).

References: Dr. Richard Kennedy, Geology Dept., Southern Utah University, Cedar City, UT.

RICH COUNTY

This county is located in extreme northern Utah and extends southward from the Idaho border at Bear Lake. Most of the county is blanketed by Tertiary sedimentary deposits within which are some interesting concretions. The Simpson Mountains near the Wyoming border are formed in Paleozoic rocks from which fossils could be collected. There are several large phosphate mines in the Simpson Mountains.

Location: Birch Creek - Woodruff Creek area

Fossils: fossil-bearing concretions

Description: The Eocene Flagstaff and Green River Formations occur as material capping ridges and filling valleys over a widespread area of northern Utah. Within these units occur concretionary zones with the concretions ranging in size from a few inches (typical) up to a foot or more in diameter. These concretions are interesting in that they often have a fossil as the core. Gastropods are common in the concretions from some areas whereas other areas may have other fossils or nondescript organic matter. The concretions occur in a wide belt whose full extent is undetermined, but it runs at least from the Causey Reservoir area in Morgan County to the Woodruff Reservoir area in Rich County, and probably extends to Bear Lake on the north and Echo to the south.

Directions: Drive about 6 miles west of Woodruff on Utah Highway 39 to the intersection with a secondary road leading south to Woodruff Reservoir. Birch Creek and Woodruff Creek meet at this point and concretions can be found along the road. Concretions litter the surrounding ridge tops, such as Cutoff Ridge and Strawberry Ridge, north of Highway 39, and the Red Mountain area south of Highway 39.

Land Status: Mixture of BLM public land, state land, and private land.

Maps: Logan (m), Ogden (m), Birch Creek Reservoirs (7.5), Meachum Ridge (7.5).

References: Dr. Richard W. Moyle, Geology Department, Weber State University, Ogden, UT.

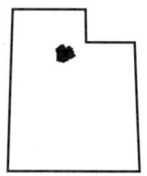

SALT LAKE COUNTY

This largely urban county still presents interesting collecting opportunities, primarily in the Wasatch Range. Dumps from many of the old mines yield interesting specimens to the collector. There are also fossil collecting sites in some of the sedimentary units.

Location: **Baby McKee Mine**

Minerals: **pyromorphite, pyrite**

Description: There are several small mine dumps and prospects on the hill southwest of and above the Cardiff Mine in Mill D South Fork off Big Cottonwood Canyon. This area, which includes the Baby McKee mine marked on the topographic map, is primarily quartzite and on the fracture surfaces of some of the quartzite can be found crystals of pyromorphite. The mineral occurs as well-formed, lime green, hexagonal crystals. They are generally small in size and best appreciated with a hand lens or microscope, but occasional lucky collectors have found thumbnail size crystals. Minor amounts of pyrite can also be found on some of these dumps although it is often partially altered to hematite.

Directions: Proceed up Big Cottonwood Canyon approximately 9.5 miles and turn right at the sign indicating Cardiff Fork or Mill D South Fork. The paved road turns to gravel after a short distance. Proceed up the gravel road. Most cars will want to park where the road crosses the creek or up the switchback nearer Doughnut Falls. Past this point the road proceeds up a rough steep hill requiring HCV/4WD. It is slightly over 2 miles to the Cardiff Mine from this point. The Baby McKee Mine group can be reached by hiking the roads that circle above the Cardiff Mine to either the left or right. Both of these roads are washed out and generally impassable to all vehicles above the Cardiff Mine. Both roads pass directly by the dumps of the Baby McKee group and link together there.

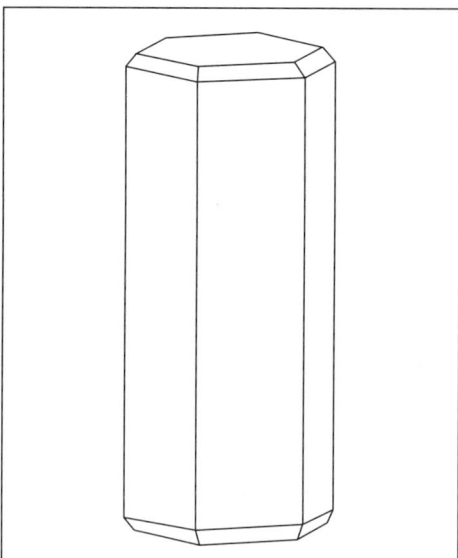

Pyromorphite crystals usually occur as simple hexagonal prismatic crystals. Sometimes the crystals are slightly hollow.

Land Status: Private land at the Cardiff Mine and National Forest lands.

Maps: Salt Lake City (m), Mt. Aire (7.5), Dromedary Peak (7.5).

References: Visited by this writer.

Location: **Flagstaff-Emma Area**

Minerals: **hemimorphite, wulfenite, cerussite, galena**

Description: This location is the series of mine dumps along the south-facing slopes above the Alta Guard Station. Approximately 100 yards past the buried water tank on the Grizzly Gulch jeep road, there is a wide gully which has washed out material from mine dumps higher on the hill. Limonite-stained rocks in this area can be broken open to reveal a stockwork of open vugs which are lined with hemimorphite. In some of the vugs bright lemon yellow crystals of wulfenite are mixed with the hemimorphite. On some of the mine dumps at higher elevation near the Flagstaff Mine are masses of limonite which have cerus-

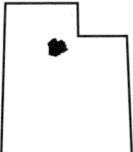

site crystals scattered on their surfaces. Mines in this area produced masses of cerussite crystals up to 12 inches across, some of which still survive in private and museum collections. Galena, usually hidden by a limonitic coating can be found on many of the dumps on this mountainside.

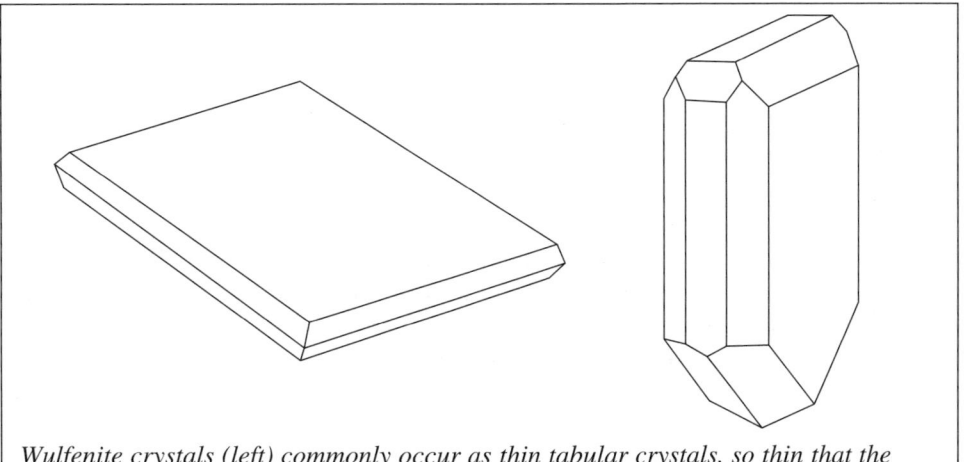

Wulfenite crystals (left) commonly occur as thin tabular crystals, so thin that the edge terminations are often not visible. Hemimorphite crystals are named for the hemimorphic habit, i.e., the top and bottom terminations are different.

Directions: Park in Alta and walk up the road that begins at the Alta Guard Station. This road circles around behind the Guard Station to the west, then switches back and heads east, gradually climbing along the slope, toward Grizzly Gulch. The mountainside is relatively open and dumps are easily seen. Numerous trails and jeep roads go up to the higher workings. This road is closed to vehicles.

Land Status: Private lands and National Forest lands.

Maps: Salt Lake City (m), Dromedary Peak (7.5).

References: Visited by this writer.

Location:	**Grizzly Gulch**
Minerals:	**garnet, vesuvianite, epidote, pyrite, calcite, forsterite, brucite, manganese oxides, serpentine**
Rocks:	**marble, massive garnet**

Description: The mines and rock outcrops in this area provide a number of interesting minerals and rocks for the collector, although well-formed crystals may be difficult to obtain. Along the road and in the general area can be found coarsely crystalline marble which has brucite as a minor constituent. Vugs in some of the marble may contain a white mineral which is lime. The trail to the right as you enter the gulch leads to an outcrop of massive garnet which contains pyrite and minor copper sulfides. Copper staining marks the rock. This outcrop continues up the creek bed to the right. Rocks on the small dump near this outcrop have areas of waxy, yellow-green serpentine which can be found as masses up to several inches across. Higher dumps to the north have boulders of manganese oxides (black sooty material) which often contain vugs of well-formed calcite crystals exhibiting rhombohedral forms. Crystals of vesuvianite and garnet can be found in the rocks up the mountainside east of the dumps. Vugs may contain well-developed vesuvianite crystals up to one half inch long. Epidote is most common as green micro-crystals on fracture surfaces, but excellent crystals are reputed to have been collected in this area.

Directions: Continue along the road from the Alta Guard Station (see previous location) until you reach

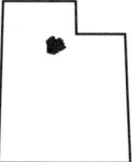 the dumps in Grizzly Gulch. These are located about one mile from the Guard Station and about 600 feet higher.

Land Status: Private land and National Forest land.

Maps: Salt Lake City (m), Dromedary Peak (7.5), Brighton (7.5).

References: Visited by this writer.

Location:	Big Cottonwood Mine
Minerals:	**ludwigite, magnetite, vesuvianite, garnet, actinolite, forsterite, serpentine, epidote, clintonite**

Description: Ludwigite is a rare magnesium iron borate which is common at this locality (and is also found at the West Spring location in Beaver County). It occurs as radiating sprays of accicular crystals frozen in matrix and associated with abundant magnetite. Both minerals are black, but the fibrous, radiating habit and silky luster distinguishes the ludwigite from the granular habit and metallic luster of the magnetite. Crude octahedrons of magnetite may also be found here. Actinolite and some serpentine can be found on the mine dump. The pale-green mica clintonite is common here and in nearby outcrops. Other skarn minerals can be found in more abundance by searching the rock-strewn gully beyond the second mine dump.

Directions: From the ski area in Brighton take the Brighton Nature Trail (follow the paved path behind the ski lifts to the sign marking the trail head). Follow the trail alongside the creek until it joins the maintenance road for the ski lift. When the road makes a sharp turn to the left, the trail leaves the road and goes right (marked by a sign saying "trail") to an overlook where the trail divides. Follow the signs and go around the west side of Dog Lake on the old mining road. The first dump has the most magnetite and ludwigite. The second dump has very little, but there are several small dumps up the hill from this point with magnetite, copper staining, garnet, etc. Continue over to the large obvious gully and examine the rock there.

Land Status: Private land and National Forest lands.

Maps: Salt Lake City (m), Brighton (7.5)

References: Visited by this writer.

Location:	Lake Solitude
Minerals:	**spinel, clintonite, epidote**

Description: Rock outcrops in the area of Lake Solitude, particularly some of the cuts along the ski lift service road, contain scattered crystals of spinel and crystals of clintonite, one of the brittle micas. Epidote may also be found in these outcrops.

Directions: Lake Solitude may be reached by hiking up the ski runs from Solitude Resort or by taking the trail from Brighton.

Land Status: Private land and National Forest lands.

Maps: Salt Lake City (m), Brighton (7.5).

References: Visited by this writer.

Location:	Maxfield Mine
Minerals:	**quartz, pyrite**

Description: Quartz crystals up to 3 inches in length have been found on the dumps of the Maxfield Mine. Crude crystals of pyrite showing pyritohedral faces have also been found here.

Directions: The Maxfield Mine is located in Big Cottonwood Canyon at the mouth of Mill A Gulch. A

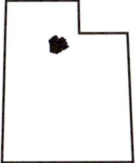
wide parking area for hikers is located on the south side of the road. Cross the road and proceed up the Mill A Gulch trail 50 yards and the dumps are visible. This is one of the most easily accessible locations in the area.

Land Status: Private land.

Maps: Salt Lake City (m), Mount Aire (7.5).

References: Visited by this writer.

Location: **Mouth of Emigration Canyon**

Fossils: **echinoderms**

Description: Small round urchins may be found in the road cut at the mouth of Emigration Canyon. Specimens can be found that have some spines intact, other rocks will have loose spines preserved.

Directions: Proceed up the Emigration Canyon Road past Hogle Zoo. At the road cut at the narrow mouth of the canyon, park and look at the rocks of the Jurassic Twin Creeks Limestone that are exposed there.

Land Status: Highway right-of-way.

Maps: Salt Lake City (m), Fort Douglas (7.5), Sugar house (7.5).

References: Bob Randolph, Salt Lake City, UT.

Location: **Summit of Emigration Canyon**

Fossils: **crinoids**

Description: The star-shaped crinoid, *Pentacrinus*, can be found in this area in the Jurassic Twin Creeks Limestone.

Directions: Proceed up the Emigration Canyon Road to the summit. A paved road with a gate branches off to the right. Walk along this road about 100 yards and look in the outcrops of limestone that occur 10 to 20 feet below the road. Some specimens can also be found in the area of recent roadbuilding activity near the oil storage tank.

Land Status: National Forest lands.

Maps: Salt Lake City (m), Mountain Dell (7.5).

References: Visited by this writer. Bob Randolph, Salt Lake City, UT.

Location: **Cephalopod Gulch**

Fossils: **cephalopods**

Description: The *Meekoceras* zone of the Triassic Thaynes Formation occurs in the gulch which was named for the abundant cephalopods that were found here.

Directions: Park in the U of U Medical Center area and hike up the foothills to the Gulch which is located directly above the Medical Center.

Land Status: Mixture of state and National Forest lands.

Maps: Salt Lake City (m), Fort Douglas (7.5).

References: Bob Randolph, Salt Lake City, UT.

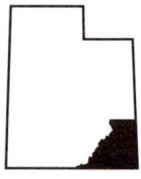

SAN JUAN COUNTY

This large county is located in the southeastern corner of the state. It includes the igneous rocks of the Abajo Mountains and part of the La Sal Mountains, but most of the rock seen in the county is Late Paleozoic or Mesozoic sedimentary rocks. Uranium mineralization is common at many areas within the county and small copper deposits occur as well.

Location: Northeast of La Sal Junction

Rock: agate

Description: A bed of agate occurs in this area that extends several miles south and at least one mile north of this point. The agate has an opaque coating and must be broken to examine the color.

Directions: Located in Sec. 28, T28S, R23E. To reach the location, start at Norhwest Pipeline Corporation's compressor station about 20 miles south of Moab on U.S. 191. From the compressor station drive south on U.S. 191 for 0.5 mile to a junction with an improved dirt road going east. Take this road approximately 0.5 mile to a junction. Stay to the left and continue for 0.7 mile to the point where the road makes a sharp turn to the left at the same time crossing a small wash. Stop here and walk up the small hill to the east.

Land Status: BLM public lands.

Maps: La Sal (m), La Sal Junction (7.5), La Sal West (7.5).

References: Stowe (1979).

Location: Chicken Corner Trail Area

Fossils: marine fossils

Description: A variety of fossils occur in a thin layer of bluish-gray limestone enclosed within the surrounding red rocks.

Directions: Located in Sec. 22, T26S, R20E. Take the Kane Creek Road where it branches off U.S. 191 near the southern edge of Moab. Follow this road beyond the end of the pavement where it leaves the river bottom, climbs over a ridge, and descends into Kane Springs Canyon. The road climbs up over Hurrah Pass and descends to the other side. The location is about 24 miles from the starting point on U.S. 191.

Land Status: BLM public lands.

Maps: La Sal (m), Moab (7.5), Through Springs Canyon (7.5), Moab (m).

References: Stowe (1979).

Location: Red House Cliffs

Rock: agate and algal balls

Description: Red agate suitable for cutting and polishing and algal balls up to 3 inches in diameter.

Directions: From the junction of Utah Highways 95 and 276 near Natural Bridges National Monument, travel southwest on Highway 276 approximately 20 miles to where the highway starts to climb out of the flat and go up over the hills. As you go up the hill watch for a cattle guard and 100 yards past the cattle guard a rough 4WD road turns off to the left. Passenger cars should park here. Go up the 4WD road about 0.8 mile and look for agate along the side of the road.

A Guide to Collecting Sites

Land Status: BLM public lands.

Maps: Navajo Mtn. (m), Clay Hills (7.5).

References: Stowe (1979)

Location: Joe Wilson Wash

Rock: agate

Description: Large pieces of agate can be found at the bottom of the wash.

Directions: Starting at La Sal Junction, drive south on U.S. 191 for 4.1 miles to Joe Wilson Wash. Park where the highway crosses the wash and hike up the wash about 0.25 mile and agate will be seen in the bottom of the wash.

Land Status: BLM public lands.

Maps: La Sal (m), La Sal West (7.5), La Sal Junction (7.5).

References: Stowe (1979).

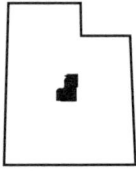

SANPETE COUNTY

This central Utah county is mainly comprised of Jurassic, Cretaceous, and Tertiary sedimentary rocks, including those of the western Wasatch Plateau. A limited number of fossil and mineral collecting sites are known.

Location: Railroad overpass

Fossils: ostracodes, gastropods, leaves

Description: The Eocene Green River Formation in this area has fossils of ostracodes and gastropods (snails). these are found in the limestone, ledge-forming units, and are often best seen on weathered surfaces of loose blocks. Shale beds within the unit may contain abundant leaf fossils.

Directions: Road cuts along U.S. 89 beginning at the railroad overpass 6.2 miles north of Fairview and extending for the next 1.5 miles northward can be searched for these fossils.

Land Status: Highway right-of-way.

Maps: Nephi (m), Fairview (7.5).

References: Rigby, et al. (1974).

Location: Mellor Canyon

Mineral: quartz

Description: Quartz crystals up to one-fourth inch in diameter occur as vein fillings and incrustations of cavities in chert within the Flagstaff Formation.

Directions: Located in the SW ¼, Sec. 26, T17S, R1E, near the head of Mellor Canyon. The road up Mellor Canyon begins about 1.5 miles north of Fayette.

Land Status: BLM public lands.

Maps: Manti (m), Hells Kitchen Canyon SE (7.5).

References: Pratt and Callaghan (1970).

Location: Sterling

Mineral: aragonite

Description: Aragonite occurs with a variety of habits in a prospect pit located on a fault zone. It occurs primarily as a white crystalline material filling fractures and lining cavities, concentric bands, mammilary forms, and massive translucent structureless material.

Directions: Located in the NW ¼, Sec. 15, T19S, R2E south of Sterling. A jeep trail leads into this area from Utah Highway 137 about 0.2 mile south of its junction with U.S. 89.

Land Status: Mixture of BLM public lands and private lands in this area.

Maps: Manti (m), Sterling (7.5).

References: Pratt and Callaghan (1970).

A Guide to Collecting Sites

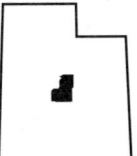

Location: Six Mile Canyon

Mineral: magnesite

Description: Boulders of magnesite occur as float in a gully in the north wall of Six Mile Canyon. Source of the boulders is unknown. Surrounding red cliffs are the North Horn Formation.

Directions: Located in the NE ¼, Sec. 30, T18S, R3E. Take the road east out of Sterling past Palisade Lake State Park and on into Six Mile Canyon.

Land Status: National Forest lands, mining claim.

Maps: Manti (m), Black Mountain (7.5).

References: Pratt and Callaghan (1970).

SEVIER COUNTY

The southern half of this central Utah county encompasses a significant part of the Marysvale volcanic complex, including the northern parts of the Tushar Mountains and Sevier Plateau. The north half of the county is underlain by a variety of Mesozoic and Cenozoic rocks such as those hosting the gypsum and salt deposits near Salina and Redmond.

Location: Salina Canyon

Fossils: plants

Description: A variety of plants including palms and sequoias are found in horizons within the Cretaceous Blackhawk Formation which, in this area, consists of a series of thin coal seams and bituminous shales, and sandstones.

Directions: Plant-bearing horizons within the Blackhawk are exposed in Salina Canyon from the vicinity of Alumbed Hollow eastward to Taylor Flats. Old U.S. 50 parallels I-70 through this area and can be used for access. Several areas have been reported as being particularly prolific: (1) On the south side of I-70 where the road to Brown's Hole climbs the hill, (2) on the north side of I-70 at the mouth of Water Hollow on the southeast side, (3) on the north side of I-70, the canyon running NNE directly across the interstate from Pipe Springs, (4) on the north side of the interstate at Taylor Flats, the ridge adjacent to the interstate.

Land Status: National Forest lands.

Maps: Salina (m), Water hollow Ridge (7.5), Steves Mountain (7.5).

References: Steve Robison, Ogden, UT. Cross et al. (1975), Parker (1976).

Location: Sigurd area

Minerals: gypsum, anhydrite, halite

Description: Wallboard plants operated by U. S. Gypsum and Georgia-Pacific are located in Sigurd and mine gypsum from tightly folded outcrops of gypsum that form ridges in the area northeast of the plants. A county road runs through this area (accessible from behind the wallboard plants or from the vicnity of Aurora) and many of the former quarries are beside the road. Collecting is permissible as long as you stay away from active mining areas where there is blasting and heavy equipment at work. Most of the material is massive gypsum and anhydrite, but groups of small crystals can be found. Halite occurs in red beds in the area and its occurrence is usually marked by a white efflorescence on the soil.

Directions: Access to the county road is from Utah Highway 24 beyond the wallboard plants or by secondary roads leading south and east out of Aurora and across the valley to the mines in the hills.

Land Status: Mixture of BLM lands and mining claims.

Maps: Salina (m), Sigurd (7.5), Aurora (7.5).

References: Visited by this writer.

SUMMIT COUNTY

This county extends from Coalville eastward to include the west end of the Uinta Mountains. An extensive area of Cretaceous rocks occurs in the vicinity of Coalville in which abundant oyster fossils can be found. Paleozoic rocks and associated fossils are found in a narrow outcrop pattern around the west end of the Uintas.

Location: Riley Canyon

Fossil: horn coral

Description: Horn corals from this area are highly prized by collectors since the corals have been replaced by red agate. There may be some claims in this area; contact claim owners before digging. Be careful digging. Do not work beneath overhangs. Three people were killed while digging in this area in 1973.

Directions: From Kamas take Utah Highway 150 (the Mirror Lake Road) east for 3 miles and turn right at the Willow Springs Trout Farm. Follow this road to Hintze Drive and turn right through the metal gate. Stay to the right at the fork and proceed to the digging area on up the mountain. HCV or 4WD is needed. The old route into this area is now closed.

Land Status: National Forest lands and mining claims by individuals and mineral clubs. Contact Utah mineral clubs for information about permission to collect on their claims and to obtain current route information.

Maps: Salt Lake City (m), Woodland (7.5).

References: Stowe (1979), various rockhounds.

Location: Chalk Creek area

Fossil: plants

Description: Abundant leaf fossils along with some stem material is found in a sandstone horizon within the Cretaceous Henefer Formation.

Directions: Go 8.2 miles east of Coalville on Utah Highway 133 to a long roadcut at the top of a hill. The roadcut is on the north side of the road and a wide parking area is on the south. The fossils occur in a horizon immediately below the obvious sandstone layer. Abundant fragmentary material can be found at the base of the slope.

Land Status: Highway right of way.

Maps: Turner Hollow (7.5).

References: Visited by this writer. Lloyd Gunther, Brigham City, UT.

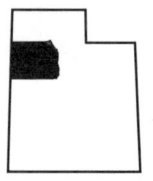

TOOELE COUNTY

This is one of the more mineral-rich counties in the state. It includes the mining districts on the west side of the Oquirrh Mountains and extends westward to the Nevada line. Important mineral collecting areas at Gold Hill, the Dugway Mountains, and the Rush Valley area lie within this county. The majority of the rocks are sedimentary rocks of Paleozoic age, but there are also interesting outcrops of igneous rock.

Location: Wendover

Rock: agate

Description and Directions: Agate occurs in the vicinity of the southern end of the Silver Island Mountains north of Danger Cave State Park. Take the road to the park and continue north on an unimproved road about 2 miles.

Land Status: BLM public lands.

Maps: Bonneville Salt Flats (m), Graham Peak (7.5).

References: Stowe (1979).

Location: Stansbury Island

Mineral: gypsum, oolitic sand

Description: Selenite crystals can be found in the mud along the western shoreline of the northern part of Stansbury Island and in the vicinity of the pumping station on the southeast side of the island. Oolitic sand dunes are found at the end of the road on the west side of the island.

Directions: Take I-80 west from Salt Lake City to the second Grantsville interchange (Utah Highway 138), approximately 30 miles west of the airport. Get off the interstate and travel west about a quarter mile past Highway 138 and take the secondary road that leads north. At about 3.5 miles a fork to the right leads to the pumping station. Drive to the pumping station and search the mud flats north of the canal. Avoid the canal and pumping station since they are private property. Back at the 3.5 mile mark, take the left fork to the north end of the island, about 10 miles, and look for crystals in the mud flats west of the road. The road is muddy and slick when wet, but generally is passable in summer.

Land Status: BLM public lands.

Maps: Tooele (m), Badger Island (7.5).

References: Stowe (1979).

Location: Timpie Mining District

Minerals: cerussite, cinnabar

Description: Mining activity in this district exposed some secondary lead minerals such as cerussite. Cinnabar occurs at some of the mines although the main area is on private property and is posted.

Directions: Take the U-138 exit off I-80 (second Grantsville exit) and follow U-138 over to the lime plant at Flux. Take a right and follow the paved road around the end of the mountain, then take the gravel road south into Timpie Valley. A HCV and/or 4WD is needed for this road. Stay off posted property.

Land Status: Mixture of BLM and state public lands, mining claims and private property.

Maps: Tooele (m), Timpie (15), Timpie (7.5).

References: Visited by this writer.

A Guide to Collecting Sites

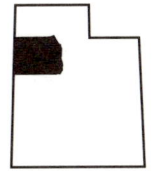

Location: **Lakeside Mountains**
Fossils: **horn coral**

Description: Limestones at the south end of the Lakeside Mountains contain horn coral up to 4 inches or more in length. They are silicified and weather out of the rock and can be found loose on the ground.

Directions: Take the Delle exit from I-80 west of Grantsville and follow the frontage road west approximately 3 miles where it turns northeastward. Continue straight after crossing the railroad tracks and proceed into the mountain area. Park and hike up the slopes to look for the horn corals.

Land Status: BLM public lands.

Maps: Tooele (m), Delle (7.5).

References: Visited by this writer.

Location: **Knolls**
Mineral: **gypsum sand**

Description: Dunes of gypsum sand mixed with some calcite oolites occur in the vicinity of Knolls.

Directions: Take the Knolls exit from I-80, approximately 80 miles west of Salt Lake City and get on the old highway just south of the freeway. The dunes are found on both sides of the road in this vicinity. Stay away from fenced areas which may have unexploded ordinance from the bombing range.

Land Status: BLM public lands, mining claims.

Maps: Bonneville Salt Flats (m), Knolls (7.5).

References: Stowe (1979).

Location: **Tooele**
Mineral: **orthoclase feldspar**

Description: Green igneous rocks with phenocrysts of orthoclase form a series of dikes visible along the hill west of Utah Highway 36 at the south edge of Tooele. The orthoclase weathers out of the rock.

Directions: Located on the south edge of Tooele, 0.7 mile from the city limits, near the electric substation in the field. A stile crosses the fence at this point. Private property. Seek permission from the owner.

Land Status: Private property.

Maps: Tooele (m), Tooele (7.5).

References: Visited by this writer.

Location: **Dry Canyon**
Minerals: **calcite, azurite, malachite, hemimorphite, aurichalcite, pyrite, galena**

Description: Located immediately north of Ophir Canyon, this was an active lead-zinc mining district, parts of which were mined as late as the 1960s. The dumps contain abundant calcite, occasionally as nice crystals and sometimes covering aurichalcite. Other minerals are less abundant.

Directions: Take Utah Highway 36 from Tooele south to Stockton. In Stockton turn left onto Silver Avenue opposite the gas station. Follow the road up the hill curving to the right and passing the softball field. Bear right across the wash from Soldier Canyon and proceed up and around the mountain into Dry Canyon, about 7 miles from Stockton. A HCV is needed for this road which has steep drop offs to one side. Dry Canyon may be entered more directly from the bottom, but the road is very narrow and rocky. A HCV and/or 4WD is needed for this route. To reach the mouth of the canyon, continue through Stockton and take Utah Highway 73 at the intersection south of Rush Lake. After about 4 miles turn left on the road into Ophir Canyon. About 0.25 mile up this road, take a gravel road to the left which leads to and up into Dry Canyon.

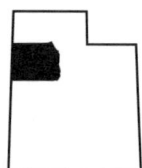

Land Status: BLM public lands, mining claims, private property.

Maps: Tooele (m), Stockton (15), Stockton (7.5).

References: Visited by this writer.

Location:	Ophir Canyon
Minerals:	pyrite, sphalerite, galena, epidote

Description: Ophir, an old mining town, now a small residential community, is located about 3 miles up Ophir Canyon. The last operating mine, the Ophir Hill Mine, was active in the 1970s and the large dump from this mine is obvious on the left as you enter town. The Ophir Hill Mine was primarily a lead-zinc producer. Substantially more silver was found in the ores from the mines on Lion Hill which is to the right as you pass through town.

Directions: From Utah Highway 73, south of Tooele, turn east on the signed road leading to Ophir. Beginning about 2.4 miles from the turnoff, material from the Ophir Hill Mine dump has been used as fill material along the road and creek. Abundant sphalerite, pyrite, and galena can be found here. Many pale green rocks, including some material with alternating green and gray stripes, are epidote rich. The dump itself is at 2.8 miles, but may be posted. After passing through the town of Ophir a gate is encountered at 3.8 miles. If you wish, you may continue up the canyon for a scenic drive (close the gate behind you) and a few mine dumps will be seen. At 4.2 miles, a turnoff to the right leads up to the summit of Lion Hill. This road is steep and narrow and requires a HCV and/or 4WD.

Land Status: Private property in Ophir. Surrounding areas are BLM public lands and mining claims.

Maps: Rush Valley (m), Stockton (15), Ophir (7.5), Mercur (7.5), Lowe Peak (7.5).

References: Visited by this writer.

Location:	Lookout Pass
Minerals:	parapierrotite, stibnite, quartz
Rock:	wonderstone

Description: Parapierrotite is a rare thallium antimony arsenic sulfosalt that is found in only a few locations in the world. At this locality it occurs as metallic grains in a dark jasperoid along with stibnite grains that mostly have been altered to antimony oxides such as stibiconite and senarmontite. Thallium is a toxic element and specimens containing this element should be handled cautiously. Do not breathe the dust while breaking the rock and do not allow children to touch the specimens.

Some of the jasperoid in this general area has interesting patterns and could be slabbed for wonderstone. Small quartz crystals are associated with some of the jasperoid.

Stibnite occurs as poorly crystallized radiating masses in similar jasperoid material at a separate location about 2 miles north of the parapierrotite location.

Directions: From Utah Highway 36 south of Tooele, take the Pony Express Road west across Lookout Pass. On the west side of the pass at a distance of 9.7 miles from the pavement, a road to the left leads south into Little Valley. At a distance of about 4 miles there is a small road on the right that was bulldozed by a mining company who drilled this location. This road leads up the ridge and is probably blocked, unless drilling is occurring, but provides a place to pull off the road and park. The occurrence is a very small area at the crest of the ridge. Look for signs of digging.

The stibnite occurrence is on the east slope of the ridge, about 150 feet below the summit, approximately 2 miles north of the previous occurrence. It is difficult to locate without a guide.

Land Status: Mining claims. Collectors have permission to collect specimens subject to activities by mining companies who may lease the claims.

Maps: Rush Valley (m), Lookout Pass (7.5).

References: Visited by this writer.

A Guide to Collecting Sites

Location: Vernon Hills

Rock: wonderstone (picturestone)

Description: Wonderstone is a rock, often sandstone or jasperoid, in which iron staining has produced designs or patterns, which show up best when the rock is slabbed.

Directions: Take Utah Highway 36 south from Tooele for 37 miles to Vernon. Continue past Vernon for 4.5 miles and take the road that turns north along the west side of the railroad tracks. Wonderstone is found in the hills to the north. There are some staked claims in the area so watch for claim posts and collect elsewhere.

Land Status: BLM public lands and mining claims.

Maps: Rush Valley (m), Vernon (7.5).

References: Stowe (1979).

Location: Thorpe Hills

Mineral: sulvanite, calciovolborthite

Description: Sulvanite is a rare copper vanadium sulfide which is known from this location, an occurrence in Mercur Canyon, and one location each in Australia and Russia. It occurs as cubic crystals embedded in a calcite and quartz matrix that cements a limestone breccia in the Cedar Fort Member of the Oquirrh Formation. Unfortunately, the mineral has excellent cleavage and it is difficult to extract unbroken crystals. Dissolving the calcite in acid reveals the crystals, but may also etch them. The mineral is seen most easily by recognizing its alteration product, calciovolborthite, which has a distinct yellow-green color. Calciovolborthite coats most grains of sulvanite.

Directions: Take Utah Highway 73 south and west from Cedar Fort and Fairfield across Fivemile Pass. Just west of the pass, take the gravel road that leads south along the west side of the Thorpe Hills. About 4 miles south a series of side roads lead into the hills. The location is at a small mine adit marked on the topographic maps in the NW ¼, Sec. 35, T7S, R3W, near the Tooele County-Utah County line.

Land Status: Mining claims.

Maps: Rush Valley (m), Fivemile Pass (7.5).

References: Visited by this writer. Dolanski (1974).

Location: Topliff area

Fossils: horn coral

Mineral: calcite

Description: A small abandoned quarry on a ridge about one mile southeast of the road intersection known as Topliff has masses of banded calcite. Further up the hill in the quarry is a dark-black limestone with white "ghosts" of horn coral. The corals are poorly preserved, but the contrast between the dark rock and the white calcite of the corals is striking and creates interesting material for slabbing.

Directions: Take Utah Highway 73 south and west from Cedar Fort and Fairfield across Fivemile Pass. Just west of the pass, take the gravel road that leads south along the west side of the Thorpe Hills. Continue southward about 6 miles to the water tank at Topliff by which time a large quarry is visible on the hill to the left (east). Take the road to this quarry, passing below it, and on south about 0.5 mile to a small quarry on a projecting ridge. This small quarry is visible from the large quarry but is not conspicuous.

Land Status: Private land with mineral rights retained by the federal government.

Maps: Rush Valley (m), Fivemile Pass (7.5).

References: Visited by this writer.

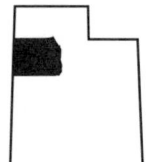

Location: Dugway Range

Minerals: pyrite, fluorite, barite, azurite, malachite

Description: The Granite mining district at the north end of the Dugway Range is characterized by pyritic copper deposits and fluorite-barite deposits. There are numerous mines and prospects in the area. Pyrite is abundant on some of the dumps and crystals to 1 inch are not uncommon. Barite and fluorite occur in many locations such as the Rainbow Mines, Cannon Mine, and at the head of Buckhorn Canyon. Barite blades up to 2 inches can be found. Fluorite is often massive or banded, but crystals can be found.

Directions: Take Utah Highway 36 south of Tooele to the Pony Express Road near Vernon. From the pavement, it is 21.6 miles to Simpson Springs, 29.0 miles to the Old River Bed, and 35.1 miles to the turnoff to the Dugway Range. This turn is marked by the Tooele-Juab County line sign. This road takes you to Fera No. 38 Well and then on to the road that goes north along the flank of the Dugway Range. This road eventually leads you into the mining district at the north end of the Dugway Range. Be careful not to stray across the Dugway Proving Grounds boundary which closely parallels the road as you reach the north end. Watch for and avoid metal objects in this area as there may be some unexploded shells dropped by pilots who strayed outside their assigned area. Rattlesnakes are common here.

Land Status: Many mining claims in the area. Most have been consolidated under one operator, currently Gold Standard, and there may be drilling or other exploration activity in the area. Stay away from any equipment or operations.

Maps: Fish Springs (m), Dugway Range (15), Dugway Range NW (7.5), Dugway Range NE (7.5).

References: Visited by this writer. Staatz and Carr (1964).

Location: Gold Hill

Minerals: arsenates (adamite, austinite, conichalcite, etc.), quartz, stibiconite

Description: The Gold Hill Mine, an open pit mine at the summit of Gold Hill about 1.5 miles west of the town, is a very important locality for Utah mineral collectors because of the wide variety of minerals that can be found there. The Gold Hill area is particularly rich in arsenic and the oxidation of the primary minerals such as arsenopyrite has created many colorful arsenates. Austinite and adamite are particularly common at the open pit mine, frequently occurring together. Austinite can be distinguished by its fluorescence. Coatings of green conichalcite occur on the rocks. Quartz is abundant in the back half of the pit and Japanese twins are often found. About halfway across the pit, on the right side, is a zone that has produced stibiconite pseudomorphs after stibnite and occasionally weathered remains of the original stibnite.

There are many mines and prospects throughout the area which can be searched for mineral specimens. The U.S. Mine, south of Gold Hill, has arsenopyrite on the dump. Mines in Lucy L Gulch have large black tourmaline (schorl), garnet, scheelite, and danburite. The Reaper and Yellow Jacket Mines (which may be active at this time) have produced very coarse actinolite with molybdenite and powellite.

Directions: Gold Hill is located south of Wendover and west of the Great Salt Lake Desert. It is reached from Wendover by paved and graveled roads. To reach the Gold Hill Mine, go north from the intersection in Gold Hill a very short distance around the first curve and take the small road to the right. This road follows an old railroad grade and an HCV is recommended. The road is seemingly blocked by a drilling site, but this can be bypassed to the left. The road curves around the hill and soon the mine and its associated dumps can be seen on the hill ahead. Vehicles without 4WD should probably park in the valley below the mine; others can drive up the narrow, steep road to a broad, flat area below the pit. Dumps, especially at the far north end of this flat area, should be examined as some interesting material has been found here. Other locations mentioned above are marked on the topographic maps and can be readily located.

Land Status: Private property, mining claims, BLM public lands. Collecting has traditionally been permitted in this area, but renewed interest in gold may stimulate mining activity and restrict access. Respect gates and posted areas. Seek permission if mining is occurring in the area in which you wish to collect.

Maps: Wildcat Mountain (m), Gold Hill (7.5), Clifton (7.5).

References: Visited by this writer.

UINTAH COUNTY

Uintah County extends southward from the crest of the Uintah Mountains along the Utah-Colorado border. Dinosaur National Monument and its famous quarry lie within Uintah County. There are a number of interesting fossil locations in the Paleozoic, Mesozoic, and Cenozoic sedimentary rocks of the county. Various types of hydrocarbons are also found.

Location:	**Threemile Canyon**
Fossil:	**algal stromatolites**
Rock:	**hydrocarbons**

Description: Stromatolites are a type of algae that originated during Precambrian time and are one of the few types of fossils found in Precambrian rocks. This particular type of algae has persisted to the present day and still occurs as columnar masses in tidal flats of coastal Australia. The algae, having no bone or shell to be preserved as a fossil, is not preserved, but layers of calcium carbonate that coated the algae are preserved and form layered masses. They occur at the Black Virgin Gilsonite Mine.

Gilsonite is a hydrocarbon that occurs in a pure form in over 15 major vein systems in Uintah County with an overall total length of 156 miles. Gilsonite in Uintah County is located at Asphalt Wash, Black Dragon Mine, Bonanza Mines, Fort Duchesne, and the Rainbow Mine. American Gilsonite Corporation, headquartered in Salt Lake City, operates the Bonanza Mines and should be contacted for permission to visit there.

Directions: Proceed south of Bonanza on Utah Highway 45 approximately 17 miles to Evacuation Creek. Continue on Highway 45 down Evacuation Creek approximately 2 miles to the mouth of Threemile Canyon. Turn right into the canyon and go approximately 1.9 miles to the Black Virgin Gilsonite Mine on the north side of the road.

Land Status: BLM public lands and private lands.

Maps: See Ridge (m), Rainbow (7.5), Dragon (7.5).

References: Stowe (1979).

Location:	**Hells Hole Canyon**
Rock:	**hydrocarbons (oil shale)**

Description: This occurence is an outcrop of the Mahogany zone of the Parachute Creek Member of the Green River Formation and is an example of an oil shale.

Directions: Take Utah Highway 45 south from Bonanza approximately 3.5 miles to bridge crossing the White River. Proceed on Highways 45 and 207 and turn left (east) on a primitive road past the corrals and go about 0.8 mile. Site is located in a small tributary to Hells Hole Canyon primarily in Sec. 20 (and 17), T10S, R25E.

Land Status: BLM public lands and state lands.

Maps: See Ridge (m), Weaver Ridge (7.5).

References: Stowe (1979).

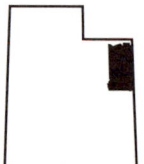

Location: Asphalt Ridge

Rock: hydrocarbons (bituminous sandstone)

Description: This location is the county asphalt pit in Asphalt Ridge. During the summer months when the rocks have been warmed, this area is an excellent location to view an oil seep. Material from the pit has been used to pave the streets of various Uintah County towns.

Directions: West of Vernal on U.S. 40 where Asphalt Ridge is cut by the highway. County pit is located in SE ¼, Sec. 30, T4S, R21E.

Land Status: County owned and operated. Obtain permission from the foreman at the site.

Maps: Vernal (m), Vernal NE (7.5).

References: Stowe (1979).

Location Brush Creek

Fossils: cephalopods (belemnites), pelecypods, gastropods, coral

Description: Belemnites are a squid-like cephalopod whose internal shell is smooth and cigar-shaped. Abundant clams (pelecypods), along with a few gastropods and coral occur in the red and green limestone of the Carmel Formation in this area.

Directions: Take Utah Highway 44 north from Vernal for 9 miles and note the geologic age markers along the road. Watch for the sign labeled "Curtis Formation" and a gravel road leading east to Brush Creek. Belemnites can be found by searching in small washes to the right of the gravel road about one mile from the highway and further along to the Forest Service sign past the cattle guard.

Land Status: National Forest lands and state lands.

Maps: Dutch John (m), Donkey Flat (7.5).

References: Stowe (1979).

Location: Jensen area

Fossils: sharks teeth

Description: Sharks teeth are fairly common in some locations. Since they are relatively small, they can often be found in ant hills where the ants have removed them as they dug their tunnels.

Directions: Cross the river east of Jensen and immediately turn north on a paved road. About 0.25 mile up the road, park and climb to the top of small hill on your right. The hill is capped with sandstone and ant hills in this area contain shark teeth.

Land Status: private

Maps: Vernal (m), Jensen (7.5).

References: Aldon Hamblin, Vernal, UT.

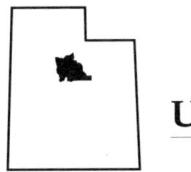

UTAH COUNTY

This central Utah county has extensive outcrops of late Paleozoic sedimentary rocks in the Wasatch Range, southern Oquirrh Mountains, and Lake Mountains. Certain horizons in these rocks are fossiliferous. Fossil-bearing Cenozoic rocks are well exposed in Spanish Fork Canyon. Utah County shares some interesting mining districts with adjoining counties. American Fork Canyon has numerous old mine dumps that extend southward from Alta in Salt Lake County and the historic Tintic mining district is at the western margin of Utah County.

Location: Pelican Point

Mineral: limonite pseudomorphs after pyrite

Description: Pyrite, iron sulfide, commonly oxidizes when exposed to air or oxygenated water, although this may be a very slow process. As it is altered from the sulfide to the oxide the external crystal shape of the pyrite may be preserved. At this locality, pseudomorphs of limonite after pyrite up to 2 inches on an edge have been found. They occur in veins and zones in the soft limey bedrock. Bryozoans are abundant in some of the horizons at this location. Massive calcite, both white and green, occurs at the entrance to a small incline about 200 feet north along the ridge.

Directions: This location is on the west side of Utah Lake near Pelican Point in the NW ¼, Sec. 6, T7S, R1E and a road leading to that point is shown on the topographic map. The site is at the top of a ridge that looks down on a small valley leading eastward toward Utah Highway 68 and the lake. A road (not shown on the map) leads up the valley from Highway 68, starting immediately opposite the explosives plant on the lakeshore. This road is rough and requires an HCV. Most drivers will wish to park at the base of the ridge and walk the last few hundred feet to the ridge summit. A better road, although longer, begins at the clay pits alongside Highway 68 south of the explosives plant. Follow this road around the south end of the clay pits (slightly rocky at this point) toward the power line running north up Enoch Canyon. Take the right fork before the first clay pit and go up to the divide and then down into Little Canyon. About 0.5 mile down Little Canyon you will see the white rock on the ridge top that marks this location and can see the road leading up to it. The road is deeply washed, but is negotiable by an HCV.

Land Status: Private lands, BLM public lands.

Maps: Provo (m), Soldiers Pass (7.5).

References: Visited by this writer.

Location: Clay Pits in the Manning Canyon Shale

Fossil: plants

Description: The Pennsylvanian Manning Canyon Shale occurs in a number of localities in north-central Utah where it is commonly exposed in quarries developed by local brick companies. The shaly units of this formation often have abundant plant material in the form of wood, stems, leaves, seeds, and fronds. The most abundant species are *Asterophyllites, Calamites, Alethopteris,* and *Neuropteris. Lepidodendron* and *Cordaites* also occur as well as many other less common species. Because of the large number of locations, they will be grouped together and listed below.

1. In the Lake Mountains near Pelican Point in the NE ¼, Sec. 13, T7S, R1W alongside Utah Highway 68, 12.1 miles south of the intersection of U-36 and U-73 west of Lehi.

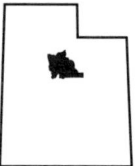

2. In the Lake Mountains near Pelican Point in the center of Sec. 1, T7S, R1W.

3. In the Lake Mountains near Pelican Point in the SW ¼, Sec. 36, T6S, R1W.

4. Powell Pit. On Lake Mountain near Burnt Canyon in the NE ¼, Sec. 3, T6S, R1W, turnoff 3.3 miles south of the intersection of Utah Highways 36 and 73 west of Lehi.

5. Clinton Pit. On Traverse Mountain in Sec. 9, T5S, R1W.

Tidwell (1962, p. 93) states: "Plants generally occur on bedding planes and vary with different types of sediments. In pink silty shale, plants are abundant, parallel bedded, and are evenly distributed over the surfaces. They are not found in definite layers in the gray-yellow clay shales, but occur sporadically and are commonly chopped off by joints or cross-laminations. Although the state of preservation in the yellowish shale is poor, fiber and cellular structure is still present in most cases, and the plants tend to deteriorate when exposed to air." These comments were with regard to sites 1-3 above.

These pits are not being mined at the time of this writing and are generally open to collectors. Brick companies or their lessees work the pits on an intermittent basis. Look over the waste rock piles, particularly at site 1, as it may be easier to find material there than in the walls of the pits. Avoid working steep walls of the pits.

Directions: Sites 1-3 are off of Utah Highway 68 along the west side of Utah Lake. Site 4 is also off of U-68 about 2 miles southwest of Saratoga Springs. Site 5 is about 2 miles west of the intersection of U-68 and U-73. All are marked on the 7.5 minute topographic maps listed below.

Land Status: Private lands, BLM public lands.

Maps: Soldiers Pass (7.5) sites 1-3. Saratoga Springs (7.5) site 4. Jordan Narrows (7.5) site 5.

References: Visited by this writer. Tidwell (1962, 1975).

Location:	American Fork Canyon
Minerals:	sphalerite, pyrite, quartz

Description: The Bog Mine is located near the head of American Fork Canyon. This mine has produced large crystals of sphalerite of a nice transparent green color. Examples can be seen on display at the Hutchings Museum in Lehi. Searching and digging on the dump of the mine can produce numerous fragments and some crystals of sphalerite. Pyritohedrons of pyrite and cleavage fragments of galena may also be found.

Large masses of pyrite have been collected in the past from the Yankee Mine area in Mary Ellen Gulch off American Fork Canyon.

Directions: Take Utah Highway 80 up American Fork Canyon past Timpanogos Cave and take the left fork off of Highway 80 to continue up the canyon.

Land Status: Patented mining claims, National Forest lands.

Maps: Brighton (7.5), Dromedary Peak (7.5)

References: Visited by this writer; Calkins, et al. (1943).

Location:	Birdseye
Rock:	Birdseye marble

Description: The Birdseye marble is an algal ball limestone of the North Horn Formation. At this location a quarry was operated in the early 1900s.

Directions: The quarry is high on the mountain east of Birdseye on U.S. 89 south of Thistle and is visible from the highway. A road to the outcrop area turns east off U.S. 89 about 1.5 miles north of Birdseye and abundant material can be found along the road on the mountainside.

A Guide to Collecting Sites

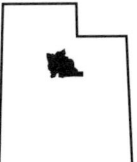

Land Status: Mixture of private and National Forest lands.

Maps: Nephi (m), Birdseye (7.5), Thistle (7.5).

References: Rigby, et al. (1974).

Location:	**Spanish Fork Canyon**
Rock:	**algal ball limestone**

Description: This is an outcrop of the Eocene Flagstaff Formation which forms ledges here. One of the units near the middle of the sequence of ledges is composed of algal balls.

Directions: This location is on U.S. 6-50, 7.9 miles east of Thistle. Park at the broad open flat and walk north to the ledges.

Land Status: National Forest lands.

Maps: Nephi (m), Thistle (7.5).

References: Rigby, et al. (1974).

Location:	**Spanish Fork Canyon**
Fossils:	**gastropods, pelecypods, ostracods, bird tracks**

Description: Fossiliferous beds of the Eocene Green River Formation occur in this area. Many of the beds have been faulted and the displacement of the layers is easily seen.

Directions: (a) 11.2 miles east of Thistle on U.S. 6-50.

(b) 14.8 - 16.0 miles east of Thistle on U.S. 6-50.

Land Status: Highway right-of-way and National Forest lands.

Maps: Nephi (m), Mill Fork (7.5), Tucker (7.5).

References: Rigby, et al. (1974).

Location:	**Tucker rest area**
Fossils:	**bird tracks**

Description: Bird tracks are found in the basal beds of the Lower Green River Formation east and west of this area. Examine ledges and weathered rocks in drainages of Starvation Creek and Clear Creek.

Directions: The Tucker rest area is located 17.7 miles east of Thistle on U.S. 6-50 in Spanish Fork Canyon.

Land Status: National Forest lands, state and private land.

Maps: Nephi (m), Tucker (7.5).

References: Moussa (1965), Rigby, et al. (1974).

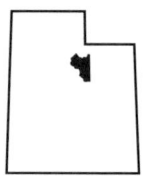

WASATCH COUNTY

This county is located along the eastern slope of the Wasatch Range and extends to the southwestern portion of the Uinta Mountains. There are a great variety of rock types in the county. Intrusive rocks and related skarns occur along the western edge of the county in the Wasatch Range while significant outcrops of Paleozoic and Mesozoic sedimentary rocks occur to the east. These are succeeded by abundant Cenozoic rocks in the southern half of the county. Fossils are abundant in many of these sedimentary units.

Location: Clayton Peak area

Minerals: spinel, garnet, vesuvianite, titanite, scolecite

Descriptions: A variety of metamorphic minerals occur in skarns associated with the Clayton Peak stock.

Directions: Take the Snake Creek Canyon road from Wasatch Mountain State Park. As you travel up this road you will see a large pile of granitic rock in a clearing to the left. Small grains of titanite can be found as an accessory mineral in these rocks. Continue up the road to a sign (missing in 1992) marking the forest boundary. Park here unless you have a HCV. A small road leads around the hill to the right (north) for a short distance to some old mine dumps. Before reaching the end of this road turn into a clearing on the left which turns into a fairly large open area often used by campers. Near the beginning of this open area a trail is visible that climbs steeply up and around the hill on the right (north). After this trail levels out on the front of the ridge, cut up through the brush to the ridge crest. As soon as you emerge from the brush the trail takes you up the ridge and then swings north into the mouth of the hanging valley (Caribou Hollow) which comes down from Clayton Peak. The trail may be obscure in the lower part of the valley, but it is fairly easy walking through forest and grassy areas to finally emerge in an open valley below Clayton Peak. Metamorphosed rocks are sparsely exposed along the north wall of the valley. Black boulders of spinel can be found as float.

This is a long steep hike, requiring about two hours of steady hiking, and should not be attempted by anyone with heart or respiratory problems.

Land Status: Mixture of private and National Forest lands.

Maps: Salt Lake City (m), Brighton (7.5).

References: Visited by this writer.

Location: Guardsman Pass

Minerals: specular hematite, quartz

Description: Road cuts at Guardsman Pass and material blasted to create the road contain abundant sprays of brilliant metallic sheets of specular hematite. They are somewhat fragile and usually are not in vugs of sufficient size to allow them to grow in an unobstructed manner, therefore, it is difficult to obtain perfect specimens. Quartz is a common accessory in the vugs and a few specimens of large (one inch) quartz crystals have been found here.

Directions: Proceed up the Guardsman Pass road from just below Brighton until you reach the parking area at the Pass. Examine the road cut and material below the road.

Land Status: Land above the highway right-of-way is private and posted.

Maps: Salt Lake City (m), Brighton (7.5).

References: Visited by this writer.

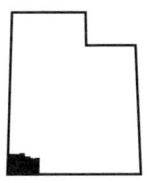

WASHINGTON COUNTY

The north part of Washington County is composed primarily of volcanic rocks and related intrusives of Cenozoic age. Cenozoic basalt flows occur at many locations throughout the county. The south half of the county is mostly Mesozoic sedimentary rocks, but in the Beaver Dam Mountains in the extreme southwest corner of the county and state are found some outcrops of Paleozoic sedimentary rocks and Precambrian rocks identical to those found at the bottom of the Grand Canyon.

Location: Hurricane Cliffs area

Rock: petrified wood

Description: Petrified wood occurs in most outcrops of the Shinarump Conglomerate in Washington County either as large log sections or as fragments. Pieces can be found on slopes, washes, and anywhere the Shinarump is exposed. The material is usually not gem quality. It is tan colored and has many holes.

Directions: There are three specific locations, as follows:

(1) Little Creek Mountain. Take Utah Highway 59 east of Hurricane for 13 miles (0.1 mile past milepost 9) until a cinder cone is visible to the right. Take the dirt road to the right and follow it for 0.75 mile and turn right for 2 miles. Wood is found throughout this area.

(2) Gooseberry Mesa. Take Utah Highway 59 east of Hurricane for 9 miles and take the road to the left up to the top of the mesa.

(3) Hurricane Mesa. Take Utah Highway 15 east of La Verkin for 5 miles. At milepost 17 a paved road to the left leads about 4 miles to the top of the mesa. Much wood is exposed to the right as the road first reaches the top of the mesa. Look along the edge of the bluff to the east edge of the mesa. There are many tracts of private land on top of the mesa so avoid posted areas.

Land Status: BLM public lands except as noted.

Maps: St. George (m), Little Creek Mountain (7.5), Virgin (7.5).

References: Stowe (1979).

Location: Leeds area

Rock: petrified wood, agate

Description: Red, maroon, white, and yellow agate occur in veins at a small knob in the Moenkopi Formation west of Leeds. The agate occurs in veins up to 2 feet wide and as large pieces scattered over the slope. Petrified wood occurs on the south side of the knob where it has weathered out of the overlying Shinarump Conglomerate.

Directions: Take the main street out of Leeds south and across I-15 and then turn north. At the T-intersection turn right and take the road to the left through the gate. The knob can be seen about 0.25 mile to the north.

Land Status: The knob is on BLM public land, but there is private land adjoining.

Maps: St. George (m), Hurricane (15), Hurricane (7.5).

References: Stowe (1979).

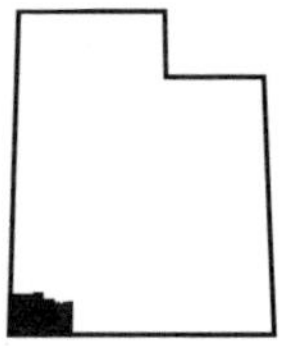

Location: Utah Hill area
Rock: alaskite (granite)
Mineral: garnet

Description: Alaskite is a name given to varieties of granite that are extremely light colored, that is, they contain few dark-colored mineral grains. Alaskites are composed almost entirely of feldspar and quartz. This particular occurrence has small garnets in the alaskite, although the garnets have been altered.

Directions: Outcrops of Precambrian intrusive rock, in which the alaskite occurs, are found in the area south and west of Utah Hill where the road from Shivwits passes through the Beaver Dam Mountains.

Land Status: BLM public lands.

Maps: St. George (m), Jarvis Peak (7.5).

References: Dr. Richard Kennedy, Geology Dept., Southern Utah University.

A Guide to Collecting Sites

WAYNE COUNTY

With the exception of Cenozoic volcanic rocks that occur in the Awapa Plateau, Wayne County is composed almost entirely of Mesozoic sedimentary rocks. Agate and petrified wood are relatively common and spectacular large crystals of gypsum have been mined from private claims. Fossils are abundant in some of the Mesozoic rocks.

Location: Caineville area

Rock: agate, jasper, chert, petrified wood

Description and Directions: Agate and colored chert are found along U-24 about 9 miles southwest of Caineville and also 6 miles east of Caineville. Jasper and petrified wood are also found in these areas.

Land Status: BLM public lands.

Maps: Loa (m), Hanksville (m), Fruita (15), Factory Butte (15), Caineville (7.5), Town Point (7.5).

References: Stowe (1979).

Location: Factory Butte

Rock: agate

Description: Red and yellow agate occur in a bed in the Curtis Formation. The Formation is greenish-gray clay and has red on both the top and bottom.

Directions: Drive west from Caineville (milepost 100) for 0.5 mile to a junction with the road to Cathedral Valley. Take this road up Caineville Wash 0.3 mile to a junction and stay to the right. At 2.2 miles is another junction with a jeep trail to the right. 4WD vehicles can take the jeep trail for 7 miles to the end of the road at an inactive uranium mine. Park at the mine and walk west for 0.5 mile to the head of the canyon to look for agate. Sec. 19, 30, T27S, R9E.

Land Status: BLM public lands.

Maps: Hanksville (m), Factory Butte (15), Factory Butte (7.5).

References: Stowe (1979).

Location: Caineville area

Fossil: oysters

Description: The oyster *Gryphaea newberryi* is extremely abundant in this area.

Directions: From the Fremont River bridge (2 miles west of Caineville) drive east on Utah Highway 12 for 0.5 mile and park. Walk 300 feet north toward a hill. The oyster shells are weathering out of the rock.

Land Status: BLM public lands.

Maps: Fruita (15), Caineville (7.5), Loa (m).

References: Stowe (1979).

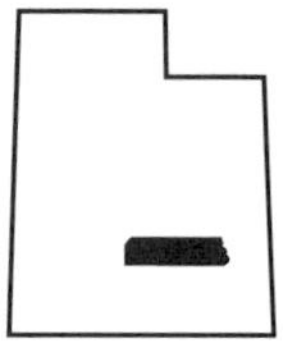

Location: south of Notom

Rock: agate

Description: Agate occurs within the Curtis Formation.

Directions: Drive 0.6 mile east from the east boundary of Capitol Reef National Park and turn south on the road to Notom. Follow this road for 3.8 miles to a junction ("Sandy Ranch 10, Henry Mtns. 28, Lake Powell 88") and turn left for 2.6 miles to a minor junction with an unimproved dirt road leading to the east. Follow the unimproved road for 0.4 mile at which time agate can be seen along the side of the road.

Land Status: BLM public lands.

Maps: Notom NE (7.5), Notom (15), Loa (m).

References: Stowe (1979).

Location: Jet Basin

Rock: jet coal

Description: Jet is a variety of lignite coal that is characterized by being relatively hard, having a strong luster, conchoidal fracture, and taking a good polish. It is usually associated with bituminous shale and probably is derived from waterlogged driftwood.

Directions: When approaching Hanksville from the east, turn left (south) at the first road after passing the Texaco station. Continue south staying to the right at the junction on the south side of Hanksville and continue 2 miles to another junction (signed "Dugout Bench, Birch Creek"). Turn right and drive 4.2 miles to another junction (signed "Dugout Bench, Birch Creek"); turn left and continue for 5.3 miles. Park close to the lower end of knoll on the right side of the road. Find a trail down into the basin and walk about 0.5 mile to begin looking for jet. Most of the jet is about 1 inch in diameter but larger logs can be found. A 6-inch coal bed is a marker, as the jet occurs below this bed.

Land Status: BLM public lands.

Maps: Mt. Ellen (15), Hanksville (m).

References: Stowe (1979).

A Guide to Collecting Sites 135

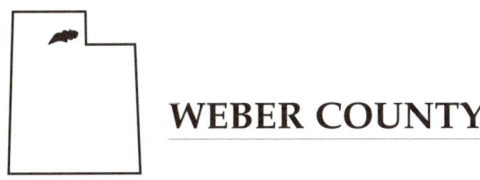

WEBER COUNTY

Western Weber County is covered by the sediments of Lake Bonneville, but in the Wasatch Range igneous and metamorphic rocks of Precambrian age are suceeded by Paleozoic sedimentary rocks. Fossils are relatively abundant in some of the Paleozoic units. East of the Wasatch are Cenozoic sediments and additional outcrops of the Paleozoic rocks.

Location: The Oaks

Fossils: plants, gastropods, bryozoans, brachiopods, crinoids, corals

Description: This location is at the contact of the Devonian Jefferson Formation and the Mississippian Beirdneau Limestone. The red-brown shale unit in the Beirdneau has worm trails and plant impressions. A variety of fossils, as listed above, can be found in the underlying Jefferson.

Directions: Beginning at the stop light at Harrison Boulevard and 12th South Street in Ogden, drive east up Ogden Canyon to the Oaks on the left (north) side of the canyon. Search the borrow pit area and the talus.

Land Status: National Forest lands.

Maps: Ogden (m), Huntsville (7.5).

References: Dr. Richard W. Moyle, Weber State University, Ogden, UT.

Location: Pineview Dam

Mineral: calcite

Description: Small nodules containing calcite crystals can be found in the roadcuts in the vicinity of Pineview Dam.

Directions: Drive up Ogden Canyon and turn left across the dam at Pineview Reservoir. Park along the highway where space permits, and walk along the roadcuts watching for white nodules in the rock. Be careful and watch for rocks and traffic.

Land Status: Highway right-of-way.

Maps: Ogden (m), Huntsville (7.5).

References: Dr. Richard W. Moyle, Weber State University, Ogden, UT.

Location: Camp Kiesel area

Fossils: brachiopods, bryozoans, crinoids

Minerals: calcite, manganese minerals

Description: Abundant fossils are found in outcrops of the Mississippian Lodgepole Limestone that occur in this area.

Directions: Take Utah Highway 39 along the south side of Pineview Reservoir, through Huntsville, and up the valley of the South Fork of the Ogden River until you reach the turnoff for Causey Reservoir and Camp Kiesel, Boy Scout camp. Follow this road along the west side of Causey Reservoir to the lake headwaters near the Boy Scout camp. Outcrops of the Lodgepole are found above the public toilets in this area.

 Additional outcrops of the Lodgepole can be found by taking the trail around the headwaters of the lake and along the east side. Also on this peninsula on the east side of the lake can be found calcite crystals and manganese minerals such as pyrolusite at an abandoned mine there.

Land Status: National Forest lands.

Maps: Ogden (m), Causey Dam (7.5).

References: Dr. Richard W. Moyle, Weber State University, Ogden, UT.

Location: Monte Cristo

Fossils: brachiopods, gastropods, corals

Description: This location is in Pennsylvanian rocks on the southwest side of Monte Cristo.

Directions: Take Utah Highway 39 from Huntsville east and north to Monte Cristo. The location is just after passing under the power lines in the Little Monte area.

Land Status: National Forest lands.

Maps: Ogden (m), Monte Cristo Peak (7.5).

References: Dr. Richard W. Moyle, Weber State University, Ogden, UT.

GLOSSARY

aa - a type of basaltic lava usually characterized by high viscosity resulting in a rough, broken, rubbly appearance to the resulting lava flow. See also pahoehoe.

accessory minerals - minerals which occur in a rock but are not minerals essential to the definition of that particular rock. Example: biotite, titanite, and zircon grains in a granite. See essential minerals.

amygdaloidal - a rock that contains amygdules, such as amygdaloidal basalt.

amygdules - small openings or vesicles in volcanic rocks which have been filled later with a mineral. Agate is a common material filling vesicles, but zeolites, quartz, calcite, and native copper are also known.

anhedral - having few, if any, well-developed crystal faces.

anion - an atom or atomic radical that has a negative charge acquired through the gain of electrons.

anticline - a geologic structure, specifically a fold in which the rocks have been arched upward by compressive forces or by material rising from below.

antimonide - a mineral which has antimony (Sb) as its principal anion. Antimonides are usually classified with the sulfides. Example: breihauptite (NiSb)

aphanitic - a textural term used to describe igneous rocks that have cooled quickly and therefore have a fine-grained appearance. If the majority of mineral grains are too small to see with the unaided eye, then the igneous rock would best be described as having an aphanitic texture. See also phaneritic and porphyritic.

arsenate - a mineral which has arsenic as part of the arsenate radical as its principal anion. These minerals are common in the oxidized zone of arsenic-bearing mineral deposits. Example: austinite $(CaZn[AsO_4][OH])$

batholith - the largest type of igneous intrusive body, defined as having a surface exposure of greater than 40 square miles. Batholiths are usually granitic in composition, have no specific shape, and are commonly associated with past or present-day mountain ranges.

borate - a group of minerals which are characterized by structures in which there are extended linkages between a highly charged boron cation and oxygen anions. These minerals are common to some evaporite deposits. Example - colemanite $(Ca_2B_6O_{11} \cdot 5H_2O)$

carbonate - any of a large group of fairly common minerals that contain the carbonate radical $(CO_3)^{-2}$. Example: calcite $CaCO_3$

cation - an atom or atomic radical that has a positive charge as a result of the loss of electrons.

chromate - any of a small group of relatively rare minerals that contain the chromate radical $(CrO_4)^{-2}$. Example: crocoite $PbCrO_4$

cinder cone - a small volcanic cone composed of pyroclastic particles, commonly of small gravel size, that accumulate as a result of fountaining of lava. May be located downwind some distance from the actual vent.

cleavage - the tendency for a mineral to break along relatively smooth plane surfaces as a result of weaknesses in the atomic bond along that direction in the mineral structure. Cleavage is described by the number of cleavage directions or the crystallographic form it might create and by a quality term such as excellent, perfect, good, fair, or poor. Example: perfect rhombohedral cleavage of calcite.

color index - in coarse-grained igneous rocks, the percentage of ferromagnesian minerals in the rock. This generally has a negative correlation with the amount of silica in the rock, i.e., a very dark rock is usually low in silica. Examples: granite, color index 10-15, very high silica; gabbro, color index 50-70, low silica.

composite cone - a volcanic cone composed of both lava and pyroclastics, often created by a series of cyclic eruptions in which pyroclastics are created by explosive eruptions until the vent is open, then lava flows occur. Most large continental volcanic cones are this type.

country rock - the rock enclosing a mineralized vein or the rock surrounding and intruded by an igneous body.

cryptocrystalline - having crystallites of such a small size that they are not visible with a normal optical microscope. Chalcedony and related materials are cryptocrystalline varieties of silica.

crystal class - one of 32 classes or point groups used in classifying crystals by grouping them by visible aspects of their symmetry.

crystal system - one of the 6 or 7 groups of the crystal classes. All classes within a crystal system can be described in terms of the same set of crystallographic axes and have some degree of similarity of crystal symmetry.

crystalline - having an orderly internal atomic structure and, therefore, the capability of occurring as a crystal.

crystallographic axes - an imaginary coordinate system which, for each crystal system, can be used to locate and describe faces, forms, and aspects of the symmetry of a given crystal.

density - mass per unit volume, such as g/cm^3. More commonly, specific gravity is used to characterize minerals since it eliminates the volume calculations.

diatreme - a brecciated mass of rock forming a volcanic pipe and having been created by an explosion of gas within the earth.

dike - a tabular intrusive body (relatively thin but extensive in the other two dimensions, book shaped) that cuts across the existing layers or structures of the rock. A very common type of intrusion. A similar body that is parallel to the existing layers or structures is a sill.

essential minerals - those minerals that are required to be present for a rock to be defined as a specific type, for example, all granites must contain orthoclase and quartz regardless of what other minerals may be present. Other minerals present in the rock are known as accessory minerals.

euhedral - having well-developed crystal faces.

evaporite minerals - those minerals which are deposited as a result of the evaporation of water. These are mostly halides and sulfates with a few oxides and carbonates. When sea water is evaporated to about 50% of its original volume, calcite and hematite form. When volume is reduced to 20%, gypsum and anhydrite are deposited, and at 10% of the original volume, halite begins to appear. Continued evaporation leads to the deposition of highly soluble, relatively rare potassium and magnesium minerals, such as sylvite, polyhalite, and carnallite.

fault - a break in the rock along which movement has occurred. Tension (pulling apart) produces normal faults such as the Wasatch Fault, whereas compression (pushing together) creates reverse or thrust faults. Shearing results in strike slip faults (horizontal movement) such as the San Andreas fault.

felsic - an igneous rock that is rich in feldspar, therefore, rich in silica, and with few ferromagnesian minerals.

ferromagnesian - containing both iron and magnesium, as in ferromagnesian minerals.

fissure eruption - a volcanic eruption from a fissure or fracture in the earth. This type of eruption was common in southern Idaho and occurs to some extent in Hawaii. It usually results in basaltic lava spreading across wide areas without producing a large volcanic cone.

fluorescence - release of energy from a mineral while it is being subjected to radiation of a shorter wave length. This results from electrons being momentarily raised to a higher energy level by the incoming radiation, then releasing the energy as they cascade back to their original state. In the most common application, an ultraviolet light causes some minerals to release energy as visible light.

foliation - a feature common to metamorphic rocks which allows them to be divided into the two groups, foliated and non-foliated. Foliation implies some degree of gneissic banding, schistosity, or slaty cleavage, i.e., a preferred orientation of mineral grains that is observable in a hand specimen of the rock.

fragmental - a textural term for volcanic igneous rocks that are composed of rock fragments created during explosive volcanism. Rocks composed of fine-grained particles such as ash are known as tuff. The name volcanic breccia is used to describe coarse-grained fragmental rocks.

gangue - rock and minerals that occur with ore but have no economic value.

glassy - a textural term for those volcanic rocks which cooled so quickly that mineral grains did not have an opportunity to form. Obsidian, pumice, and perlite are the most common examples. Some porphyritic rocks have a glassy groundmass and are known as vitrophyres.

gneissic banding - a type of metamorphic foliation in which quartz and feldspar typically form light-colored bands which alternate with dark bands of tabular or elongated grains such as biotite or hornblende. Gneissic banding can be quite faint as in a granitic gneiss when the original rock did not have many dark-colored minerals. Gneisses are formed during regional metamorphism and, in most cases, it is doubtful that the banding is the result of original bedding in the parent rock.

habit - the form, shape, or common mode of occurrence of a mineral or mineral aggregates.

hardness - the ability of a mineral to scratch another substance or be scratched, expressed in comparison to the ten minerals that make up Moh's Scale. More accurate means of measuring hardness are available in mineral laboratories, but are usually not necessary for identification.

halide - any of a group of minerals whose major anion is one of the halogen elements (Cl, F, Br, or I). Example: halite NaCl

hexagonal - a crystal system which is characterized by 6-fold symmetry, commonly resulting in 6-sided prismatic crystals (beryl, apatite) or occasional dipyramids. Some crystallographers also include the trigonal crystals in this system as a separate division.

hydroxide - any of a group of minerals, commonly formed by weathering processes, in which hydroxide $(OH)^{-1}$ is the major anionic group. Example: gibbsite $Al(OH)_3$

intermediate - said of an igneous rock that is intermediate in composition between felsic and mafic.

ion - a non-specific term for any atom or atomic group that carries a charge as a result of either the loss or gain of electrons.

isometric - a crystal system which is characterized by equidimensional forms and a high degree of symmetry. Cubes (pyrite, galena, halite), octahedrons (fluorite, pyrite), dodecahedrons (garnet), and other forms are common.

joint - a fracture or break in the rock.

laccolith - a type of igneous intrusion with a flat bottom and domed top, similar to a bowl turned upside down. This type of intrusion, along with associated stocks, forms the core of the Henry, La Sal, and Abajo Mountains of Utah.

lithology - a description of a rock, especially one based on the properties that can be seen in a hand specimen.

lithophysae - small to moderate-sized openings in siliceous volcanic rocks such as rhyolite and obsidian that are filled with concentric shells of material composed of quartz and feldspar. These are common in rhyolites of the Thomas Range where topaz, hematite, and other minerals are found in the lithophysae.

luster - the appearance of a mineral as it reflects light. Luster is divided into metallic, submetallic, and nonmetallic categories. Since most minerals are nonmetallic, these are usually further described by a descriptive term such as vitreous (glass-like reflections), dull, silky, adamantine (hard bright reflections), and others.

mafic - igneous rocks rich in magnesium- and iron-bearing minerals, thus a dark-colored, low silica rock.

miarolitic - a term that describes irregular-shaped cavities that occur in intrusive rocks, particularly granitic rocks, in which crystals of rock-forming minerals such as quartz and feldspar line the walls and protrude into the cavity.

microcrystalline - having crystallites that are so small a microscope would be necessary to observe them.

mineral - simply defined as a chemical compound that occurs in nature. A more precise definition would be a naturally occurring, homogeneous solid, formed by inorganic processes, and having an orderly atomic structure and a definite chemical composition. Minerals are the discrete grains that compose rocks.

molybdate - a small group of minerals in which the anionic group is the molybdate radical $(MoO_4)^{-2}$. Example: wulfenite $PbMoO_4$

monocline - a geologic structure, specifically a fold, in which the rock layers are horizontal, then inclined, then horizontal again. Examples are the Waterpocket Fold in Capitol Reef National Park and Comb Ridge in southeastern Utah.

monoclinic - a crystal system characterized by one inclined crystallographic axis, resulting in crystals that usually have an obvious slanted direction and relatively low symmetry. One of the most common crystal systems for minerals.

native element - a term used to designate those minerals which occur as a single chemical element. Examples: gold, copper, silver, diamond and graphite (carbon), and sulfur.

nitrate - a small group of minerals in which the anionic group is the nitrate radical $(NO_3)^{-1}$. Example: niter (saltpeter) KNO_3

orthorhombic - a crystal system characterized by blocky or tabular crystals and relatively simple forms such as prisms, dipyramids, and pinacoids. One of the most common crystal systems for minerals.

oxide - a large group of common and important minerals containing oxygen as the anion. Examples: hematite Fe_2O_3, magnetite Fe_3O_4, cuprite Cu_2O

pahoehoe - basaltic lava of low viscosity so that it flows easily and smoothly. Solidified flows are characterized by smooth, ropey, undulating surfaces. Pahoehoe flows sometimes turn into the more viscous aa flows as the lava cools and loses gases.

paleontology - the study of fossils.

petrology - the study of rocks.

phaneritic - coarse-grained texture in igneous rocks. Mineral grains are clearly visible to the unaided eye.

phantom - used to describe the appearance of outlines of former crystal forms within a crystal, usually a result of changing conditions as the crystal grew, and occasionally marked by the presence of foreign minerals. Common examples are smoky phantoms within quartz and amethyst.

phenocrysts - the larger grains in an igneous rock with a porphyritic texture.

phosphate - a group of minerals which are characterized by having the phosphate radical $(PO_4)^{-3}$ as the major anionic component. Example: apatite $Ca_5(PO_4, CO_3)_3(F, Cl, OH)$

phosphorescence - the emission of light from a mineral after it has been exposed to a source of radiation such as ultraviolet light. In contrast to fluorescence, phosphoresence occurs after the energy source has been removed. The light is created by excited electrons returning to their original energy state. The phenomenon is usually quite faint and requires complete darkness to be seen.

pillow lava - a lava flow that has rounded or tube-like masses making up its surface as a result of having occurred underwater where each emerging surge of lava was rapidly cooled to create the distinct shapes.

point group - crystal class; one of the 32 ways in which points can be arranged around an object.

polymorphism - the occurrence of a chemical compound (mineral) in more than one structural arrangement. Examples: calcite (trigonal) and aragonite (orthorhombic), argentite (isometric) and acanthite (monoclinic)

porphyritic - an igneous rock with two distinct grain sizes. The larger grains are referred to as phenocrysts. Porphyritic textures are very common in volcanic rocks because the magma began cooling slowly within th earth and formed some large grains which were later erupted onto the earth's surface with the remaining liquid which then cooled rapidly to form an aphanitic groundmass.

pseudomorph - a mineral that has been replaced by a second mineral, but the external crystal form of the first mineral has been preserved. Example: limonite pseudomorphs after pyrite.

pseudosymmetry - the appearance of a higher degree of symmetry than the mineral actually possesses. Quite often this may be the result of twinning or the random intergrowth of crystals.

pyroclastics - the solid particles emitted during a volcanic eruption. Large particles are referred to as blocks (if solid when ejected) or bombs (if molten when ejected). Other particles, in order of decreasing size, are lapilli, ash, and dust. Cinders is a general term which has no specific size associated with it. Tephra is a common synonym for pyroclastics.

scepter - a crystal having a second stage of growth which formed a larger crystal around the termination of the original crystal. Quartz scepters are most common, but other minerals exhibit this habit also.

schistosity - a form of metamorphic foliation in which the rock is composed primarily of tabular or elongate minerals arranged in parallel planes. Most schists are dominated by micas or chlorite, but amphiboles such as hornblende, tremolite, or actinolite also form schists.

selenide - a small group of rare minerals that have the element selenium as the anion. They are usually classified with the sulfides. Example: tiemannite $HgSe$

silica - silicon dioxide (SiO_2) as a mineral forms quartz, but is an important chemical constituent of igneous and metamorphic rocks in the form of silicate minerals.

silicate - a large group of important minerals, many of them rock-forming minerals, which result from extended linkages between silicon atoms and oxygen atoms. Extensive substitution of aluminum for silicon and hydroxyl (OH) for oxygen, among others, leads to a tremendous number of mineral species.

sill - a tabular intrusion of magma that occurs parallel to existing layers or structures. A similar intrusion that cuts across layers is known as a dike.

slaty cleavage - a form of metamorphic foliation in which the rock breaks along relatively smooth surfaces; flat in the case of slate and curved or crenulated in the case of phyllite.

specific gravity - a unitless number, the ratio between the weight of a mineral and an equal volume of water. Usually determined using Archimedes' principle of buoyancy by the formula $G = Wa/(Wa-Ww)$ where Wa is the weight of the mineral in air and Ww is the weight of the mineral while suspended in water.

stock - a large intrusion, but smaller than a batholith, thus less than 40 square miles of surface exposure. Stocks are quite common and are usually slightly more mafic in composition than are batholiths.

stratovolcano - a volcano with a composite cone, formed by layers of lava and pyroclastics. Most large continental volcanoes are this type. Examples: Mt. Rainier, Mt. St. Helens.

streak - the color of a mineral's powder when rubbed across a piece of unglazed white porcelain. This is an identifying characteristic which works best for dark-colored metallic and submetallic minerals.

sulfate - any of a group of relatively common minerals which contain the sulfate $(SO_4)^{-2}$ radical. Sulfates may result from the oxidation of sulfide minerals in ore deposits, or from the oxidation of pyrite in sedimentary rocks, or in evaporite deposits. Examples: gypsum $CaSO_4 \cdot 2H_2O$, barite $BaSO_4$, anhydrite $CaSO_4$

sulfide - a common and important group of minerals which contain the element sulfur as their principle anion. Many of these minerals are important as a source of a particular metal such as zinc, copper, or nickel. Examples: sphalerite ZnS, galena PbS

sulfosalt - a small group of minerals which differ from the sulfides in that the semi-metals (arsenic and antimony) occur as cations rather than as anions. Examples: enargite Cu_3AsS_4, proustite Ag_3AsS_3, tetrahedrite $(Cu, Fe)_{12}Sb_4S_{13}$

subhedral - having some crystal faces, but not particularly well developed.

syncline - a geologic structure, specifically a fold in which the rocks have been arched downward as a result of compressive forces.

telluride - a small group of minerals that contain tellurium as their major anion. These minerals are usually classified with the sulfides. Examples: sylvanite $(Au, Ag)_2Te_4$, krennerite $AuTe_2$

tephra - a synonym of pyroclastics, the solid particles ejected by a volcano.

tetragonal - a crystal system in which all classes have one unique crystallographic axis which is associated with 4-fold symmetry. This results in crystals that are elongated or flattened in one direction and have either a square or octagonal cross section.

triclinic - a crystal system distinguished by very little, if any, symmetry.

trigonal - a crystal system, or a division of the hexagonal system, in which the unique axis has 3-fold symmetry. Crystals may have either three or six sides.

twin law - a statement of the planes of reflection or composition involved in a twin operation. The more common twin laws are given common names, such as Japan twin, Carlsbad twin, and Iron Cross.

ultramafic - an igneous rock that is extremely rich in magnesium- and iron-bearing minerals, with low silica, and usually no feldspar. Most such rocks contain olivine and/or pyroxene as the major minerals.

vanadate - a small number of minerals which have the vanadate radical $(VO_4)^{-3}$ as their major anion. Example: vanadinite $Pb_5(VO_4)Cl$

vesicles - small bubbles in volcanic rocks created by escaping gases. When filled by later mineral deposits they become amygdules.

viscosity - the resistance to flow possessed by a fluid. In reference to lavas, viscosity is controlled by the temperature (high temperature = low viscosity), dissolved gases (high gas content = low viscosity), and silica content (high silica = high viscosity).

xenolith - literally a "foreign rock." A fragment of country rock that has fallen into the magma and was not melted, because it was composed of minerals with a high melting point, thus the magma solidified around it. Most xenoliths are fragments of mafic rock surrounded by a felsic or intermediate magma.

REFERENCES CITED

Abou-Zied, S. (1973) Geology of the Milford Flat quadrangle, Star district, Beaver County, Utah *in* Geology of the Milford area: Utah Geological Association Publication 3, p. 43-48.

Baer, James L. (1962) Geology of the Star Range, Beaver County, Utah: Brigham Young University Geology Studies, v. 9, part 2, p. 29-52.

Baer, James L. (1973) Summary of stratigraphy and structure of the Star Range, Beaver County, Utah *in* Geology of the Milford area: Utah Geological Association Publication 3, p. 33-38.

Barosh, P. J. (1960) Beaver Lake Mountains, Beaver County, Utah: Their geology and ore deposits: Utah Geological and Mineral Survey Bulletin 68, 85 p.

Braithwaite, L. F. (1976) Graptolites from the Pogonip Group (lower Ordovician) of western Utah: Geological Society of America Special Paper 166, 106 p.

Bryant, Bruce (1988) Geology of the Farmington Canyon Complex, Wasatch Mountains, Utah: U. S. Geological Survey Professional Paper 1476, 54 p.

Bullock, Kenneth C. (1981) Minerals and mineral localities of Utah: Utah Geological and Mineral Survey Bulletin 117, 177 p.

Butler, B. S. (1913) Geology and ore deposits of the San Francisco and adjacent districts, Utah: U. S. Geological Survey Professional Paper 80, 212 p.

Butler, B. S., Loughlin, G. F., Heikes, V. C., and others (1920) Ore deposits of Utah: U. S. Geological Survey Professional Paper 111, 672 p.

Calkins, F. C., and Butler, B. S. (1943) Geology and ore deposits of the Cottonwood-American Fork area, Utah: U. S. Geological Survey Professional Paper 201, 152 p.

Callaghan, Eugene (1973) Mineral resource potential of Piute County, Utah and adjoining area: Utah Geological and Mineralogical Survey Bulletin 102, 135 p.

Cobban, W. A. (1976) Ammonite record from the Mancos Shale of the CastleValley-Price-Woodside Area, east-central Utah: Brigham Young University Geology Studies, v. 22, part 3, p. 117-126.

Crawford, A. and Buranek, A. (1945) The tungsten deposits of the Mineral Range, Beaver County, Utah: Utah Engineering Exp. Station, Bulletin 25, 48 p.

Cross, Aureal T., Maxfield, E. Blair, Cotter, Edward, Cross, Christopher (1975) Field guide and road log to the western Book Cliffs, Castle Valley, and parts of the Wasatch Plateau: Brigham Young University Geology Studies, v. 22, part 2, 132 p.

Dietrich, Richard V. and Skinner, Brian J. (1979) Rocks and rock minerals: John Wiley & Sons, Inc., New York, 319 p.

Doelling, Hellmut H. and Davis, Fitzhugh D., with Brandt, Cynthia J. (1989) The geology of Kane County, Utah, geology, mineral resources, geologic hazards: Utah Geological and Mineral Survey Bulletin 124, 192 p., 10 pl.

Dolanski, J. (1974) Sulvanite from the Thorpe Hills, Utah: American Mineralogist, v. 39, nos. 11-12, p. 908-928.

Donnay J. H. and Nowacki W. (1955) Geological Society of America Memoir 60, as cited *in* F. D. Bloss (1971) Crystallography and Crystal Chemistry: Holt, Rinehart and Winston, Inc., New York, 545 p.

Duttweiler, Karen A. and Griffits, Wallace R. (1988) Geology and geochemistry of the Broken Ridge area, southern Wah Wah Mountains, Iron County, Utah: U. S. Geological Survey Bulletin 1843, 32 p.

Erickson, M. P. (1966) Igneous complex at Wah Wah Pass, Beaver County, Utah: Utah Geological and Mineralogical Survey Special Studies 17, 14 p.

Gunther, L. F., and Gunther, V. G. (1981) Some Middle Cambrian fossils of Utah: Brigham Young University Geology Studies, v. 28, part 1, 81 p.

Hansen, Wallace R. (1957) Geology of the Clay Basin quadrangle, Utah: U. S. Geological Survey Map GQ 101.

Hintze, Lehi F. (1973) Geologic road logs of western Utah and eastern Nevada: Brigham Young University Geology Studies, Studies for Students No. 7, v. 20, part 2, 66 p.

Hintze, Lehi F. (1974a) Preliminary geologic map of the Conger Mountain quadrangle, Millard County, Utah: U. S. Geological Survey Map MF-634.

References Cited

Hintze, Lehi F. (1974b) Preliminary geologic map of the Crystal Peak quadrangle, Millard County, Utah: U. S. Geological Map MF-635.

Hintze, Lehi F. (1974c) Preliminary geologic map of the Notch Peak quadrangle, Millard County, Utah: U. S. Geological Survey Map MF-636.

Hintze, Lehi F. (1974d) Preliminary geologic map of The Barn quadrangle, Millard County, Utah: USGS Map MF-633.

Hintze, Lehi F. (1987) Esceptionally fossiliferous lower Ordovician strata in the Ibex area, western Millard County, Utah: Geological Society of America Centennial Field Guide, v. 2, p. 261-264.

Hintze, Lehi F. (1988) Geologic history of Utah: Brigham Young University Geology Studies Special Publication 7, 202 p.

Holfert, John (1977) A field guide to Topaz and associated minerals of Topaz Mountain, Utah: Privately published, 41+ pages.

Hose, Richard K., and Repenning, Charles A. (1959) Stratigraphy of Pennsylvanian, Permian, and Lower Triassic rocks of Confusion Range, west-central Utah: American Association of Petroleum Geologists Bulletin, v. 43, no. 9, p. 2167-2196.

IAPG (1951) Guidebook Number 6, Geology of the Canyon, House, and Confusion Ranges, Millard County, Utah.

Kerr, P. F., Brophy, G. P., Dahl, H. M., Green, Jack, and Woolard, L. E. (1957) Marysvale, Utah uranium area: geology, volcanic relations, and hydrothermal alteration: Geological Society of America Special Paper 64, 212 p.

Mackin, J. H. (1954) Geology and iron ore deposits of the Granite Mountain area, Iron County, Utah: U. S. Geological Survey Mineral Investigations map MF-14.

Mackin, J. H. (1968) Iron ore deposits of the Iron Springs district, southwestern Utah *in* Ore deposits of the United States, 1933-1967: American Institute of Mining Engineers, Graton-Sales volume, New York, v. 2, p. 922-1010.

Mason, Brian, and Moore, Carleton B. (1982) Principles of geochemistry: John Wiley & Sons, New York, 344 p.

Moore, Raymond C., Lalicker, Cecil G., and Fischer, Alfred G. (1952) Invertebrate fossils: McGraw-Hill Book Company, Inc., New York, 766 p.

Morris, H. T. (1968) The Main Tintic mining district, Utah *in* Ore deposits of the United States, 1933-1967: American Institute of Mining Engineers, Graton-Sales volume, New York, v. 2, p. 1043-1073.

Moussa, Mounir Tawfik (1965) Geology of the Soldier Summit quadrangle, Utah: Ph.D. dissertation, University of Utah, Salt Lake City, Utah. 129 p.

Parker, Lee R. (1976) The Paleoecology of the fluvial coal-forming swamps and associated floodplain environments in the Blackhawk Formation (Upper Cretaceous) of central Utah: Brigham Young University Geology Studies, v. 22, part 3, p. 99-116

Philpotts, Anthony R. (1990) Principles of igneous and metamorphic petrology: Prentice-Hall, Englewood Cliffs, New Jersey, 498 p.

Pratt, Alan R. and Callaghan, Eugene (1970) Land and mineral resources of Sanpete County, Utah: Utah Geological and Mineralogical Survey Bulletin 85, 72 p.

Rigby, J. Keith (1952) Geology of the Selma Hills, Utah County, Utah: Utah Geological and Mineralogical Survey Bulletin 45, 107 p.

Rigby, J. Keith, Hintze, Lehi F., and Welsch, Stanley L. (1974) Geologic guide to the northwestern Colorado Plateau: Brigham Young University Geology Studies, Studies for Students No. 9, v. 21, part 2, 117 p.

Rigby, J. Keith (1978) Porifera of the Middle Cambrian Wheeler Shale, from the Wheeler Amphitheater, House Range, in western Utah: Journal of Paleontology, v. 52, no. 6, p. 1325-1345.

Rigby, J. Keith (1983) Sponges of the Middle Cambrian Marjum Limestone from the House Range and Drum Mountains of western Millard County, Utah: Journal of Paleontology, v. 57, p. 240-270.

Robison, R. A. (1964) Late Middle Cambrian faunas from western Utah: Journal of Paleontology, v. 38, no. 3, p. 510-566.

Rodriguez, Joaquin, and Gutschick, Raymond C. (1978) A new shallow water Schizophoria from the

Leatham Formation (Late Famennina), northeastern Utah: Journal of Paleontology, v. 52, no. 6, p. 1346-1355.

Rogers, John C. (1984) Depositional environments and paleoecology of two quarry sites in the Middle Cambrian Marjum and Wheeler Formations, House Range, Utah: Brigham Young University Geology Studies, v. 31, part 1, p. 97-116.

Sadlick, Walter (1965) Biostratigraphy of the Chainman Formation, eastern Nevada and western Utah: unpublished Ph.D. dissertation, University of Utah, 227 p.

Sargent and Zeller (1984) Sand calcite crystals from Garfield County, Utah: U. S. Geological Survey Bulletin 1606, 15 p.

Skedros, John G. (1985) The trilobites of Antelope Springs, Utah: Senior Honors Project, University of Utah, 221 p.

Staatz, M. H., and Carr, W. J. (1964) Geology and mineral deposits of the Thomas and Dugway Ranges, Juab and Tooele Counties, Utah: U. S. Geological Survey Professional Paper 415, 188 p.

Stokes, W. Lee (1982) Essentials of earth history, fourth edition: Prentice Hall, New York, 577 p.

Stokes, William Lee (1986) Geology of Utah: Utah Museum of Natural History (Occasional Paper No. 6) and Utah Geological and Mineral Survey, Salt Lake City, UT, 280 p. plus appendices.

Stowe, Carlton H. (1979) Rockhound guide to mineral and fossil localities in Utah (field checked by Lee I. Perry): Utah Geological and Mineral Survey Circular 63, 79 p.

Stringham, Bronson (1964) Altered areas south of the Horn Silver Mine, Beaver County, Utah: Utah Geological and Mineralogical Survey Special Studies 9, 18 p.

Swensen, A. Jaren (1962) Anisoceratidae and Hamitidae (Ammonoidea) from the Cretaceous of Texas and Utah: Brigham Young University Geology Studies v. 9, part 2, p. 53-82.

Tidwell, William D. (1962) An Early Pennsylvanian flora from the Manning Canyon Shale, Utah: Brigham Young University Geology Studies, v. 9, part 2, p. 83-101.

Tidwell, William D. (1975) Common fossil plants of Western North America: Brigham Young University Press, 197 p.

Tidwell, William D., Jennings, James R., and Call, Victor B. (1988) Flora of Manning Canyon Shale, Part III: Sphenophyta: Brigham Young University Geology Studies, v. 35, p. 15-32.

Trimble, Larry Merc (1977) Geology and ore deposits of the San Rafael River mining area, Emery County, Utah: M.S. thesis, University of Utah, Salt Lake City, UT, 264 p.

Trimble, Larry M. and Doelling, Hellmut H. (1978) Geology and uranium-vanadium deposits of the San Rafael River mining area, Emery County, Utah: Utah Geological and Mineral Survey Bulletin 113, 122 p.

Walcott, C. D. (1886) Second contribution to the studies on the Cambrian faunas of North America: U. S. Geological Survey Bulletin 30, p. 1-369.

Welsh, John E. (1973) Geology of the Beaver Lake Mountains and Rocky Range, Beaver County, Utah *in* Geology of the Milford area: Utah Geological Association Publication 3, p. 49-54.

Whelan, J. (1965) Hydrothermal alteration and mineralogy, Staats Mine and Blawn Mountain areas, central Wah Wah Mountains, Beaver County, Utah: Utah Geological and Mineralogical Survey Special Studies 12, 31 p.

Williams, J. S. (1958) Geologic atlas of Utah, Cache County: Utah Geological and Mineral Survey Bulletin 64, 98 p.

Wray, William B., Jr. (1973) Geology and mineralization of the Rebel Mine area, Star Range, Beaver County, Utah *in* Geology of the Milford area: Utah Geological Association Publication 3, p. 39-42.

INDEX

acanthite 61
actinolite 112
adamite 124, C-9
adularia 58
agate 60, 75, 76, 79, 81, 83,
    84, 85, 86, 89, 94, 114, 115, 120, 131, 133, 134
    after barite 84
    black 89
    grape 75
alaskite 131
algal balls 114, 129
algal stromatolites 125
alunite 60, 61, 106
ammonites 76, 101
andalusite 67
anhydrite 60, 118
anthophyllite 72
apatite 88
aragonite 64, 90, 101, 116
aurichalcite 65, 121, C-8, C-14
austinite 124
autunite 61
azurite 59, 61, 69, 121, 124, C-12, C-13, C-15
barite 62, 63, 124, C-10
belemnites 126
beryl 72, 91, C-2
    aquamarine 63
bird tracks 129
bixbyite 91, C-3
blastoids 101
bornite 58, 59
brachiopods 67, 69, 70, 99, 100, 101, 103, 135, 136
brochantite 59, C-11
brucite 111
bryozoans 69, 135
calciovolborthite 123
calcite 59, 61, 62,
    63, 77, 81, 88, 90, 91, 105, 106, 107, 111, 121, 123,
    135, C-8, C-14
cassiterite 91
celestite 77, C-14
cephalopods 71, 82, 100, 113, 126
cerargyrite 61
cerussite 110, 120, C-7
chabazite 106, 107
chalcedony 60, 87, 91
chalcopyrite 58, 59, 60, 61, 102
chert 133
chlorite 58
chrysocolla 58, 59, 61, 66
cinnabar 120
clays, copper-bearing 66
clinkers 80
clintonite 58, 112, C-6
coal 71
concretions 79, 109
conichalcite 124, C-9
connellite C-9
copper 66, C-5, C-12
coral, horn 70, 119, 121, 123
corals 67, 69, 99, 101, 126, 135, 136
cornwallite C-12
corundum 108
crandallite C-13
crinoids 69, 95, 99, 113, 135, C-12
cuprite 59, 61, 66
diopside 58, 61, 102
dolomite 69
durangite 91, C-4
echinoderms 100, 113
enargite 90
eocrinoids 68
epidote 58, 61, 62, 111, 112, 122
feldspar
    orthoclase 64, 121, C-11
    plagioclase, albite 103
    plagioclase, labradorite 101
fish 66, 68
fluorite 58, 61, 87, 91, 106, 124, C-10, C-15, C-16
forsterite 111, 112
galena 59, 61, 62, 63, 69, 110, 121, 122
gar fish 74
garnet 61, 67, 72, 91, 102, 103, 111, 112,
    130, 131, C-3, C-4
    grossular 58, 62
    rock 111
gastropods 82, 116, 126, 129, 135, 136
geodes 77, 89, 105
gneiss 73
graptolites 99
gypsum 66, 80, 82, 118, 120, 121, C-13, C-14
halite 118, C-13
hematite 61, 87, 91
    specular 60, 62, 130
hemimorphite 110, 121, C-7, C-8
heulandite 106, 107
hornblende 80
hyrocarbons 125, 126

ilmenite..91
jasper..............................76, 77, 81, 94, 133, C-14
jet coal...134
kaolinite..60
kyanite...67, 72
laumontite..58
leaves..76, 116
limonite...60, 61, C-9
   after pyrite......................................67, 127, C-16
   after siderite..60
ludwigite...59, 112
magnesite...59, 117
magnetite...58, 61, 63, 88, 112
malachite........58, 59, 61, 63, 69, 121, 124, C-12, C-15
manganese oxides.................................107, 111, 135
marble...111
   birdseye...128
migmatite..73
mixite..C-9, C-12
molybdenite..59, 102
mordenite...106, 107
muscovite...61
nepheline..108
obsidian..102
opal..60
ostracods...103, 116, 129
oysters..133
parapierrotite...122
pegmatite..73
pelecypods (also see oysters)..............71, 76, 82, 88, 95, 126, 129
petrified wood.....................................75, 79, 81, 83, 84, 85, 94, 95, 131, 133
philipsburgite..C-9
plant fossils............................71, 118, 119, 127, 135
pseudobrookite...91, C-4
psilomelane..107
pyrite......................59, 60, 61, 62, 90, 105, 110, 111, 112, 121, 122, 124, 128, C-5, C-6, C-10
pyromorphite..110, C-7

quartz................58, 60, 61, 77, 87, 102, 103, 106, 107, 112, 116, 122, 124, 128, 130, C-5, C-9, C-10, C-11
   smoky...64, 103
   amethyst..61, 88, 91, 103, 108
   tourmalinated...60
rhyolite...108, C-3
ripple marks..105
rosasite...C-8
sandstone, banded...64
scheelite..62, 103
scolecite...106, 107, 130
septarian nodules..82, 94
sericite..61
serpentine...58, 111, 112
shark teeth..126
siderite...88
sphalerite...106, 122, 128, C-6
sphene...58
spinel...108, 112, 130
sponges..98
staurolite...67, 72
stibiconite...124, C-5
stibnite...80, 122, C-16
stilbite...106, 107
sulfur..60, C-16
sulvanite...123
sunstone...101
szaibelyite..59
tellurides..61
titanite..130
topaz...87, 91, C-1, C-2, C-3
tourmaline..60, 72
tremolite..59, 60
tridymite...C-4
trilobites.............................65, 68, 97, 98, 99, 100, 103
uranophane...61
variscite..C-13
vesuvianite..102, 111, 112, 130
wollastonite..58, 59
wonderstone..122, 123
wulfenite..62, 63, 65, 110, C-7, C-15